WHAT MADE FREUD LAUGH

In her characteristically engaging style, Nelson explores a topic that has fascinated and frustrated scholars for centuries. Initially drawn to the meaning of laughter through her decades of work studying crying from an attachment perspective, Nelson argues that laughter is based in the attachment system, which explains much about its confusing and apparently contradictory qualities.

Laughter may represent connection or detachment. It can invite closeness, or be a barrier to it. Some laughter helps us cope with stress; other laughter may serve as a defense and represent resistance to growth and change. Nelson resolves these paradoxes and complexities by linking attachment-based laughter with the exploratory/play system in infancy, and the social/affiliative, conflict/appeasement, sexual/mating, and fear/wariness systems of later life. An attachment perspective also helps to explain the source of different patterns and uses of laughter, suggesting how and why they may vary according to attachment style, and explaining the multiple meanings of laughter in the context of the therapeutic relationship. As she discovers, attachment has much to teach us about laughter, and laughter has much to teach us about attachment. This lively book sheds light on the ways in which we connect, grow, and transform and how, through shared humor, play, and delight, we have fun doing so.

Judith Kay Nelson, MSW, PhD, is the former dean and currently on the faculty of the Sanville Institute for Clinical Social Work and Psychotherapy, California. She also teaches attachment and neurobiology in the clinical social work doctoral program at Smith College, Massachusetts. She has taught and presented throughout the United States and Europe on topics related to crying, grief, laughter, and attachment.

WHAT MADE FREUD LAUGH

An Attachment Perspective on Laughter

Routledge
Taylor & Francis Group

NEW YORK AND LONDON

First published 2012
by Routledge
711 Third Avenue, New York, NY 10017

Simultaneously published in the UK
by Routledge
27 Church Road, Hove, East Sussex BN3 2FA

Routledge is an imprint of the Taylor & Francis Group, an informa business

Library of Congress Cataloging in Publication Data

Nelson, Judith Kay, 1941–
  What made Freud laugh : an attachment perspective on laughter / by Judith Kay Nelson.
    p. cm.
  Includes bibliographical references and index.
  1. Laughter.   2. Attachment behavior.   I. Title.
  BF575.L3N45   2012
  152.4'3—dc23   2012005595

ISBN: 978-0-415-99832-1 (hbk)
ISBN: 978-0-415-99833-8 (pbk)
ISBN: 978-0-203-10326-5 (ebk)

Typeset in Bembo
by Apex CoVantage, LLC

SFI Certified Sourcing
www.sfiprogram.org
SFI-00453

Printed and bound in the United States of America
by Edwards Brothers, Inc.

For Aurelia June and Leo Cassady

CONTENTS

ACKNOWLEDGMENTS

I once read that only a person with no sense of humor would attempt to write a book on laughter. The following people are responsible for helping me keep mine alive and well while working on this project, and I extend a hearty thank you to each of them and wish for them much laugher and happiness.

George Zimmar at Routledge has been a supportive and understanding editor. His patience and words of encouragement have kept me steady and on track throughout. I also greatly appreciate the help of Marta Moldvai, who has been a steady presence during the publication process.

My team of writing helpers has also been amazing. The time, effort, and sheer brain power they have donated have made all the difference in preparing this book. For help on the front lines, I thank Cynthia Nelson, Rose Jade, Marcia Hoogstra, and Lori Pesavento for standing by at all hours to read and edit, and Greta Christina, Ingrid Nelson, and Russ Nelson for fielding my editing questions by return e-mail. My colleagues/readers—Maureen Adams, Ann Cameron, Yvette Esprey, and Charles Rizzutto—have been responsive, helpful, supportive, and generous as they diligently read and responded to the chapters I sent along at regular intervals. I appreciate their generosity and their individual and collective wisdom and know that the work is more solid because of them.

To the many colleagues who have shared anecdotes, brainstormed about ideas and theories, and generally supported and encouraged me, I am grateful beyond measure: Cynthia O' Connell, Lise and Neal Blumenfeld, Suzanne Bennett, Allan and Judy Schore, Kate White, and Merle Davis. Colleagues and students from The Sanville Institute for Clinical Social Work and Psychotherapy have been standing by with ideas, examples, and much good old-fashioned laughter. I especially thank Gregory Bellow, Jo Ann Bellow, Mary Coombs, Tina Casenza, Angeleen Campra, Deborah Levine, Silvio Machado, Lonnie Prince, and the Sanville students who worked on the laughter project: Hillary Dreyfuss, Michelle Frisch, Paula Holt, Sidney Mullen, and Cazeaux Nordstrom. Several Smith College School for Social Work doctoral students also contributed ideas and examples. Thank you especially to Sally Comer and Maria Oliva.

I would also like to thank some of the dear friends who have helped to make this project both fun and funny. To the Women's Group—Margo Arcanin, Margaret Ballou, Barbara Miller, Judy Morhar, Donna Rosenheim, Susan Sandler, and Ruth Sands—I offer my gratitude for the deep bonds of friendship, closeness, loyalty, and confidence over so many years. Thank you, too, to the Women's Potluck Group—Pattie Howard, Cindy Black, Trudi Elm, Cathy Parker, Brenda Adams, and Diane Fischer—for the regular infusions of creative energy and good food.

Laughter, for me, began in my family. Thank you to my sister, Marcia, who has been giggling with me since childhood, to the new kids in the family, Ava and Cecilia, Tanner and Wyatt, for reminding me about childhood, and to the former kids, Corrie Hoogstra, Dirk Hoogstra, and Ingrid Nelson, for demonstrating developmental changes and entertaining me in the process. Thank you also to Craig Hoogstra who likes to tell jokes, Russ Nelson for playing second string on the "yo-yo" team, my mother, Lucille Baker, who had the loudest laugh in the world, and my father, Kenneth Baker, who could insert odd jokes and facts in the funniest places. I am grateful also to Uncle Jack, Aunt Pauline, and the McDermott cousins who taught me about true wit and kept it coming; the rest of the Payne cousins in Michigan, Joan and Jerry Horne, Larry, David, and Barbara Payne, for making childhood fun; the Payne cousins in Mississippi for all the good times on the farm; and the Baker cousins in Mississippi, especially Dorothy Jean Latham and Sonny Latham, for keeping the southern storytelling traditions alive. I would also like to thank my in-laws of the past 25 years, Dick and Jeri Williams, for the good company and warm winter hospitality, Ellen Pesavento and Teri and Michael Miranti for being family, and Derek and Jordan Miranti for all that kid energy and playful good fun.

I would like to thank my immediate family—the San Francisco branch, Ingrid Nelson and Greta Christina, for their enthusiasm and understanding of what it takes to get this done, and the Portland branch, Cynthia Nelson, Dusty Reske, Aurelia, and Leo, for making every day for play and laughter.

Lori Pesavento has managed to be my primary support squad, my primary attachment figure, and my best laughmate throughout this process, and for that, "thank you" only scratches the surface.

INTRODUCTION

"Laughter," comedian Victor Borge once said, "is the shortest distance between two people." A simple behavior, common to all human beings and quite a few of our close animal relatives, laughter is nonetheless mysterious, profound, complex, and confusing. Philosophers, theologians, psychologists, scientists, and humorists of all stripes are drawn to study it and formulate theories, yet most who try are humbled by the process. Freud, writing about jokes and humor almost 100 years ago, said he would not even attempt to consider everything that had been written about laughter. He quotes the preface to a book on the psychology of laughter published a few years earlier (Dugas as cited in Freud, 1905/1983):

> There is no action that is more commonplace or that has been more widely studied than laughter. There is none that has succeeded more in exciting the curiosity both of ordinary people and of philosophers. There is none on which more observations have been collected and more theories built. But at the same time there is none that remains more unexplained. (p. 146)

A student of laughter in the 21st century is even more inundated by theories and scientific studies on the subject. During the decades when I was studying crying from an attachment perspective and working out a theory to explain its meaning throughout life, I kept thinking that focusing an attachment lens on laughter could help to clarify some of the confusion and controversy among the prevailing theories and help psychotherapists navigate some of the tricky aspects of laughter in psychotherapeutic treatment. I determined that as soon as the dust had settled from the completion of my book *Seeing Through Tears: Crying and Attachment*, I would begin work on building an attachment theory of laughter. I felt confident that the same principles I had applied to crying would also apply to laughter and that, as with crying, doing so would prove useful in expanding our developmental and clinical understanding of both attachment and laughter.

I had spent a quarter century studying crying, and I assumed that much of that work would translate into a similar attachment theory of laughter. As with crying, however, I was faced with the contradictory elements of laughter, along with the absence of any direct studies looking at the relationship between laughter and attachment. As I searched, this time with the benefit of far-reaching computer databases unavailable during the early years of my crying research, I kept coming up empty-handed. Furthermore, I discovered to my shock that laughter does not appear on any of the usual lists of attachment behaviors. Clearly there was much work to be done in order to complete a companion volume to the crying book.

As I read back through the literature on attachment behaviors, it became clear that although attachment theorists include smiling on their lists of attachment behaviors, crying is considered the default attachment behavior. I, too, had been of that mind all through my years of research on crying, assuming crying to be the "key" behavior linking infant and caregiver. From the standpoint of modern attachment theory, where the focus is on the dyadic regulation of attachment, I assumed, as do most theorists (Cassidy & Shaver, 2008), that the caregiver's interactive regulation in soothing the infant's distress is the primary building block for secure attachment.

My awakening to the equal importance of positive arousal and its regulation came about when I began to study the neurobiology of interpersonal relationships in books such as those by Schore (2003a, 2003b) and others (Cozolino, 2006) that describe and integrate the findings from many relevant scientific studies. Over and over, positive arousal appears to be on equal footing with negative arousal when it comes to establishing a secure attachment bond between infant and caregiver and to influencing the development of the infant's nervous system and its propensities toward certain characteristic patterns of affect arousal and regulation. This realization brought me from casually thinking I should write a book about laughter and attachment to having a sense of mission about it. I had found a gap: attachment theory, while acknowledging that smiling is an attachment behavior, had nonetheless positioned distress and crying as foundational even though studies increasingly show that initiating, prolonging, and monitoring levels of positive engagement associated with smiling and laughter play key roles as well (Schore, 2003a; Tronick, 2007).

In order to address the gap, I felt it necessary to first establish that laughter is indeed an attachment behavior, albeit one that is directly linked to the exploratory and play systems in infancy. I felt it necessary to first establish that laughter is indeed an attachment behavior, though, as we will see, it is linked to the exploratory and play systems in infancy and to other systems of behavior later in life. Chapter 1 therefore begins with examples of laughter that demonstrate its direct tie to the attachment system, in infancy and throughout life, and argues for classifying it as an attachment behavior linked to the system of exploration and play.

Chapter 2 begins the task of untangling the confusing and contradictory aspects of laughter and showing how they can be explained by the links between laughter and other systems of behavior, as well as by the distinction increasingly being made in research between Duchenne (spontaneous belly laughs associated with positive arousal) and non-Duchenne laughter (conversational inserts that can be associated with either positive or negative arousal). Chapters 3 and 4 complete Part 1 by looking at the attachment aspects of the major theories of laughter (Chapter 3) and a survey of laughter research (Chapter 4).

Once the attachment foundation for laughter is laid out in the first four chapters, Part 2 moves on to the particulars of how an attachment perspective informs our understanding of laughter in infancy (Chapter 5), and how laughter in infancy informs the development of attachment security or insecurity (Chapter 6). The unfolding of laughter during childhood and into adolescence is the focus of Part 3, beginning with Chapter 7. Chapter 8 applies an attachment perspective on laughter to clinical work with children, exploring its relevance in assessing attachment style and affect arousal and regulation, as well as exploring how it informs aspects of the psychotherapeutic relationship with children.

Part 4 begins in Chapter 9, which provides an attachment perspective on the complexities of laughter in adult life and relationships. Chapter 10 focuses on applying an attachment perspective on laughter to the clinical assessment of adult attachment style and history, and further explores the many meanings and uses—or misuses—of laughter in psychotherapy with adults.

The final section, Part 5, is on transcendent laughter. An attachment viewpoint helps to position laughter within the larger human context, including how comedy and humor at times enable people to transcend their own particular quirks and circumstances and move to a level of attachment and connection with all of humankind, nature, the universe, and, in some instances, the divine. Laughter in literature, film, and poetry also serves as a means of transforming individual grief and pain, moving us from loss to love—and on certain fortunate occasions, to transcend personal loss and connect us with universal love.

I have stayed engaged in my study of crying for so many decades—drawn in by its complexities and depth—because all along I sensed that the meaning of crying was all rolled up in the meaning of life. I confess that I did not come to my study of laughter with the same conviction about its centrality in human experience, but in the end, I realized I had remade the same "discovery": the meaning of laughter, like crying, boils down to love and loss. The path to understanding laughter led me to the love and loss that is at the core of the attachment system and spiraled me back to the love and loss that is also at the core of the meaning of life.

Part 1

A Theory of Laughter

1

LAUGHTER AS ATTACHMENT BEHAVIOR

Foundations of a Theory

During a visit to the Museum of Indian Arts and Culture in Santa Fe, New Mexico (September 2008), I read the following oral history in a display case:

> Babies usually laugh for the first time at 3 months. It is best for a baby to laugh to a relative who is good-natured. The person who makes a baby laugh for the first time has to host a party to celebrate the baby's successful transition into the adult world. This person provides food, treats, and natural salt. Relatives and friends come to the baby's first–laugh party to assure there will always be togetherness. Lillie Lane; Diné (Navajo)

Every baby's first laugh is cause for celebration, but the reason is often assumed to be because it means the baby is "happy" or enjoying a playful moment. If pressed, we might say that it was joyful for the caregiver, too, and that it was fun and made her feel good. What is often missing, however, is the idea that laughter is first and foremost about togetherness and community. Not so with the Navajo tradition, which points directly to the relational significance of laughter in infancy. First, it joins the caregiver and the infant in a community ritual, conferring special honor and responsibility on the person who first "makes" the baby laugh. Second, it marks the laughter as the beginning point of the baby's transition into the adult relational world. The party is the way for the baby's familial community to carry forward his or her best wishes that, as in the first experience of laughter, the child will always know togetherness—in good times (the special foods) and bad (the natural salt), in love and in loss.

We are born to attach; we are equipped from birth with behaviors that enable us to make the connections with our caregivers, and that make attachment possible. Infants need caregivers to help soothe them in times of distress, and for that we have crying, the inborn attachment behavior that makes a baby's negative arousal clear and creates a corresponding negative arousal in caregivers. It is designed to keep caregivers in close proximity or bring them back quickly when the baby is in distress. Within the first two or three months of life, however, the infant develops another of our inborn attachment behaviors: laughter. Laughter is designed to connect infants with their caregivers when they are not stressed, at times when they are open to new and unusual experiences. From the beginning, laughter is linked to play with the caregiver, as crying is linked with separation from the caregiver. Both are important to our future attachment security, and both represent crucial experiences of affect arousal and regulation. Upbeat, well-modulated, easy laughter shared by infant and caregiver serves to solidify their early connection. Repeated cycles of playful arousal and positive engagement, fed by the laughter of both caregiver and infant, help to initiate, support, and maintain the caregiver-infant bond we know as attachment.

Laughter like this is a warm, fuzzy attachment behavior enticing caregiver and baby to stay close and keep coming back for more, whereas crying is an aversive attachment behavior—we come to help and stay close so we can get it to stop. Both are powerful behaviors infants can do on their own—from birth in the case of crying, and within the first three or four months in the case of laughter. Both behaviors are recognizable in infant-parent pairs the world over.

In order to establish the foundation for an attachment theory of laughter, we will begin by looking at the type of baseline, genuine, unfiltered laughter that occurs in optimal caregiver-infant relationships, and in positive, humorous, connected experiences between adults. This is the type of laughter that is firmly rooted in the attachment system and linked with the exploratory/play system. In the remaining chapters in Part 1, we will use this foundation to round out a classification of different types of laughter based on the links between the attachment system and other systems of behavior, such as conflict/aggression, fear/wariness, and mating/sex. In subsequent chapters, we will establish an attachment-based prototype for exploring laughter in infancy, childhood, and adulthood, then look at how it is associated with the development of attachment security and insecurity, and finally look at the ways in which it can inform our clinical understanding and interventions at each developmental level.

Laughter as Connection

Freud recalled with great fondness an important but normally very serious professor of his who walked in to class one day laughing. He told the class a simple joke that had amused him and burst into laughter again at its conclusion. Freud recalled that the joke itself had not impressed him; rather it was the hearty laughter of his professor that stood out in his memory. He seemed to say that because he and his fellow students idealized their serious teacher, they were both surprised and pleased to see him acting out of character, relating to them on a less serious and perhaps more personal level. When the professor shared the joke with the students, even though they did not find the content especially humorous, his laughter made them feel more connected to him—significantly enough that Freud recalled that event fondly years later.

In his oft-cited book *Jokes and Their Relation to the Unconscious,* Freud (1905/1983) mentions laughter frequently—though he makes it clear that laughter is not his focus—and in it he quoted Dugas, a French philosopher, who said that there is "no behavior that remains more unexplained" (as cited in Freud, 1905/1983, p. 146). As I reread Freud's book with laughter in mind, however, I was struck by the number of times that Freud reported on something like the above that made *him* laugh. In fact, he said that was one of the criteria he used for selecting the jokes to include in his analysis. As he put it, "It is natural that we should choose as the subjects of our investigation examples of jokes by which we ourselves have been most struck in the course of our lives and which have made us laugh the most" (p. 15). Tipped off by that personal reference, I could not help noticing that not only the jokes he collected, but also the contexts in which he recalled laughing at them, were more about his attachment relationships than about the jokes themselves.

Elsewhere in his book, Freud described laughter at a dinner party where he was a guest. At the end of the meal, a complicated dessert known as a roulade was served. Someone asked, in German, whether it was homemade. The host replied by saying that indeed it was a "home-roulade," a pun that combined the name of the French dessert with the English term "home-rule," which was at the time part of a political controversy being much discussed in the press. Freud (1905/1983) wrote, "When those of us present heard this improvised joke it gave us pleasure—which I can clearly recall made us laugh" (p. 94). This instantaneous, multilayered, multilanguage pun was a reply to a serious question asked by a guest in German. It juxtaposed the name of the French dessert with an English word "rule," while simultaneously making reference to a political controversy involving the English.

Freud (1905/1983), having looked deeply at jokes for their unconscious meaning, was mystified by this particular one, which he notes is like countless other "improvised" jokes where the "hearers' feeling of pleasure cannot have arisen from the purpose of the joke or from its intellectual content" (p. 94). He was left to conclude that the "feeling of pleasure" must be connected "with the technique of the joke" (p. 94). The "technique" that seems most in evidence, however, is almost purely relational: relying primarily on the intimacy and proximity of the guests. This complex "in-joke" is a perfect example of one where "you had to be there" to find it funny. The quip was expressed in three shared languages among a group of friends sitting together at the end of a meal in one of their homes. In a flash of wit that certainly could not have been prepared or planned in advance, the host responded to a simple question and everyone was transported simultaneously into shared laughter. Everyone got it: each knew the French dessert, the political reference, and the three languages, along with the intended meaning of the original question.

Spontaneous laughter at an in-joke helps to create, maintain, and acknowledge group connectedness. *"We* all get it," is the clear message, but instead of nodding appreciatively or responding with a polite comment, there is, without thought, mutual arousal of each individual's attachment system, exhibited as a burst of un-planned, nonverbal, implicitly understood attachment behavior: laughter.

Freud (1905/1983) elsewhere in the book called punning *Kalauer,* the "lowest" form of humor (p. 45), by which he seems to mean the least intellectually and technically challenging and the least analytically interesting. Yet here he recalls the whole group joined in laughter at the complex pun in this special moment of togetherness, enjoying food and each other's company.

While many people have commented on Freud's sense of humor and love of jokes (Oring, 1984), I found myself understanding him here in the context of his friendships rather than simply recognizing his ability to appreciate "joke tech-nique" intellectually or his analysis of intrapsychic pleasure. I like knowing that Freud had good friends and sat around the dinner table and laughed with them at a clever remark. Picturing his attachments and laughter, I feel connected to Freud the person, rather than just to his brilliant mind.

I found another example highlighting the relational aspects of laughter for adults when I began to read about the practice of Laughter Yoga and Laughter Clubs. Laughter Yoga is a series of laughter exercises originated in 1995 by Madan Kataria (2008) in India. The first Laughter Club founded by Dr. Kataria had five members, though that number has now grown to an astounding 6,000 clubs in 60 countries. Laughter not only draws individuals together, it is also contagious. Laughter creates a communal, connected experience that crosses gender, age, and cultural barriers.

As part of the research for this book, I arranged to visit a Northampton, Mas-sachusetts, Laughter Yoga group to check it out for myself. I had expected some-thing like the usual yoga practice where individuals are on mats doing their poses while facing the teacher. Instead, we were instructed to do all of the laughter exercises while walking around the group looking directly into each other's eyes. As awkward as we felt, we nonetheless served as momentary partners in the prac-tice of laughter, signifying its relational core. Togetherness, even with strangers, stimulates laughter far more successfully than trying to laugh alone; we are, in fact, 30 times more likely to laugh when in the company of others (Provine, 2000). A YouTube video (Kataria, 2006) titled "Benefits of Laughter Yoga With John Cleese" shows a Laughter Yoga group in action, including the interactive engage-ment of participants, which was engaging enough even on video to make me laugh right along with them.

When searching on the Laughter Yoga website trying to learn more about its philosophy and techniques, I came across a discussion about the problem of what to do with the desire to practice Laughter Yoga while alone in public. Kataria (2008) said that he had faced this problem while stranded in the Hamburg airport waiting for a flight. His solution was simply to open up his cell phone and hold it to his ear as if talking with someone. As long as it looked to others as if he were engaged in a telephone conversation, he felt comfortably inconspicuous laughing uproariously for as long as he wished. Kataria knew instinctively, as do most of us, that laughing alone out loud in public would be certain to attract attention. Without the cell phone, his solitary laughter might well have been considered somewhere between strange and downright mad, and would no doubt have made his fellow passengers take notice and be a bit leery of him.

The Case for Viewing Laughter as an Attachment Behavior

As with most other relationship behaviors, such as those associated with caregiving, mating, or affiliation, it makes sense to search out laughter's roots in the attachment system. John Bowlby (1969) first defined the human attachment system and enumerated the inborn behaviors that help to support and maintain the attachment bond. His list of behaviors includes "crying and calling, babbling and smiling, clinging, non-nutritional sucking, and locomotion as used in approach, following, and seeking" (p. 244).

Since laughter is not on that list, I combed through all of Bowlby's writings and was amazed to find not one mention of the word laughter. I e-mailed colleagues in London, one of whom had been a close associate of Bowlby's, to ask about this omission, and they put me in touch with Sir Richard Bowlby, John Bowlby's son. Both my friends and Bowlby's son said that Bowlby certainly appreciated humor, yet they could not account for his never having mentioned laughter in his writing. Sir Richard Bowlby agreed with my suggestion that his father may have been influenced by Darwin's view, that smiling and laughter exist as one behavior differentiated only on a continuum of intensity.

> My father would have considered laughter to be a natural extension of smiling in which he was very interested. He was a synthesizer of other people's work, and at the time he was working he did not have people like Panksepp [a laughter researcher] tickling his rats, he had to rely on existing publications and was probably more influenced by Darwin. (R. Bowlby, personal communication, October 20, 2008)

Sir Richard Bowlby also graciously wrote that his father was always interested in new ideas and research that might have some bearing on attachment.

I also took heart from the fact that Bowlby inserted a qualifier before his list of attachment behaviors: "Attachment is mediated by several different sorts of behavior of which *the most obvious are* [italics added] . . . ," which I take to mean that he left room for the inclusion of other related behaviors, as well. Other theoreticians and researchers who have written about attachment behaviors (Cassidy, 1999; Marvin & Britner, 2008; Sroufe, 1995; Sroufe & Waters, 1977) have generally worked from Bowlby's list. Ainsworth (1964), Bowlby's collaborator and an attachment researcher, also left room for additions to her list when she wrote, "This catalogue is probably incomplete" (p. 57). Sroufe and Waters (1977) pointed out that both separation/distress and engagement/positive behaviors such as "smiling, clinging and signaling" are functionally related in that "all lead to the same predictable outcome—caregiver-infant proximity." Both, they wrote, "are used by the infant in the service of proximity or physical or psychological contact" (p. 1189).

During the years I was studying the meaning of crying and attachment, I would write the word "laughter" in the margin next to ideas about other attachment behaviors that seemed equally to relate to laughter. For example, Bowlby (1969) wrote, "An infant often calls persistently and, when attended to, orients to and smiles at his mother or other companion. Later, he greets and approaches her and seeks her attention in a thousand attractive ways" (pp. 203–204). Laughter certainly seemed to qualify as one of those "thousand attractive ways" an infant uses to initiate and prolong playful engagement with caregivers.

My efforts to study crying, a difficult and multilayered behavior, were inextricably linked to my understanding of it as an attachment behavior throughout life (Nelson, 2005). Crying clearly functions as a powerful signal beckoning the caregiver: "Come here, I need you." Based on this understanding, I was able to look at crying through the lens of attachment; that was the key to unlocking its mysteries, developmentally, clinically, socially, and even spiritually. I was also able to classify different types of crying and inhibited crying and to speculate about how attachment styles and early caregiving experiences are related to later crying behavior. Crying, I learned, from an attachment perspective, is about love and loss, about separation and grief, about hope and healing.

When the time came to turn that same lens onto laughter, I was confident that attachment would also be the key to unlocking its mysteries. Initially, I thought many of the same insights I had developed about crying would also apply to laughter, but I encountered some unexpected difficulties. The first was the fact that laughter was not on any list of attachment behaviors, and the second was that, as a behavior, it is far more diverse than crying.

Before I could attempt an attachment classification of laughter throughout life, therefore, I needed to determine with some level of confidence that laughter does indeed originate in the attachment system. I was eventually able to do so through careful study of attachment behavior literature and research, with a particular focus on smiling and the findings of neurobiological attachment research described below. Further confirmation regarding the link between laughter and attachment came from careful study and analysis of the many theories about laughter in philosophy, psychology, and psychoanalysis, and from general laughter research, the subjects of the next two chapters.

Attachment Characteristics of Smiling That Also Apply to Laughter

Though Darwin thought that smiling and laughter are the same behavior on a continuum of intensity, a number of other writers, including myself, disagree

(Gervais & Wilson, 2005; Keltner, 2009; Nelson, 2008; Sroufe & Waters, 1976; Wolff, 1987). Wolff (1987), an infant emotion researcher, distinguishes between the two behaviors based on the fact that each one employs different motor and respiratory components, facial muscles, and vocal patterns: smiling is silent, and laughter is vocalized. In addition, he points out, smiling and laughter have different developmental pathways, are elicited by different stimuli, and create different responses in companions and observers.

While I agree that smiling and laughter are different behaviors, I am struck by how many of Bowlby's ideas about smiling as an attachment behavior also apply to laughter. Because Bowlby, as his son pointed out, did not have access to later research and depended on Darwin's view that smiling and laughter are the same behavior on a continuum of intensity, we may assume that his ideas about smiling are also relevant to building a case for laughter as an attachment behavior.

Here, for example, are a few of Bowlby's (1969) ideas about smiling that apply equally to laughter. If the word "smiling" is replaced with "laughter," the statements still hold true.

1. The smile of a human infant is so endearing and has so strong an effect on his parents that it is no surprise to find that it has engaged the attention of a great many workers from Darwin (1872/1965) onwards. (Bowlby, 1969, p. 280)

Here we have no problem making all the same assertions about laughter. In fact, compared to crying, the mountains of attention given to laughter, both theoretical and research, are astounding. People—and I have to include myself—are not only drawn to sharing it, they are also drawn to thinking about it and studying it.

2. The stimuli eliciting smiles in our evolutionary past were "far more likely to come from a baby's mother-figure and from other people in his family than from any other source, animate or inanimate" (Bowlby, 1969, p. 280).

The Navajo first-laugh party confirms the idea that infant laughter is generated by a familiar caregiver, bestowing that person with special honors and with responsibilities for the baby's future well-being. Subsequent infant laughter research (Nwokah, Hsu, Dobrowolska, & Fogel, 1994; Reddy, 2008; Sroufe & Wunsch, 1972) supports the conclusion that early infant laughter is evoked by close caregivers. Early laughter occurs in the bosom of the close attachment circle and rarely occurs in isolation (Reddy, 2008).

3. The smile "has the full functional consequence of leading the baby's companion to respond to him in a playful and loving way" (Bowlby, 1969, p. 281).

4.   The baby's smile acts as a social releaser, the predictable outcome of which is that the baby's mother (or other figure smiled at) responds in a loving way that prolongs social interaction between them and increases the likelihood of her exhibiting maternal behavior in the future. (Bowlby, 1969, p. 280)
5.   The function of a baby's smile is that of increasing interaction between mother and baby and maintaining them in proximity to each other. (Bowlby, 1969, p. 280)

Numbers 3, 4, and 5 all stress variations of the fact that laughter and smiling not only increase proximity, like crying, but they also make it so much fun (unlike crying, which is anything but fun) that caregivers keep coming back for more.

6.   The face of the caregiver elicits a more immediate and generous smile than unfamiliar people or masks. (Bowlby, 1969, p. 280)
7.   Familiar figures are smiled at freely, especially during play or in greeting. Strangers may instead elicit fearful withdrawal or reluctant greeting or an almost self-consciously sociable smile usually given from a safe distance. (Bowlby, 1969, p. 281)

A defining characteristic of all attachment behaviors is that they target a specific caregiver or caregivers rather than occurring indiscriminately with any person. In fact, as Bowlby points out and every parent knows, strangers may cause the child to withdraw or cry rather than smile or laugh, even though they may make strenuous efforts to communicate positively and in friendly manner.

8.   When her baby smiles and babbles a mother smiles back, "talks" to him, strokes and pats him, and perhaps picks him up. In all this each partner seems to be expressing joy in the other's presence and the effect is certainly one of prolonging their social interaction. (Bowlby, 1969, p. 246)
9.   When the caregiver "is tired and irritated with her infant, his smile disarms her; when she is feeding or otherwise caring for him, his smile is a reward and encouragement to her. In strict scientific terms, her infant's smile so affects a mother that the future likelihood of her responding to his signals promptly and in a way favoring his survival is increased." (Bowlby, 1969, p. 246)

Smiling and laughter invite affect arousal and regulation from the caregiver toward the baby—talking, patting, stroking, picking up—a core feature of attachment behaviors. Here we see that laughter invites positive caregiving gestures toward the baby. In addition, the infant's laughter and clowning also up-regulate or intensify the positive arousal of a caregiver who is "tired and irritated," as Bowlby put it. My grandson Leo, at 9 months, will make eye contact and just start laughing out of the blue, inviting us to join the fun, which is no stretch at all, no matter how distracted we might be at the moment.

Bowlby (1969) points out that being able to positively engage a dysregulated or depressed caregiver is definitely in the child's best interest. Recently, a colleague told me of a still-face video (Tronick, 2007) where the infant tried every trick to reengage the frozen-faced mother. After all else had failed, the infant laughed, and in spite of the mother's determination to follow the instructions to keep her face still, she could not control herself and burst out laughing, to the presumed relief of the baby.

By the time I finish reading Bowlby's list describing the attachment power of smiling/laughter, I am smiling myself. I am happy, not only because it convinces me that Bowlby would agree that laughter is an attachment behavior, but because just reading the description of the various ways that smiling/laughter promote engagement makes me feel good. I, too, am reenergized and up-regulated.

Neurobiology and Attachment

The literature and research on the neurobiology of attachment provided important scaffolding for my earlier work on crying and attachment. In it I found confirmation of my belief that repeated cycles of negative arousal and crying met by caregiver attunement and regulation were at the heart of the formation of the attachment bond. While I was reading and studying about crying, however, another idea kept leaping out at me, one that had not previously registered in my consciousness. That is, that positive arousal and the ways that caregivers respond—or do not respond—are equally at the core of the attachment process. For example, I read the following regarding the anterior cingulate area of the human medial-frontal cortex: it is "a region involved in play and separation behaviors, *laughing and crying* [italics added] vocalizations" (Schore, 2003a, p. 158). It is laughter *and* crying, play *and* separation that are responsible for maintaining contact between mothers and their offspring. Not only are both attachment behaviors but both also initiate points of mutual contact between caregiver and infant. Laughter and crying also represent what we might call the yin and yang necessary to maintain the balance required for maintaining security while exploring the new and unfamiliar.

Laughter is specifically mentioned from time to time throughout interpersonal neurobiological literature, along with the related positive affects, elation and mutual delight. In Schore (2003a), for example, I read that "stable attachment bonds that transmit high levels of positive affect [laughter] are vitally important for the infant's continuing neurobiological development" (p. 10). Positive arousal is important for several reasons. First of all, it has been "well established both that [positive arousal] is the affective state that underlies and motivates attachment behavior and that the combination of joy and interest motivates attachment bond formation" (p. 10). Further, as Schore (2003a) also points out, positive arousal promotes "a symbiotic entrainment between the mother's mature and the infant's immature nervous systems" (p. 10). "Symbiotic entrainment" refers to the mutual engagement of the nervous systems of caregiver and infant. In other words, when either initiates a smile or a laugh, it triggers a response in the other, and the party begins. A caregiver makes a funny face, the baby giggles, and the caregiver does it again. Everybody is having a good time, laughing, smiling, and feeling positively aroused, and everybody keeps coming back for more good times and good feelings. The baby may instigate the fun, too. Maybe he or she puts a finger on the caregiver's nose and makes a cute sound. The caregiver smiles and the baby smiles back. Positive arousal, like negative, is mutual and contagious.

Ainsworth (1964) describes this process of mutual entrainment as occurring because the behaviors of the infant are designed to evoke a response from the caregiver and thereby set off "a chain of interaction which serves to consolidate the affectional relationship" (p. 51). Sroufe (1995) goes further in defining this "chain of interaction" as "the dyadic regulation of emotion" (p. 172). Initiating positive arousal is mutual play; regulating the arousal at comfortable levels is mutual as well. Both are two-person or dyadic relational experiences. Dyadic or interactive emotional regulation not only helps to consolidate the attachment bond, but it is also "a harbinger of the self-regulation that is to come" (p. 172). Looking at attachment formation with these new neurobiological glasses, I began to see how when a caregiver makes a funny noise and the baby giggles, the moment of shared delight is not only intense and important for the child's developing sense of security and play, but it is also important for the child's developing nervous system and future ability to regulate affect.

Up-regulation or intensification of positive arousal is accomplished through the symbiotic entrainment that helps the baby or caregiver go from a quiet or even slightly distressed state to a playful, positive one. When my grandson Leo, at 6 months old, started to get fussy at the beach while his mother and sister were swimming, I took him over and dangled his feet in the water on the shore. He went in a flash from fussing and squirming to splashing his feet and laughing. On the other side of the equation, if there are too much excitement and overstimulation, a little down-regulating or de-escalation of positive arousal would be in order. That happened one time when Leo laughed so hard at his mother's silly noises that he got the hiccups. At that point his mother switched over to talking with him in a bemused but soothing tone and nursed him for a bit so he could calm and be ready for more play.

When a baby cries, it signals negative arousal and engages the caregiver by creating a parallel state in that person (another example of the "symbiotic entrainment" mentioned by Schore). Soothing or regulating the baby's negative affect similarly soothes and quiets the internal state of the caregiver. It is the repetition of these mutual ongoing arousal, attunement/misattunement, and interactive regulation/repair cycles—positive and negative, up-regulating or intensifying and down-regulating or de-intensifying—between infant and caregiver that results in attachment bond formation during the first year of life.

Crying in infancy is prototypically triggered by *separation* from the primary caregiver; it is a calling for the return of the caregiver's presence in order to receive the soothing touch and words of comfort that will regulate or de-intensify the negative arousal. On the other hand, the warm, fuzzy attachment behaviors such as smiling, laughter, and cooing take place almost exclusively *in the presence* of the caregiver. Both attachment behaviors exist to increase proximity between child and caregiver and both require ongoing affect attunement and regulation. Crying brings and keeps the caregiver close so that the crying will stop, whereas smiling and laughter signal the child's interest in interaction, thereby encouraging and prolonging contact. The end point of both attachment behaviors, however, is proximity and positive arousal.

Characteristics of Laughter as Attachment Behavior

Laughter as Connection

While infant laughter prototypically occurs in response to playful interactions with familiar caregivers, sometimes it represents a simple wish to be connected with the caregiver(s). When my granddaughter Aurelia was about 7 or 8 months old, she was sitting on the kitchen floor with her head deep inside the cupboard playing with pots and pans. Her parents and I were standing right next to her talking about politics and we started laughing. She promptly pulled her head out of the cupboard, looked up at us, and started laughing, too. She wanted, it appeared, to join with us even though she had no visual or other interactive cues (beyond the auditory ones) that would have elicited her laughter. By contrast, a few months later, I was taking care of her in an empty classroom next door to one full of a lively group of adult students. Although loud laughter repeatedly came from the group in the next room, Aurelia did not even look up from the book we were reading or acknowledge the laughter in any way. Apparently, the only laughter she was interested in joining was that of her attachment figures, not that of strangers; this is another hallmark of attachment behaviors.

Laughter in infancy is about initiating and reinforcing playful togetherness with familiar caregivers. It is a signal of and strong hook inviting positive engagement organized around a wide variety of interactive play and games, from funny faces and silly noises, to peekaboo, bouncing balls, or horsy rides. Even tickling, that dependable infant laugh inducer, requires the participation of a safe caregiver, since, as Darwin (1872/1965) pointed out, we are unable to tickle ourselves. An unfamiliar tickler, or one not convincingly vetted by soothing parental looks or sounds, will engender fear and crying rather than laughter. Laughter researchers Panksepp and Burgdorf (2003)—who literally tickles rats and makes them "chirp" with laughter, which can be seen on YouTube (Panksepp, 2007b)—wrote that the response integration system for laughter is evolutionarily prepared to respond to certain environmental events, such as tickle and friendly surprising stimuli, so as to facilitate social interactions and to take them in positive directions in ways that promote bonding and cooperative activities. (p. 543)

Panksepp and Burgdorf (2003) also wrote that "one might imagine laughter and mirth to be global attractor processes that captivate widely reverberating ensembles of neural networks within the brain of one individual that can spread infectiously among interacting individuals" (p. 543). Certainly more than 56 million hits (as of March 2012) would qualify the YouTube video entitled, "Twin boys laughing at each other" (wildminer, 2007) as a "global attractor." These little guys, age 4 months, are lying on their sides facing each other. During moments of direct eye contact, one would start laughing and the other would giggle right along with him. It happens repeatedly in the space of this short clip and speaks to nothing more directly than the bond between the two, as neither has a toy or a tickle or a joke to offer, just the gaze and the giggle and those "neural networks" spreading the joy of connection from brother to brother—and to more than 56 million strangers (and counting) on the Internet.

Freud (1905/1983) made particular note of another attachment aspect of laughter: the familiar compulsion to share a joke or a laugh. The flourishing networks of online joke sharing give daily evidence of this. So did my friend Pattie when we were sitting a few seats apart at a Teresa Tudury house concert. When the singer came to the line "I want to talk to Mrs. God," from her song "The Phone Call," a tongue-in-cheek social and religious protest song that I found hilarious, I glanced down the row to find Pattie leaning forward to make eye contact with me so we could share our laughter. The well-known bonding experience of communal laughter is familiar to almost all adults, in groups (comedy clubs, business meetings, church congregations) and in individual relationships, ranging from lovers to friends and even occasionally with strangers. The "bonding" aspects of hostile laughter are also well-known and will be discussed from an attachment perspective in later chapters.

Laughter as the Link Between Attachment and Exploratory Systems

Proximity to the attuned caregiver provides more than literal protection from danger. It also provides a different kind of safety, the kind that enables the child to begin to explore new objects, experiences, people, and places. Engaging with a caregiver in playful, positive interactions through laughter is the beginning stage in learning how to interact and make one's way in the world of social relationships and also in learning about the affects those interactions generate. One of the primary purposes of the attachment bond is to provide a sense of safety and security in the infant; the bond with the attachment figure/caregiver serves "as a secure base for exploration" (Sroufe & Waters, 1977, p. 1186), enabling the infant to move beyond what is safe and explore the unfamiliar. The need for exploration and play is central for learning about and adapting to our environment, which is necessary for learning and survival.

Aurelia, my little research n of 1, for example, demonstrated the connection between laughing, exploratory learning, and the caregiver as secure base when at 6 months she was riding in the baby carrier facing away from her daddy's chest. I had given her a new blue ball, and he would bounce it on the floor and catch it right in front of her. Each time he caught it, she giggled delightedly. What better "secure base" could she have had for enjoying this new experience than the proximity and physical touch of her father? Her laughter signaled her delight and her wish to continue the fun, thus creating a moment of mutual delight between father and daughter.

In the current view of attachment as being the dyadic regulation of affect, proximity is, of course, necessary in order for interactive regulation to occur. "Active parental participation in state regulation is critical to enabling the child to shift from the negative affective states of hyperaroused distress or hypoaroused deflation to a reestablished state of positive affect" (Schore, 2003b, p. 11). Likewise, the infant requires the presence of the caregiver to encourage, prolong, and heighten positive encounters. It does not seem possible to any significant degree for the infant to create or intensify her own positive arousal in isolation any more than it is possible to tickle yourself.

Laughter as Affect Regulation

Gentle laughter sometimes signals that negative arousal has decreased and positive arousal has occurred, and sometimes laughter helps to bring that about. To help a child recover from a minor tumble, for example, a parent might say, with a lighthearted, sympathetic chuckle, "Did that old sidewalk try to take a bite out of your knee?" Or, once the crisis is over and the Band-Aid applied, a lighthearted comment might help the child up-regulate her positive arousal and return to play.

I was not trying to make Aurelia laugh at the playground when she was an 11-month-old tired and crying for her mother. I hugged her as we sat on the bench and explained that we would have to wait a little longer for Mama to return. When she stopped crying and was sitting quietly in my lap, I asked if she wanted a rice cracker, to which she nodded yes. She was speedily chomping through the cracker and I said, "Does that cracker feel good on your toofeys?" She started to laugh. With my help (proximity and regulation in the language of attachment), she had been able to come back from negative arousal to positive, signaled by her laughter.

Affect regulation does not always refer to a return to positive affect from negative arousal. It also includes the generation of or up-regulation to heightened positive affect through play. The caregiver uses a variety of techniques to help stimulate smiling and laughter. One of the "laughing baby" videos on YouTube (Spacelord72) that I frequently play for my classes to illustrate infant laughter (and it consistently up-regulates everyone's affect) shows a child of about 10 months breaking into irresistible belly laughs every time his dad makes a particular guttural throat sound. When the baby's laughter winds down and stops, he looks around for more. As soon as the sound recurs, the baby starts a laugh cycle all over again.

Sroufe and Wunsch's (1972) infant laughter research turned up numerous other examples of parent-evoked laughter in infants, including mothers popping their lips, putting a washcloth in their mouths and shaking it, or pretending to suck on the baby's bottle—all particularly effective laugh-inducing behaviors for babies under 1 year of age. Aurelia's mother's wing-flapping chicken dance that kept her laughing for a few months near her first birthday could be added to this list along with quite a few innovative parental moves I found on the Internet, such as "Baby laughing hysterically over ripping paper" (BruBearBaby, 2011), the paper being his dad's job rejection letter (not only Dad and baby, but also more than 39 million viewers, as of March 2012, have been up-regulated by this video). Laughter in the early months of life, as in these examples, is primarily parent/caregiver generated with lively, appealing laughter assuring mutual interaction and shared positive arousal in both the parental and infant partners. It goes a long way toward evoking positive arousal for the rest of us, too.

Laughter as Attachment Behavior Throughout Life

In order to make the case that laughter is an attachment behavior, as we have seen, it is necessary to locate it squarely in the attachment system in infancy—as an inborn behavior that occurs spontaneously in the development of all infants somewhere between the third and fourth months of life. However, Bowlby (1969) also said "attachment behavior does not disappear with childhood but persists throughout life" (p. 350) in modified, less intense, or more complex forms. Researchers have pointed out that infant laughter and adult laughter strongly resemble each other; both rely on similar devices for humor and both consistently link laughter with exploration and play. Gervais and Wilson (2005) make the further point that not only are infant and adult laughter related behaviors, both also share much common ground with primate laughter (though there is a different acoustical pattern):

> Taken together, the laughter of nonhuman primates, the spontaneous laughter of human infants, tickling, and formal adult humor all share what is essentially a phylogenetically and ontogenetically-conserved structure and context here referred to as nonserious social incongruity. (p. 399)

Laughter, like other attachment behaviors, is inborn and interpersonal, but how we relate to each other—and what we find funny—is highly influenced by social context. Laughter is "inhibited and elicited in accordance with display rules and varying norms and customs" (Gervais & Wilson, 2005, p. 400) meaning that an instance of laughter is codetermined by biology and culture. Physical comedy, however, is the one type that may transcend cultures. Stick a red ball on your nose and people anywhere in the world, if they feel safe, will laugh at you. Tell a joke about American politics, however, and only those who follow the details—and probably only those who agree with your political views—will laugh with you. Hours after an earthquake struck Washington, DC, on August 25, 2011, Internet jokesters were declaring that it occurred on a heretofore unknown fault line called "Obama's fault." People of all parties and persuasions found that laugh-out-loud funny, if for different reasons. However, in a few decades, if not sooner, this particular humor may be lost on everyone.

An attachment classification of laughter in adulthood is the foundation for understanding laughter throughout life. A broader classification of laughter from an attachment perspective, however, must be able to incorporate a number of dichotomies, paradoxes, and apparent contradictions while building on that foundation. In the following chapter, we will explore the ways in which laughter in the attachment system links with other systems of behavior, such as the hostility/conflict system and the sexual/mating system, and at how distinguishing between genuine, shared Duchenne laughter and the titters, chortles, chuckles, and guffaws of non-Duchenne laughter will enable us to begin to formulate an understanding of laughter throughout life in all its forms and complexities.

2

TYPES OF LAUGHTER

Human laughter, as Keltner (2009) points out, is "stunning in its diversity and complexity."

> There are derisive laughs, flirtatious laughs, singsongy laughs, embarrassed groans, piercing laughs, laughs of tension, silent, head-lightening laughs of euphoria, barrel-chested laughs of strength, laughs that signal the absurdity of the shortness of life and the extent to which we care about our existence, contemptuous laughs that signal privilege and class, and laughs that are little more than grunts or growls. (p. 125)

The first way to account for this incredible diversity, while staying grounded in an attachment perspective, is to distinguish between involuntary belly laughs, known as Duchenne laughter, and manufactured, low-key conversational laughs, known as non-Duchenne laughter, both named for the French neurologist in the 1800s who first made the distinction. The second is to understand the ways in which laughter bridges from the attachment system to other systems of behavior.

Duchenne and Non-Duchenne Laughter

Duchenne laughter is the genuine, uncontrolled, involuntary expression of positive affect. Non-Duchenne laughter, on the other hand, is more of a conversational insert appearing without conscious forethought—though it can be voluntarily produced or inhibited—and representing a variety of positive or negative affects. The two types of laughter can often be distinguished by context as well as by some of their emotional and physiological attributes.

The primary distinction between the two types of laughter is based on work distinguishing types of smiles (Frank, Ekman, & Friesen, 1993). The physiological differences between Duchenne and non-Duchenne smiles are coded by measuring the action of the zygomatic major muscle and the orbicularis oculi muscles around the eye. These muscles, along a quality known as "eye brightness," produce the effect sometimes known as "smiley eyes" (Keltner & Bonanno, 1997; "Smile," 2008).

There appear to be acoustic differences between the types of laughter, as well. Duchenne laughs are "voiced" and have a measurable frequency that sounds tonal and song-like, whereas non-Duchenne laughs are "unvoiced" and sound atonal and noisier (Hudenko, Stone, & Bachorowski, 2009). From an affective standpoint, Duchenne laughter is thought to be more directly and consistently related to the experience of positive affect (Hudenko et al., 2009), whereas certain unvoiced laughs, such as the "grunt-like laughs" that suggest affirmation, may be only "loosely coupled with an individual's internal affective state" (p. 1394). Responses to the two types of laughter have been found to differ, with Duchenne laughter having a more positive impact on listeners (Bachorowski & Owren, 2001; Keltner & Bonanno, 1997). In addition to representing different emotional expressions, these two types of laughter may have different evolutionary pathways and developmental trajectories (Gervais & Wilson, 2005).

According to some research, the two types of laughter may have different neuro-biological coordinates and pathways, as well (Wild, Rodden, Grodd, & Ruch, 2003). The first, Duchenne laughter, is "an 'involuntary' or 'emotionally driven' system that involves the amygdala, thalamic/hypo- and subthalamic areas and the dorsal/tegmental brainstem. The second, non-Duchenne or so-called 'voluntary' laughter (in the sense that it can be volitionally produced and inhibited, though only rarely is that done with consciousness) originates in the premotor/frontal opercular areas and leads through the motor cortex and pyramidal tract to the ventral brainstem" (p. 2121). With some brain injuries or pathologies, one of these two pathways may work when the other does not, meaning that spontaneous eruptive laughter may occur in the absence of the ability to laugh voluntarily and vice versa (Wild et al., 2003).

Duchenne laughter is easily recognized as the belly laugh, the giggling fit, the doubling-over, tear-producing, spontaneous eruption of playful, audible, contagious positive affect. If this genuine, warm, joyous, love-filled laughter of connection is, as some theorists and researchers suggest, the evolutionary prototype of laughter (Gervais & Wilson, 2005), its link with the attachment system seems most clear. Likewise, the fact that it is an inborn skill appearing spontaneously within the first three or four months of life, promoting proximity and positive engagement, argues for its belonging to the attachment system, as we saw in the previous chapter's example about the Navajo ritual celebration of the infant's first laugh that celebrates these very qualities.

Non-Duchenne laughter is the most frequently occurring type of adult laughter, comprising about half of the laughter in typically developing young adults—and more in older adults (Bachorowski & Owren, 2001). Of the 1,200 examples of laughter Provine (2000) recorded in natural settings, most seem to be non-Duchenne, though he does not make that distinction. The laughter-inducing comments recorded were by and large triggered by "you-had-to-be-there" comments: "'I should do that, but I'm too lazy'; 'I try to lead a normal life'; or 'What can I say?'" (pp. 40–41). In fact, Provine's research team found that most of the conversation preceding the laughter they observed was "like that of an interminable television situation comedy scripted by an extremely ungifted writer" (p. 42).

Non-Duchenne laughter—sometimes meant to be humorous, sometimes not—greases the wheels of social relationships in a variety of ways. It can appear as chuckles, giggles, and guffaws accompanying affectionate teasing or joking around with friends and family. It also can be laughter that is nervous, flirtatious, appealing, or amused. Much non-Duchenne laughter is a conversational insert that helps to facilitate friendliness and avoid misunderstandings. It helps to fill in pauses, encourage conversations to keep rolling, maintain the interest and attention of a partner, disguise embarrassment, or offer an apology.

All of these subtle cues wrapped up in a non-Duchenne giggle or chortle are, like all laughter, part of our implicit, procedural system of relating to each other and operating out of conscious awareness. We rarely *decide* to laugh—it is spontaneous and unscripted—even in moments when no humor exists. Non-Duchenne laughter could be stopped volitionally if necessary, unlike Duchenne laughter, though most of the time we are not even aware that we have inserted a laugh into the conversational mix.

At its best, non-Duchenne laughter bolsters cohesion in families, among friends and even strangers (Foot & Chapman, 1996), and is a powerful tool we use for the dyadic regulation of affect. It helps us in monitoring, attuning, and regulating our own and other's affects. At its worst, non-Duchenne laughter that is mean, critical, or bullying crosses over from the attachment system to the conflict system, promoting detachment—or enabling one group of people to attach at the expense of another group, a topic for our consideration below.

Laughter Linked to Other Behavioral Systems

Another way to account for different types of laughter throughout life is to look at the ways in which laughter migrates into, or bridges between, attachment and other behavioral systems. Sroufe (1995) argues that no behavior "in the service of attachment" is "exclusively an attachment behavior" (p. 175). Beginning with laughter and the exploration/play system and ending with laughter and the conflict/appeasement system, the following sections briefly introduce the links between the relevant behavioral systems and laughter as attachment, which will be discussed and illustrated in greater detail in subsequent chapters.

The Exploration/Play System

Laughter researcher Panksepp (2000) has said that laughter is the evolutionary relative of play. The inborn exploratory/play system is motivated by our urge, beginning in infancy, to experience the novel, the unexplained, and the unexpected. This description dovetails with the incongruity theory of laughter, which postulates that novelty and surprise are key ingredients for much of our laughter. At 6 months old, my grandson Leo liked the incongruity of gentle tummy kisses, ice cubes in a bowl, and the goofy antics of his big sister jumping around on the bed. Personally, I laughed while reading an unexpected headline in the newspaper about an 83-year-old man being injured by an exploding bottle of prune juice and, a few days later, about a woman whose mother's ashes were stolen when she took them to a bingo game for good luck. Leo is still learning about the world and other people through safe encounters with the incongruent and surprising—so, apparently, am I.

Sroufe (1995) stresses the importance of the exploratory system saying that it is "as much a part of human survival as attachment itself, given the role of environmental mastery in human adaptation" (p. 175). Ainsworth stresses the interplay between the attachment and the exploratory/play system. As she puts it, "The dynamic equilibrium between the two behavioral systems is even more significant for development and for survival than either in isolation" (as cited in Cassidy, 2008, p. 8).

The link between the two systems is most in evidence when the child uses the caregiver as a secure base for exploration. Grossman, Grossman, Kindler, and Zimmerman (2008) point out that in order to learn about new environments and try new skills, a young child must be able to balance "appropriate fear of novelty and danger" (p. 858) with a feeling of security. It is the attuned caregiver who provides a safe, protective circle for the child and who first successfully helps the infant to expand his or her exploratory frontiers. It is the caregiver who initiates the surprises, as in peekaboo or "I'm gonna getcha." The caregiver provides the secure base, the stamp of approval, so the baby feels safe enough to embrace incongruity and express playful delight through laughter. Negative arousal and exploration as well as negative arousal and play simply do not go together. Positive arousal and security are a prerequisite for both exploration and play.

Laughter and the Sociability/Affiliative System

The affiliative system, sometimes called the sociability system, represents the "desire to do things in company with others" (Bowlby, 1969, p. 229). It includes the behavioral expressions of friendliness and goodwill that support this aim. Most affiliative behaviors originate in the attachment system—smiling, friendly approach, laughter, hugging, touch, affectionate kissing, and interactive affect regulation—making the link between the two systems a particularly direct one. Affiliative bonds are often playful as well, revolving around positive arousal and laughter. Aurelia, at age four, met up with some new children on the beach and soon they were building sand castles and giggling as they squashed them with their bare feet. An acquaintance-on-the-way-to-becoming-a-friend recently entertained me with a funny, profanity-laced political tirade that had me in stitches and wanting more: more laughter and more time with him.

Affiliation refers to the broader circle of friendships that begin with the network of playmates in childhood. It grows outward from the original playmates—caregivers, grandparents, siblings, and other well-known adults and children in an infant's safe circle. Also, from an evolutionary survival standpoint, there is safety in numbers when it comes to the need for protection. Exploration is also more fun—and safer—with one's age-mates, making affiliation an attractive and pleasurable way to engage with and master one's environment.

Certain types of non-Duchenne or conversational laughter also indicate and produce pleasure, thereby prolonging social contact, encouraging ongoing connection, and, in close relationships, increasing intimacy (Keltner & Bonanno, 1997). Provine (1993) points out that the speaker in a conversation laughs up to 46% more than listeners, presumably because he or she is motivated to promote a positive connection and smooth over awkward or potentially conflicted interactions. It colors how the words are received and invites connection by making togetherness playful and fun, and keeps it that way by preventing misunderstandings and regulating potential negative affect.

Laughter and the Caregiving System

Caregiving behaviors include all of the ways that caregivers approach and respond to infants. The list of caregiving behaviors I compiled when I was writing about crying includes smiling, gazing, singing, talking, cuddling, laughing, snuggling/nuzzling, carrying, kissing, hugging, rocking, and holding, all of which require physical contact or proximity (Nelson, 2005). The primary focus in the attachment literature, however, has been on caregiving behaviors for purposes of down-regulating too much negative arousal, primarily distress and crying.

A caregiver who initiates a playful interaction designed to intensify and up-regulate positive arousal and produce laughter is also engaging in caregiving behavior. Positive arousal, as we have seen, plays a key role in the formation of secure attachment, affect regulation, and neurological development, though this aspect of caregiving behavior has been under-discussed in the attachment literature. Positive engagement between caregiver and infant has been always acknowledged, particularly in regard to smiling, but the emphasis has remained on responding to and down-regulating or soothing negative arousal.

When the attachment system is defined, as it has been classically, as consisting of behaviors that encourage proximity for purposes of protecting an infant from danger, it follows that a, if not *the*, primary goal of caregiving is to restore security by responding to or down-regulating and de-intensifying negative arousal or distress (Bowlby, 1969). Modern attachment theory, however, expands the definition of attachment to include the dyadic (two-person) or mutual regulation of all affect, both negative and positive. This means that the caregiver is a necessary partner in all types of arousal. Based on insights and knowledge gained from neurobiological research, we see that the attachment/caregiving system serves both these functions: attuning to and regulating positive and negative arousal. Gazing, smiling, holding, and cooing are all important caregiving behaviors that down-regulate negative arousal, such as when we hug an upset, crying little grandson Leo. However, attuned caregiving responses to positive arousal are equally important, as when we nuzzle Leo's neck and smile when he laughs at us.

Smiling and laughter are, at times, attuned caregiving behaviors that help down-regulate negative arousal as well as attuning to and up-regulating positive arousal or helping to regulate it when the infant is overstimulated in play. The affect regulation is not always unidirectional from caregiver to infant. Just as a crying infant can create negative arousal in a caregiver (Nelson, 2005), an infant can also do something cute and unexpected, arousing laughter and helping to up-regulate positive arousal in a caregiver who is out of sorts. In fact, sometimes when I am having a frustrating day, I invite Aurelia and Leo over to play and experience an upsurge in positive arousal immediately.

Laughter and the Sexual/Mating System

As Bowlby (1969) pointed out, the attachment and the sexual systems are distinct, but "there is good evidence also that they are apt to impinge on each other and to influence the development of each other. This occurs in other species as well as in man" (p. 233). Clinging and kissing, he points out, are common to both systems. Laughter, rooted in attachment, similarly finds its way into the sexual mating system in the form of flirtatious or seductive laughter. Laughter researcher Panksepp (2007b) points out that laughter may "index willingness for social engagement, similar to human infantile laughter, which may mature into productive adult socio-sexual behaviors" (p. 231).

A German researcher, Karl Grammer (2005), has analyzed laughter in opposite-sex encounters. Laughter, together with bodily postures and movements, conveys messages "that range from sexual solicitation to aversion" (p. 209). Gender differences in frequency of laughter have also been noted by researchers. Most studies show that females laugh far more frequently than males, while males lead the way in frequency of eliciting laughs. While status and power issues may influence this difference, some as-yet-unidentified differences in our reproductive systems, hormones in particular, may also play a possible role. In an analysis of personals ads, Provine (2000) found that 13% of the ads studied mentioned laughter or laughter-related behaviors as being desirable. Females were 62% more likely to mention it than men.

Of course the overlap between sex and humor is well-known, in regard to so-called off-color jokes, labeled by Freud (1905/1983) as "tendentious" jokes. He writes, "A non-tendentious joke scarcely ever achieves the sudden burst of laughter which makes tendentious ones so irresistible" (p. 96). Of course, his comment raises questions about the role that both culture and gender play in who laughs how much and when at tendentious jokes. When Freud writes, "A person who laughs at smut that he hears is laughing as though he were the spectator of an act of sexual aggression" (p. 97), he is not specifically referring to either gender or culture. Nonetheless, pointing out this particular overlap between laughter and the sex/mating and conflict/aggression systems does imply a connection, one that is well-known among feminists and others who study acts of sexual aggression.

Laughter and the Conflict/Aggression/ Appeasement System

The link between laughter and aggression is also acknowledged in the familiar distinction we make between laughing *with* someone and laughing *at* someone. While laughing *at* someone can lead to the opposite of attachment, which is *detachment*, it can also promote attachment to one's confederates.

Hostile laughter, as perhaps all of us know, is sometimes a great bonding element between intimates. In college, my like-minded classmates and I called our, to us hilarious, joking around "mocking," and it was our staple of humor. We had nicknames for college administrators and theological concepts; we called our religious school's theological orientation "fundy," short for fundamentalist. We entertained ourselves with outrageous humorous fantasies of broadcasting our apostasies, all venting our rebellious hostility at our parental and *in-loco-parentis* caregivers. It separated us from them and bound us inextricably to each other as we marched together toward individuation.

The link between laughter and the conflict/aggression system may have evolutionary roots. Darwin (1872/1965) pointed out that the expressions for the sneer, the snarl, and the grin have in common bared teeth. The snarl is a fighting signal among primates and canines, accompanied by bright, fierce eyes. The friendly grin also involves bared teeth, but the eyes are bright and playful rather than hostile. The sneer is a cross between the two; it is laughter in a hostile manner. Darwin wrote, "Our semi-human progenitors uncovered their canine teeth when prepared for battle, as we still do when feeling ferocious, or when merely sneering at or defying [or laughing at] someone, without any intention of making a real attack with our teeth" (p. 252).

Although it seems more likely that laughter evolved separately through playful encounters between safe caregivers and age-mates, the overlap between the expressions is interesting. Somehow, a behavior designed to advance and enhance attachment can at times also engender detachment. Sometimes called "dark laughter" (Panksepp, 2000), this usually mirthless laughter is used for derision, ridicule, put-downs, establishing dominance, bullying, cruelty, mocking, scapegoating, shaming, and scorn. Dark laughter occurs in aggressive, nervous, or hierarchical contexts, functioning to manipulate, exclude, judge, deride, or subvert the victim. Perpetrators also use cruel laughter to increase their own positive arousal, making them feel better and more in control. They also manipulatively use the bonding power of laughter to recruit allies, perhaps out of fear that they, too, might become a target, or because they have been one in the past.

Some dark-side laughter may also be trauma-based dissociated affect, broken off from its original function in order to deflect, derail, or numb unbearable pain. The evil, destructive laughter of the Joker in *Batman*, who was aimed at destroying the people of Gotham City, is probably the most iconic example in popular culture. It will be taken up as a case study in a later chapter.

Another permutation of laughter in its relationship to the conflict/hostility system is appeasement aimed at avoiding or signaling the end of conflict. The "I was only kidding" dodge, often accompanied by a non-Duchenne laugh, is one such example. Sometimes, the non-Duchenne laugh alone suggests the same thing. Laughter, as many couples know, can also help to derail an argument. Welcome is the moment in my relationship when one of us sees the humor in our disagreement and manages to successfully derail the conversation. We have even designated a few humorous signals to help us lighten up in tense moments, "TOV" (tone of voice) being one of the most effective. Laughter not only helps to bring about the resolution, but it can also signal its arrival to the relief of everyone.

Appeasement behaviors used to avert the eruption of overt conflict are also considered part of the conflict/hostility system. Laughter, particularly Duchenne laughter, is often used in that way. It serves as a sign that the person should take one's comments lightly or with a grain of salt rather than literally. Laughter, too, may signal the end of an argument, a kind of makeup behavior that signals a return to connection and good spirits between foes or combatants.

Laughter and the Fear/Wariness System

There is a natural link between the fear/wariness system and the attachment system. Anxiety and fear are the primary forms of distress that trigger attachment behaviors and call for regulating, soothing responses from caregivers. Early in life, crying would be the primary link to the fear/wariness system, as fear in an infant would preclude laughter.

Later in life, however, anxious laughter appears. It is a common phenomenon, serving both to defensively ward off fear, and, at times, also as an attachment appeal to caregivers for soothing it. Nervous laughter can mean everything from "I need help" to "I'm harmless," to "I hope you are harmless," or "Please be nice to me." It can be a signal to the other person that no harm is intended and the interaction is a safe one. It sometimes overlaps with laughter as a sexual behavior, such as when people approaching potential romantic partners giggle nervously. This laughter indicates interest coupled with the vulnerability to rejection in making an approach or being approached (Grammer, 2005). Defending against while communicating vulnerability may also occur in other social contexts where power differentials are an issue.

Viewing laughter as an attachment behavior with primary ties to the caregiving and exploration/curiosity/play systems offers a way to understand its core meaning and its diverse presentations. Understanding that laughter is an attachment behavior linked to other systems of behavior helps make it possible to begin to define and classify different types of laughter. The impact of these various systems and their respective functions will become clearer throughout the following chapters on laughter and infancy, childhood, and adult life, as well as in the chapters on laughter in the therapeutic relationship and the clinical hour.

3

THEORIES ABOUT LAUGHTER FROM AN ATTACHMENT PERSPECTIVE

The Psychology of Laughter and Comedy (Greig, 1923) lists a total of 94 different theories of humor and laughter. The list begins with Plato in 388 BCE and ends in 1921 CE when the manuscript was completed. The list would be considerably longer if we were to add the theories that have appeared in subsequent years.

For a writer attempting to outline a new attachment-theory approach to laughter, this abundance of theories is a nice problem to have—quite unlike the one I faced when applying attachment theory to crying. Then, with the exception of a limited one-dimensional discharge theory, I was almost completely in uncharted theoretical territory. With laughter, I have had the luxury of looking through the history of the theories and seeing where they broached attachment concepts and where their blind alleys and unsatisfactory conclusions could be explained using an attachment approach.

Strictly speaking, it is a misnomer to call the theories on Greig's list theories of laughter, although many of theorists do so. Laughter is often mentioned in them, but most often laughter is subsumed under the larger, related—though different— topic of humor, jokes, or comedy. Laughter is considered a by-product of humor or comedy or as evidence of their existence or success. Most humor and comedy theories focus on cognitive and verbal aspects rather than on the underlying implicitly understood and relational qualities that relate to laughter itself. For the most part, they also overlook the spontaneous, mutually created moments of shared laughter in the discourse of daily life, focusing instead on laughter evoked in the course of stage plays, films, stand-up comedy routines, or in response to set-piece jokes.

Humor, jokes, and comedy are the cognitive backdrop of laughter to which intellectual analysis and theorizing is naturally more drawn. Reddy (2008), however, strongly suggests (and I agree) that humor is also relational:

> The science of humour is probably better built through an explication of the structure of its processes than through trying to build processes out of

its supposed structures. Fundamentally, then, it takes an engagement between two people (at least) for funniness to begin to exist. Painting humour
as a textual phenomenon—focusing on it primarily as the structure of a
joke—is destructive, not only for understanding when it begins, but also for
understanding how it exists even in adults. Funniness exists only in relation.
(p. 214)

If observed from a relational standpoint, most theories of humor and the comic
do recognize that an audience of some type is required for humor to succeed, if
not for it to exist in the first place. As we will see, this is true of each of the three
primary categories of humor theories: the superiority or disparagement theory,
incongruity theory, and discharge theory. We will look at each of these theories to
see what they tell us about laughter and attachment, and then, reversing the lens,
see what an attachment viewpoint explains about the strengths and weaknesses of
these theories.

The Superiority or Disparagement Theory

The superiority or disparagement theory of humor and laughter held sway for
almost 2,000 years. It is, simply put, the theory that laughter aimed at another
person is a way to put them in their place. Plato takes issue with this kind of
status-enhancing laughter at others. He points to people who laugh at a person
whom they consider "ridiculous" because "he entertains a false conceit of his
wealth, beauty, or wisdom," though he is not so powerful as to be dangerous or in-
cite fear. When these conditions are met, "his friends take a malicious pleasure in
laughter at him; they express the spite, malice, or offense excited by his pretensions
in laughter" (Gardiner, Metcalf, & Beebe-Center, 1937, p. 19). Plato considered
derisive laughter such as this to be rude and immature. He cautions in the *Republic*
(360 BCE/1957) that public officials "ought not to be ready laughers." Poets, too,
he enjoins not "to represent men of repute as overcome by laughter, much less to
represent the gods in such a case" (p. 388).

When Plato takes an ethical position against ridiculing the foibles of high-
minded people, he is recognizing that laughter is an interpersonal issue. His arguments run parallel to those used in discussions of laughter that accompanies hostile
teasing and bullying where the relationship power of laughter is turned upside
down. Hostile derisive laughter is often used to evoke shame and negative arousal
(in the victim) and create distance/detachment (from the victim) on the one hand,
and bonding (with fellow ridiculers) on the other, rather than promoting positive
arousal and positive connection.

Aristotle, in the same vein as Plato, is apparently suspicious of laughter, when he
calls the ridiculous "a species of the ugly" (as cited in Morreall, 1987, p. 14). He
counsels tact, propriety, and respect for the feelings of others in regard to humor
and laughter, all social values that enhance attachment and affiliative connections

of all kinds, from the intimate to the casual acquaintance. He also distinguishes between dramatic comedy and "invective or injurious personal satire," making room for the former (Paddington, 1933, p. 153). In successful dramatic productions, comedic techniques create a powerful connection among the playwright, actors, and audience. Laughter serves as both a means of connection (affiliation, attachment) and an affirmation that it exists.

When Aristotle describes laughter as a physiological process that is "independent of the will" (Fudge, 2003, p. 280), he is also pointing to an attribute of other inborn attachment behaviors. Deep, unfeigned, Duchenne laughter, like crying, is, for the most part, outside of voluntary control, even in adulthood.

Foreshadowing present-day neurobiological attachment research, Aristotle also touches on the interpersonal affect-regulation potential of laughter when he refers to Gorgias's idea that "one should destroy one's opponents' seriousness with laughter, and their laughter with seriousness." In a similar vein, he notes that laughter is used to "win one's audiences' amused approval and thus to manipulate the mood of a public gathering in one's own favour" (as cited in Halliwell, 1991, p. 293). Quintilian, a Greek philosopher and educator who died in 100 BCE, also touches on laughter as a means of regulating affect by "dissipating melancholy impressions . . . unbending the mind from too intense application, . . . renewing its powers and recruiting its strength, after being surfeited and fatigued" (as cited in Paddington, 1933, p. 227).

A modern proponent of what he calls the normative superiority theory, Buckley (2003) argues that there is a positive moral connotation in the humor of disparagement that may promote social conformity in a good way. He suggests that the three-sided relational equation of jester, listener, and "butt" of the joke can be a good-natured means of coaching the butt of the joke about social expectations for the good of the group rather than necessarily being about hostility. He correctly points out that there is often a tie of solidarity in the laughter of the listener and the jester. "Coaching" the butt about social expectations also implies a relationship. He wrote, "In identifying a butt, laughter's message is both negative and positive. We are told what not to do if we wish to avoid becoming a butt, and also what to do if we wish to immunize ourselves against laughter" (p. xii).

Along this line, it would seem that pointing out minor foibles or missteps through affectionate teasing can also be a way of expressing closeness appreciated by both partners. What couple does not have their in-jokes at one another's expense? Is one partner always rushing around in a frenzy before guests arrive? Is the other a stickler for square corners on the sheets, and towels hanging in perfect alignment? Good-natured teasing about individual peculiarities is both a corrective and a way of easing some hostility over minor irritants. Sometimes laughter, approaching ridicule, may be a signal and perhaps a corrective for attachment relationships that are unbalanced due to excessive self-involvement or "power trips" on the part of one member.

Sharing laughter at the expense of others can also be a way of emphasizing and enhancing one's sense of belonging to an "in-group," thus contributing to attachment or affiliation bonds. It can also be a way of expressing hostility toward others with whom we have differences, or of preempting hostile attacks. When friends and confederates joke about or make fun of others, it ranges from detached and hostile victimization to healthy protest against injustices; in either case, however, it can draw the instigators closer together. Of course the presence or absence of the "butt" is a big variable, the assumption being that a butt who does not hear the jokes does not suffer. At times, humor is a form of protest against harsh treatment, or prejudice, or stereotyping that helps to bond and bolster the victims. Laughter and poking fun at one's enemies is a means of expressing pain while also transforming it to something laughable.

Freud (1905/1983), for example, was a well-known collector of Jewish jokes, which he said amused him greatly. "We make no enquiries about their origin but only about their efficiency—whether they are capable of making us laugh and whether they deserve our theoretical interest. And both these two requirements are best fulfilled precisely by Jewish jokes" (p. 49). He was laughing as a Jew, identifying with other Jews—or sometimes at the expense of certain subgroups of Jews. He laughed on both sides of the in-group/out-group equation, joining simultaneously, if paradoxically, with both groups.

Freud distinguishes stories "created by Jews and directed against Jewish characteristics" (p. 111) from those about Jews that are "brutal comic stories" created by people who regard Jews as "comic figures" (p. 111). He points out that while Jews recognize this anti-Semitic element, they also recognize their real faults and the "connection between them and their good qualities" (p.111). He is also aware of the indirect expression of hostility these jokes represent when "the person concerned finds criticism or aggressiveness difficult so long as they are direct, and possible only along circuitous paths" (p. 142).

The Incongruity or Surprise Theory

In 1658, the theory of French physician De la Chambre, in contrast to seven different psychological theories of laughter in his day, expressed his view that for laughter to occur the "soul must be 'taken in' and surprised" in a gentle and agreeable manner (as cited in Gardiner et al., 1937, p. 138). Emphasizing the surprise of the soul is a poetic way of describing the implicit, nonconscious, interpersonal aspects of laughter. Further emphasizing its relational qualities, he insisted that a further condition for laughter is that there must be witnesses to it (Gardner et al., 1937, p. 138).

Immanuel Kant (in his *Critique of Judgment* published in 1790, as cited in Paddington, 1933) wrote that laughter is "an affection arising from the sudden transformation of a strained expectation into nothing" (p. 169). In other words, laughter is generated by a surprising, unexpected outcome. By way of an example, he says that a story about a man whose hair turns gray overnight as a result of a misfortune would not be funny. However, if the story were that overnight the man's *wig* turned gray, the unexpected twist would render it funny. (He was right in my case as I did laugh at the surprise twist.)

Arthur Schopenhauer, writing in the early to mid 1800s, believed that his carefully reasoned incongruity theory solved the problem of laughter's meaning. "The cause of laughter in every case is simply the sudden perception of the incongruity between a concept and the real objects which have been thought through it in some relation, and the laugh itself is just the expression of this incongruity" (as cited in Greig, 1923, pp. 253–254). Laughter, according to this theory, is the reaction that occurs when things that appear congruous are in fact not congruous (i.e., the hair and the wig in the example above).

Schopenhauer had another way of describing the pleasure in laughter at the ludicrous, which he believed represents the "victory of knowledge of perception over that of thought" (as cited in Paddington, 1933, p. 174). I rather like Schopenhauer's formulation and see it as moving from a cognitive exploration of intellectually crafted ideas to the implicit, nonlinear manifestations of playful and usually unplanned silliness. From the standpoint of the incongruity or surprise theories, laughter is not about formal jokes, humor, and comedy, but rather about procedural, implicit forms of knowing and relating that are consonant with present-day attachment theory and interpersonal neurobiology. Laughter represents moments of connection between two or more people, thereby creating and affirming the presence of the connection—as with Freud and his friends laughing over the "home-roulard" joke after dinner.

The other aspect of incongruency theory and laughter is that it supports the link between security in the attachment system and the exploratory system. Only when a child is comfortable and unafraid in the company of trusted caregivers will laughter at something unexpected occur. If a child, or for that matter an adult, is insecure, novelty and incongruity trigger fear and crying, not laughter.

The Discharge/Relief Theory

The laughter theory most cited in the 20th century, first described in the work of Herbert Spencer, is based on the idea that laughter results from the arousal of a large amount of nervous energy that is "suddenly checked in its flow" and thus "discharges itself" in some other direction. The result is "an efflux through the motor nerves to various classes of the muscles, producing the half-convulsive actions we term laughter" (as cited in Darwin, 1872/1965, p. 198). Freud, the primary source for the contemporary discharge theory of laughter, relied on Spencer's ideas and, early on, linked affective expressions such as crying and laughter to drive energy. His view was that some obstacle such as a defense or inhibition or social prohibition would "dam up" the affect related to drive energy—sexual or aggressive—and that a joke (and presumably laughter) would release or discharge that energy, bringing pleasure.

In his book looking at humor, wit from the standpoint of drive and discharge theory, Freud (1905/1983) focused his attention on jokes and their meaning and on the question of why certain word combinations evoke laughter. "What has happened to the thought… in order to turn it into a joke that made us laugh so heartily?" (p. 18). The joke in this particular instance is about a character named Hirsch-Hyacinth of Hamburg, a lottery agent and extractor of corns (pretty funny setup!) who boasts about his relationship with the wealthy Baron Rothschild. The punch line is, "Rothschild treated me quite as his equal—quite famillionairely" (p. 16). Though Freud says the remark made him laugh out loud, the laughter is treated as a by-product of the joke, as evidence that it is indeed funny. Freud immediately turns to cognitive, explicit analysis of the humor: "There can be no doubt that it is precisely on this *verbal structure* [italics added] that the joke's character as a joke and *its power to cause a laugh* depend" (p. 18). The power is seen to be in the cognitive gymnastics of the joke, not in the laugh, which is treated as the physical concomitant of humor.

Freud goes on to brilliantly analyze "joke technique," applying the psychoanalytic principles of condensation, economy, and substitute formation, which parallel the principles used to understand dreams. To Freud's credit, he understands that, while these principles are indeed at work and analyzable, the vehicle of the joke's laughter-compelling effect is "not made in any way clearer by our discovery of the joke-technique." He remains puzzled and asks, "In what way can a linguistic process of condensation accompanied by the formation of a substitute by means of a composite word, give us pleasure and make us laugh? This is evidently a different problem" (p. 20). Here Freud put his finger directly on the limitations of the explicit, cognitive, verbal approach to trying to understand laughter by understanding humor, jokes, wit, and the comic. Jokes are what evolutionists call the "proximate cause" or immediate precipitant of the laughter, but they tell us nothing about the "ultimate cause" of why we as a species laugh in the first place.

Freud does acknowledge the implicit procedural aspect of laughter when he writes, "Laughter is in fact the product of an automatic process which is only made possible by our conscious attention's being kept away from it" (p. 154). He recognizes in himself the implicit process involved in turning a "thought into a joke." In order to do so, it is necessary to "select from among the possible forms of expression the precise one which brings along with it a yield of verbal pleasure. We know from self-observation that this selection is not made by conscious attention" (p. 177). As we know and Freud understood, this is a lightening quick process that, as my former office partner used to joke, "skips upstairs," referring to its unconscious, as opposed to cognitive, origins.

The social power of jokes did not escape Freud's notice either: "A new joke acts almost like an event of universal interest; it is passed from one person to another like the news of the latest victory" (p. 15)—and that was before the Internet, where jokes get passed around social networks with lightning speed, linking us all together in cyber-laughter. Freud was also perfectly well aware that a funny joke is pleasurable to both the individual who makes it *and* the person who hears it. This recognition, however, left him with a confusing problem. How does viewing laughter as a discharge of drive energy account for its interpersonal aspects? For a joke to be successful, both the joker and the audience must feel pleasure, meaning that there must be discharge for all involved. He expressed the dilemma this way: "The process in the humorist must tally with the process in the hearer," though "in the hearer we must assume that there is only an echo, a copy, of this unknown process" (Freud, 1927, p. 162).

Freud's comment shows his awareness of the dilemma that occurs when a one-person discharge theory tries to explain mutual discharge of the type that takes place with jokes. The awareness of that contradiction points Freud toward 21st-century interpersonal affect theory, which looks at the mutuality of affect arousal and regulation. He also recognized, though using different language, that humorous exchanges occur at an implicit level rather than as a consciously understood and directed, explicit verbal exchange. His work, though focused on laughter as discharge, foreshadowed both an attachment view of laughter and a regulation theory approach to it as well.

As Freud continued to puzzle just how jokes work this magic, his list for categorizing joke technique grew to include condensation, substitution, double meaning, overstatement, analogies, displacement, faulty reasoning, absurdity, shifting of psychical emphasis, indirect representation, and representation by the opposite. As with others who have attempted categorizations of humor, the list goes on with no unifying themes visible. His dissatisfaction with the growing list is palpable when he writes, "The technical methods of joking which we have earlier described—displacement, indirect representation and so on—thus possess the power of evoking a feeling of pleasure in the hearer, though we cannot in the least see how they may have acquired this power" (Freud, 1905/1983, p. 95).

Freud is at his best in his analysis of what he calls "tendentious jokes," those that are hostile (aggressive) or obscene (sexual) in nature and therefore most clearly associated with drive discharge. Such jokes, he noted, elicit a "burst of laughter," indicating pleasure. However, he says, "We are not in a position to distinguish by our feeling what part of the pleasure arises from the sources of their technique and what part from those of their purpose. *Thus, strictly speaking, we do not know what we are laughing at*" (Freud, 1905/1983, p. 102; italics are as Freud made them in the original German version). Even when the technique is wretched, he says, these jokes may still provoke much laughter. Cognitive analysis, even at a complex symbolic level, left him with many questions unanswered. As others have pointed out, Freud's concept of the preconscious is one that, in part, parallels implicit, procedural thought processes. His description of comedy in this regard might also be applied to laughter: "Such processes, which run their course in the preconscious but lack the cathexis of attention with which consciousness is linked, may aptly be given the name of 'automatic.' The process . . . must remain automatic if it is to produce comic pleasure" (p. 220). Here he is pointing to the fact that explaining a joke's origins explicitly is almost impossible and doing so to the extent possible robs it of its comedic effect.

Furthering his foreshadowing of an attachment view of laughter, Freud was interested in the fact that tendentious jokes usually involve at least three people: the joke-maker, the object of the aggression, and the listener, who partakes of the pleasure by laughing at the joke. The joke-maker, Freud suggests, will "bribe the hearer," using the offered pleasure of the joke, into "taking sides" (p. 103). This, he notes, is well expressed in the common German phrase *die Lacher auf seine Seite ziehen,* which translates as, "to bring the laughers over to our side," an exact description of the attachment function of disparaging laughter. Freud is perplexed, however, about whose hostile or sexual drive is being expressed—the joker, the laugher, or both. He says that it is obviously the joker whose internal obstacle is being circumvented by the "lustful or hostile" joke: the joker draws pleasure from the instinct otherwise blocked. However, it is paradoxically the laugher who shows the enjoyment—or at the very least, as Freud put it, "bears witness by his laughter" (p. 103).

At times, Freud's gift for explicit verbal analysis fails him and he is left with a joke he says is beyond (or beneath) technique, clearly in the realm of the implicit, procedural form of responding and relating. He writes, "We may for a time be quite baffled by this analysis and may even think of taking refuge in denying that the anecdote—*though it made us laugh* [italics added]—possesses the character of a joke" (Freud, 1905/1983, p. 50). Other jokes, the ones that are "short-lived" and woven into our conversation, "will not bear being uprooted from their original soil and kept in isolation" (p. 79). Freud is here referring presciently to what current laughter researchers have found—that the majority of laughter is not at formal jokes at all, but rather at conversational "quips" (in context) such as "nice coat" or "see you later," which, as Freud points out, have no visible cognitive standing at all. To deal with this problem, he suggests separating the "thought content" from the "joke-work" (p. 94). Nonetheless, it would appear that time and again, like so many other writers about humor, Freud is drawn back into the "thought content" and, though he is a master at verbal analysis, finds himself coming up short.

As Freud connects with some of his reader's potential frustration about these limitations, he made me laugh out loud: "If at this point a reader should become indignant at a method of approach which threatens to ruin his enjoyment of jokes without being able to throw any light on the source of that enjoyment, I would beg him to be patient for the moment" (p. 24). Here Freud was able to connect with me, his reader, by making me laugh! In that moment, I felt attached to him as a person and I felt completely with him as he continued to describe his thinking. Furthermore, his comment made me feel that he was interested in me and in what I am thinking, too. In fact, I do feel attached to Freud through our mutual love of, and interest in trying to understand, the power of humor and laughter. I love following his complex, multilayered arguments, and I have the utmost respect for his openness to holes in his thinking and his sensitivity in looking for gaps in his analysis. The title of this book seeks to honor his pioneering work, his intellectual prowess in analyzing this topic, his prescience in anticipating both interpersonal neurobiology and attachment theory, and, perhaps most of all, his sense of humor.

Overall, the three primary theories of laughter suggest that it is an interpersonal behavior. None of them conflict with an attachment viewpoint on laughter and, in fact, each contributes something to our understanding of the links between the attachment system and other systems of behavior. The superiority/disparagement and the discharge theory both suggest that laughter links the attachment and conflict/hostility systems. The incongruity theory links the attachment and exploratory/play systems, a primary partnership first established in infancy that persists throughout life. The incongruity theory arguably represents the most frequently occurring and healthy form of humor throughout life. It may also turn out, when more research is available, that laughing at incongruities may be the most prevalent type of humor in those who are securely attached. In the following chapter, we turn from theories to look at laughter research in terms of the light it may shed on an attachment perspective of laughter.

4

LAUGHTER RESEARCH
AND ATTACHMENT

In 1897, G. Stanley Hall, the first president of the American Psychological Association, coauthored an article on laughter saying, "We are persuaded that all current theories [of laughter] are utterly inadequate and speculative, and that there are few more promising fields of psychological research" (G. S. Hall & Allin, 1897, p. 40). Judging by the voluminous literature now available, Hall's challenge was taken up with a vengeance, though the credit no doubt goes more to the appeal and magnetism of laughter itself than to his call for professionals to take up the cause.

The research on laughter uses techniques ranging from surveys and diaries to experimental designs and naturalistic/observation studies. Laughter research has also been undertaken by multiple disciplines—evolution, ethology, physiology, philosophy, psychology, theology, sociology—and from different standpoints—interpersonal neurobiology, medical pathology, stress reduction, health, and well-being. In addition, laughter's social, interpersonal, and contagious aspects are explored developmentally, cross-culturally, and linguistically. Further research looks at the development of laughter through infancy and childhood, and at individual, gender, and cultural differences in frequency, precipitants, and etiquette. There is also a small but growing body of research looking at laughter in psychotherapy.

The related list of research on smiles and smiling, not to mention humor, is at least as extensive as that for laughter and perhaps more so. Unlike crying, laughter is a popular and familiar topic for research. It is easier to create ethically under experimental conditions and easy to identify when it occurs. And, unlike crying, laughter can be fun for researchers and participants alike.

Evolution and Ethology

Evolutionary and ethological perspectives on laughter seem especially pertinent for our purposes because the attachment system, including attachment behaviors like laughter, is believed to have evolved as part of our innate push toward parent/ infant bonding and social connectedness. Cross-cultural emotion research has shown that laughter is a universal expression, known and recognized in all cultures, and this finding supports the attachment view that it is a social behavior hardwired into all human beings. As Darwin wrote, "with all the races of man, the expression of good spirit appears to be the same and is easily recognized" (1872/1965, p. 211). From an evolutionary standpoint the question about laughter is twofold. The first asks why a person laughs in a given instance in a given culture (what evolutionary theorists call the proximate cause) and the second why we laugh as a species (what they call the ultimate cause).

Laughter Acoustics

It is noteworthy that the sound of laughter is stereotyped between individuals, programmed by the human nervous system and vocal track. This factor points to the universality of laughter behavior and further supports the idea that its roots are in the attachment system. Because laughter sounds are acoustically similar in all humans, laughter, like crying, is an immediately recognizable social signal anywhere in the world. Provine (1996) writes, "The species-wide distribution of laughter and its stereotypical (and simple) structure suggests that the behavior has strong genetic and neurophysiological-based qualities attractive to those who wish to understand the mechanisms and natural history of behavior" (p. 38).

The universality of the human ability to produce and recognize the laughter signal (though not, of course, the socially constructed humor that evokes it) is an argument for categorizing laughter as an attachment behavior because such behaviors, according to attachment theory, should be shared by human infants across cultures (van IJzendoorn & Sagi-Schwartz, 2008). Attachment behaviors are also subject to experience and learning, which explains individual and cultural differences in the contexts for, and interpretations of, laughter. Because laughter patterns, if not laughter sounds, are so strongly impacted by experience, the importance of better understanding laughter's developmental and relationship functioning is underscored, both of which are enhanced by taking an attachment perspective.

Darwin speculates that it is important from a survival standpoint that playful laughter sounds be as different as possible from the sounds of distress, which they are. Laughter sounds consist of long *broken* voiced expirations interspersed with short, deep inspirations, whereas distress cries are *prolonged* voiced (in infancy, though often silent in adulthood) expirations also punctuated with brief inspirations. He noted, "The whole expression of a man in good spirits is exactly the opposite of that of one suffering from sorrow" (1872/1965, p. 211).

If crying sounds evolved as distress cries for help from a caregiving other, laughter sounds are believed to have evolved as a call for playmates to join in play—or to signal playful intent. From an attachment standpoint, having a pronounced difference between negative and positive arousal makes sense. Helpless infants use loud crying as a signal to end separation and to seek soothing from the caregiver, but they also need to have an inborn means for eliciting positive engagement. Crying is a loud, intense, not easily ignored sound that not only communicates dysregulation and distress, but also creates it in the caregiver, thus assuring efforts to terminate the infant's distress. Playful laughter, on the other hand, beckons to the caregiver for frolicking and fun, and creates a sense of pleasure in both partners.

In the early weeks of life when low arousal is optimal for the infant, silent smiling is a highly effective engagement bid to the caregiver (Bowlby, 1969). The vocalized intensity of laughter becomes possible with greater maturation—when a more stimulating connection is sought and welcomed. Grotjahn (1957) states the attachment behavior case for laughter's sounds by saying simply, "Laughter is loud because it calls for company" (p. 33).

Darwin (1872/1965) also points specifically to the attachment function of laughter when he writes that it is "employed as the means for a joyful meeting between the parents and their offspring and between the attached members of the same social community" (p. 205). Animal behaviorist Lorenz (1963) believed that laughter evolved as a greeting ceremony designed to blunt aggressive reactions that might follow even brief separations. He states the attachment case as follows: laughter "tends to create a bond" and "shared laughter not only diverts aggression but also produces a feeling of social unity" (p. 179).

Laughter in Primates and Other Species

Evolutionary theorists Gervais and Wilson (2005) point to the pant-like vocalizations of the great apes in tickling and chasing. They suggest, "A rudimentary precursor to human laughter has distant evolutionary origins in the common primate ancestor of humans and the other great apes at least 6.5 million years ago" (p. 398). A study of bonobo laughter lends support to the hypothesis that laughter originated in primates as "a universal signal of well-being in a playful situation to help regulate social interactions" (Zimmerman as cited in Beale, 2003, para. 8).

Certain primates—for example, infant bonobos and pygmy chimpanzees— laugh when they are tickled, with vocalization patterns and facial expressions quite like those of human infants. Ethologists in Hanover, Germany, compared the laughter sounds of bonobos and human infants in the first year of life and found that they follow roughly the same patterns in frequency changes and intensity, though the bonobo's laugh is at a higher pitch (Beale, 2003).

Provine and Yong (1991) believe laughter to be "an ancient mode of prelinguistic vocal communication that is performed in parallel with, but has not been displaced by, modern speech and language" (p. 122). Provine (2000), in studying chimpanzee laughter, noted that chimpanzees and human infants have similar facial expressions, known as the "relaxed open-mouth display," and produce laughs in the same contexts, tickling, or "rough-and-tumble play." The biggest similarity between human and chimpanzee laughter, however, is its rhythmic structure—the "sonic bursts occur at regular intervals" (p. 79). The "sonic bursts" of chimps, however, occur at about twice the speed as those of humans. The breathy, fast, in-out quality of chimpanzee laughter is due to the fact that chimps vocalize on each in and each out breath, whereas human laughter only occurs on the exhale, and is often prolonged. Provine (2000) and others see this difference as possible evidence for the fact that human vocalizations, including laughter sounds, are dependent on walking upright. The theory is that breathing patterns in animals that walk on all fours have to be coordinated with their locomotion so that the lungs are full of air when the forelimbs hit the ground. As a result, chimpanzees' laugh sounds occur and are vocalized directly in rhythm with each inhalation and exhalation, as opposed to human laughter which breaks exhalations into discrete "ha, ha, ha," sounds. In other words, being bipedal has given humans the freedom to breathe in and out irrespective of gait, and hence to generate more complex sounds.

Primate laughter may also serve an attachment function at reunions as well as at play. Darwin (1872/1965) notes that chimpanzees "make a kind of barking noise, when pleased by the return of anyone *to whom they are attached* [italics added]" (p. 131). He also mentions a monkey species known as the *Cebus asaræ* who, "when rejoiced at again seeing a beloved person, utters a peculiar tittering sound. When this noise, which the keepers call a laugh, is uttered, the lips are protruded" (p. 132).

Darwin provides a detailed description of chimpanzee and monkey laughter when they are tickled. "The corners of the mouth are then drawn backwards; and this sometimes causes the lower eyelids to be slightly wrinkled." Their teeth are not exposed, "but their eyes sparkle and grow brighter" (p. 132). Significantly, Darwin's observation of bright eyes in primate laughter points toward a parallel between human Duchenne laughter and that of other primates. (I presume primates do not use non-Duchenne laughter to indicate they are "only kidding" when they make a hostile gesture, though perhaps we underestimate them.)

In analyzing the details of human laughter, Darwin found the sparkling eyes puzzling and confessed to being flummoxed by what more poetic writers might describe as a kind of brightly shining inner light that is unmistakable in genuine laugher. He speculated that the sparkle might be due to moisture squeezed out of the lacrimal glands, but discounted the idea because eyes moist from grief, quite the opposite, "become dull" (p. 132).

Panksepp and Burdorf (2003) have also identified what seems to be laughter in the chirping of rats. Their article is titled "'Laughing' Rats and the Evolutionary Antecedents of Human Joy?" Note the careful inclusion of the question mark in the title, presumably a sign of caution about anthropomorphizing animal behavior. It is hard not to do, however, given their finding that both play- and tickle-induced "ultrasonic vocalization patterns" or "chirps" in rats "may have more than passing resemblance to primitive human laughter" (p. 53). A video of Panksepp (2007a) tickling the rats is available on YouTube and is quite heartwarming as well as interesting. (I never would have guessed that hearing a rat laugh would make me feel so warmly connected with it, my ideas about laughter as an attachment behavior notwithstanding!)

Panksepp and Burdorff (2003) summarize "a dozen reasons for the working hypothesis that such rat vocalizations reflect a type of positive affect that may have evolutionary relations to the joyfulness of human childhood laughter commonly accompanying social play" (p. 533). They also suggest that being able to express playfulness through laughter, what they call one of our "neurobehavioral tools," promotes "social bonding and the development of social skills," thus linking laughter as an attachment behavior to the exploratory/play system (p. 534).

Smiles and Laughter

As noted in Chapter 1, Darwin, who influenced Bowlby, was of the opinion that a smile is a close relative of the laugh, with the difference between a broad smile and a gentle laugh being simply one of intensity. He noted that the smile precedes the laugh in individual development, but theorized that from an evolutionary standpoint, the laugh preceded the smile because

> the habit of uttering loud reiterated sounds from a sense of pleasure, first led to the retraction of the corners of the mouth and of the upper lip, and to the contraction of the orbicular muscles; and that now, through association and long-continued habit, the same muscles are brought into slight play whenever any cause excites in us a feeling which, if stronger, would have led to laughter; and the result is a smile. (Darwin, 1872/1965, p. 209)

However, others (Nwokah, Hsu, Dobrowolska, & Fogel, 1994) have suggested, and I concur, that while smiling and laughter are related, it makes more sense to study them as separate phenomena—to think of them more as cousins than siblings. Nowokah, Hsu, Dobrowolska, and Fogel write, "Although laughter and smiling both usually indicate positive affect and often converge, the interactive and communicative features of laughter in dyadic interaction may be more clearly determined by studying laughter separately as a unique phenomenon of vocal, facial, and sometimes postural modes" (p. 24). Lockard, Fahrenbruch, Smith, and Morgan (1977) argue that smiling and laughter were originally two different displays in nonhuman primates. They believe that smiling originated in the "silent bared-teeth submissive grimace of primates," while laughter evolved from the "relaxed open-mouth display of play" (p. 183). They point out that in primates such as chimpanzees who can both smile and laugh, the two are distinct behaviors, being neither temporally nor categorically related (p. 183).

Lockard et al. (1977) also point to a similar distinction in the smiles and laughter of children because each occurs in different contexts. Vocalized laughter is associated with rough-and-tumble play, whereas smiles are used for greeting and affirming approachability. In adults, too, this distinction holds. In observing

141 adult dyadic interactions at work, on breaks, during chance encounters, or leisure-time activities, they found that most smiling took place in greetings and departures (clearly an attachment behavior), whereas "frank laughter" (Duchenne, presumably) occurred almost exclusively at play or in a recreational context. "If frank laughter does occur in the other social situations, it is usually during the later stages of the interaction, prior to termination when the exchanges had grown more informal" (p. 185). They speculate that if the smile is a submissive display evolved to prevent hostile aggressive encounters, it would logically be associated with affiliative, friendly intentions. Smiling serves as an invitation to approach and become playful, while laughter is the sound that signifies and accompanies interactive play.

Lockard et al. (1977) also noticed that in certain social contexts, especially in formal situations like reception lines or friendly interactions between superiors and subordinates, forced laughter is likely to occur. They see forced, or non-Duchenne laughter, as possibly being an "acquired blending of the two displays," smiling and laughter (p. 185). Non-Duchenne laughter, "through convergence, learning, or both, would create the appearance of a continuum of graded signals concealing originally discrete displays of different phyletic origins" (p. 185). In other words, it is Duchenne and non-Duchenne laughter that form the continuum of intensity, not laughter and smiling.

Smiling is also contrasted with laughter in that it is more difficult to inhibit but easier to produce voluntarily. Provine (2000) says, "The voluntary smile is an important evolutionary adaptation that provides increased flexibility and conscious control over facial behavior" (p. 52). He also notes that smiles require close face-to-face contact for communication, whereas laughter sounds can reach an audience in the dark or over the telephone. (My friend Pattie and I can attest to this distinction based on our experience getting hysterical, unstoppable giggles during what was supposed to be a quiet ritual in an intensely dark cave in Hawaii. We only wished the others present had not been able to hear our laughter sounds, as their annoyance with us, though silent, penetrated the darkness.)

Neurobiological Laughter Research

The central importance of laughter as an attachment behavior in infancy rests on its role in neurological, and hence social development during the first 18 to 24 months of life. Positive engagement between infant and caregiver contributes not only to attachment bond formation, but also to the infant's neurobiological development. Positive arousal, attunement, and regulation between infant and caregiver promote what Schore calls "a symbiotic entrainment" between the caregiver's mature and the infant's immature nervous systems. "Entrainment" refers to the process of emotional contagion or looping that joins the two nervous systems. With positive, playful input from the caregiver, the child is pulled into "a similar state of heightened sympathetic activity and resultant positive affect, alert activity, and behavioral activation" (Schore, 2003a, p. 10). This nervous-system-to-nervous-system transactional connection between caregiver and infant is crucial for the development of the child's ongoing ability to successfully regulate affect and to negotiate social relationships beginning with family and friends. The importance of this neurobiological foundation based in positive arousal, attunement, and regulation will be discussed in greater detail in the following chapters on laughter in infancy.

Laughter throughout life is nonverbal and most attempts to translate the humor behind laughter into words eradicate the inclination to laugh. Laughter is part of our imagery-forming, nonverbal, intuitive, primarily right hemisphere–based ability to perceive and act without conscious thought, what has been called our system of "implicit procedural knowing" (Lyons-Ruth, 1998). In this procedural way of perceiving, processing, and relating, we draw on what we know without consciously thinking it through, and we act on that socio-emotional knowledge regularly. We recognize faces, expressions, and tones of voice, and instantaneously "get" social nuances, including funny comments, without needing—and often without being able—to articulate why or how.

As we know, our best jokes are spontaneous, shared creations that arouse our own unmediated laughter responses, as well as laughter in those around us. Provine (2000) points out that formal jokes and spoken word comedic humor are responsible for only a tiny fraction of laughter and represent "only recently evolved cognitive and linguistic stimuli for laughter" (pp. 342–343).

Provine's (2000) discovery that laughter occurs primarily at the end of statements or questions, and almost never mid-phrase, further supports the association between laughter and our nonconscious, implicit, attachment-forged ways of knowing and relating. In his study more than 1,200 laugh episodes were observed, and virtually no speaker phrases (less than 1%) were interrupted by audience laughter, nor did the speakers interrupt themselves to laugh. Laughter consistently and predictably followed complete statements or questions rather than being randomly scattered throughout the speech stream. This consistent placement of laughter at the end of conversational phrases is called "the punctuation effect," and indicates, according to Provine, "that a lawful and probably neurologically based process governs the placement of laughter in speech" (p. 37). He further suggests that this is a neurological mechanism whereby "*the brains of speaker and audience are locked into a dual processing mode*" (p. 38), an example of the "symbiotic entrainment," mentioned above. The shared rhythm of laughter-inducing comments and responses—comment/laughter . . . comment/laughter, similar to a call-response pattern in gospel music—suggests a powerful, neurologically based attachment/affiliation dance in action, such as that described by Stern (1998).

Others have noted, and Temple Grandin has described in her autobiography on dealing with her own autism, what happens when there is a glitch in this processing mode. Grandin says that being autistic has meant she is not able to follow the social rhythm of laughter. Other people "will laugh together and then talk quietly until the next laughing cycle." She inadvertently interrupts or starts laughing at the wrong places (as cited in Provine, 2000, p. 39).

Gervais and Wilson (2005) further suggest that the nonconscious but consistent grammatical placement of laughter might be used to distinguish Duchenne from non-Duchenne laughter. "Conversational [non-Duchenne] laughter is being used strategically like speech as a metacommunicative marker," they suggest, "as opposed to being 'uncontrollable' like Duchenne laughter" (p. 400). They point to research that suggests that "spontaneous stimulus-induced laughter [Duchenne] and volitional laughter [non-Duchenne] do indeed arise from separate neural systems" (p. 400).

One complicating factor in making a distinction between the two types of laughs is that most laughter research does not define or treat them separately. The assumption seems to be that the laughter under study is Duchenne laughter that is genuine, unforced, uncalculated, and largely beyond conscious control (Keltner & Bonanno, 1997). A few researchers, however, are beginning to make a distinction between the two types of laughter with interesting results. Hudenko, Stone, and Bachorowski (2009), for example, separate the two types into what they call "voiced" (most similar to Duchenne) and "unvoiced" (most similar to non-Duchenne) laughs in autistic children. They found that autistic children are able to appropriately produce voiced (Duchenne) laughter at things they find genuinely funny, whereas they run into difficulties of the type Grandin describes when it comes to the appropriate use of unvoiced, non-Duchenne laughter.

Laughter Contagion

The fact that laughter is so often contagious provides more evidence for understanding it as an implicit (that is, unmediated, unpremeditated), primarily right-hemisphere brain function. In an airport restaurant recently, I saw a brother and sister about 10 and 12 begin laughing hysterically at the plight of their mother whose fingers had gotten stuck trying to retrieve some hand wipes from their plastic container. As their father tried to free their mother's fingers from the teeth inside the lid and one remedy after another failed, the children laughed even harder. Soon those of us at nearby tables were making eye contact with each other and starting to laugh, too, quite hard in my own case. Even though I sympathized with the mother whose fingers were stuck, the comical laughing response of the children was contagious and prevailed over my respect for their mother's feelings.

Researchers in London (Trust, 2006) studied fMRI brain responses in people listening to laughter tracks. Whereas any sound triggered a response in the premotor cortical region that prepares the muscles in the face to respond accordingly, "the response was greater for positive sounds, suggesting that these were more contagious than negative sounds" (para. 4). The researchers suggest that this response in the brain primes us to smile or laugh and "provides a way of mirroring the behaviour of others, something which helps us interact socially. It could play an important role in building strong bonds between individuals in a group" (para. 5).

Provine (2000) suggests that our brains have both a laugh-generator, a neural circuit that produces laughter behavior, and a laugh-detector. "Once triggered, the laugh-detector activates ('releases') a *laugh-generator,* a neural circuit that produces" what we identify as laughter (p. 149). In other words, "laughter has the innate capacity to trigger laughter" (p.149).

Humor Appreciation

While certain left-hemispheric cognitive processes no doubt help us figure out whether something is funny or not, Shammi and Stuss (1999) stress that intellectual understanding is not sufficient to explain how we do that. Appreciating humor, they point out, "requires an affective response" and, for that, we need right hemispheric "holistic and simultaneous processing style" more than the semantic retrieval and explicit analysis of the left hemisphere (p. 664).

Shammi and Stuss (1999) point out that the punch line of a joke is a novel "problem-solving" task in which the incongruity "must be detected and then reconciled" (p. 663). In order to decode a punch line, to "get the joke," the brain has to keep all kinds of knowledge in play simultaneously, make sense of it in a microsecond and then, almost in the same instant, burst into laughter. Otherwise, the moment is lost and the joke is not funny—there is no time for careful, conscious, linear thinking. For the split-second analysis of humor, we depend on our right hemisphere–based ability to recognize, organize, integrate, and interpret "abstract/non-literal... and indirect forms of communication, such as irony, affective intonation and sarcasm" (p. 663). It seems a miracle that our brains spark quickly enough for us to burst out laughing practically within the same second we hear something funny—and do it together with others if we are in a group. We have our attachment systems and our attuned caregivers, working in concert with our acquired cognitive skills, to thank for giving us this wonderful and powerful ability to make associations and connections so quickly, bypassing the need for conscious processing of the "joke."

Shammi and Stuss (1999) found that brain-injured individuals with damage to the anterior portion of the right frontal lobe show the highest level of interference with the ability to understand and appreciate humor and the ability to smile or laugh in response to it. Noninjured subjects or patients with injuries in other parts of the brain were able to correctly rate a joke or cartoon as humorous. Laughter and smiling were deficient only in the group with right frontal deficits.

Other studies have found that patients with right-hemisphere damage show "a dissociation between their cognitive and affective responses" (Shammi & Stuss, 1999, p. 664). When given a verbal joke setup, they could not identify the punch line. They were drawn to surprise/slapstick endings that were only peripherally connected to the humorous intent. They also were unable to explain why a joke was funny. They could relate to surprise elements but could not establish coherence, meaning that they could appreciate slapstick humor more than other types.

Humor production is also impacted when there is frontal lobe damage. People with damage to the frontal lobes often have what is known as *"Wizelsucht* (addiction to telling jokes, usually inappropriate in content when they are produced), *moria* (silly, euphoric behaviour), and inappropriate laughter" (Shammi & Stuss, 1999, p. 662).

Perception and Affect Regulation

Beginning in infancy, positive engagement signified by laughter with a caregiver, in addition to play, can also serve as a means of de-intensifying or down-regulating negative arousal and up-regulating positive. It is a visible and visceral process that optimally carries forward throughout life. The widespread belief that well-timed laughter can help to de-intensify negative arousal throughout life relies on experiential anecdotes, for most of us, along with research about laughter's mitigating effects on stress.

One such study by Kuiper and Martin (1998) analyzed self-reports of laughter in relationship to stress over a 3-day period. Surprisingly, they found no direct correlation between the amount of laughter and the amount of felt stress. However, individuals whose stressful life events increased, but who laughed more in spite of it, did not show the expected higher levels of negative affect. The authors speculate that laughter during stressful times is linked with effective appraisal and coping techniques in general. These, in turn, have been found to be highly associated with attachment style (see Mikulincer & Shaver, 2007), meaning that early interactions with caregivers continue to have an impact affect on regulation throughout life. "Symbiotic entrainment" between laughing, engaged, and attuned caregivers and infants appears to pay off over a lifetime in increased affect regulation abilities in the face of stress.

Not only is laughter related to how a person appraises stress, but another study shows that it can actually change how a person perceives a drawn figure (Lowinger, 2005). The findings are based on a simple experiment with an ambiguous line drawing called a Necker cube that was performed by an Australian professor, Jack Pettigrew. Normally, in looking at the Necker cube, the brain switches back and forth between two competing perceptions, a mechanism known as binocular rivalry. By accident, Pettigrew discovered that during laughter, the brain blends the images together so that the illusion is lost and only a flat two-dimensional drawing is seen. "If you see both images together you can be pretty sure you're seeing from both hemispheres at the same time," he says (as cited in Lowinger, 2005). He performed his experiments using a joke to prime laughter. I tried it with forced laughter and was surprised to see that the images converged then, as well.

Laughter and Health

Research into the relationship between laughter and health has been widespread ever since 1979 when Norman Cousins laughed his way through and out of a painful, life-threatening illness and wrote a book about it. There is even a Cousins Center for Psychoneuroimmunology at the UCLA medical school.

Laughter, research has shown, is good for our hearts, our vascular, immune, and respiratory systems, and for our mood and our relationships. Laughter also has been shown to lower the level of stress hormones (cortisol, norepinephrine, DOPAC, and growth hormone) and can temporarily lower blood pressure and reduce pain. One study (Beckman, Regier, & Young, 2007), for example, looked at the effects of 15-minute daily sessions of guided "non-humor dependent laughter" on 15 consecutive workdays. They found significant increases in "self-regulation, optimism, positive emotions, and social identification" (p. 167). The Laughter Clubs and Laughter Yoga groups that began in India have now spread throughout the world, including to the U.S. People gather in groups, make eye contact, and do mutual laughter exercises, vouching for the health and mood benefits of laughter.

A recent study in Israel (Szalavitz, 2011) focused on the impact of laughter on 219 women undergoing an IVF procedure. Thirty-six percent of those exposed to a "medical clown" for 15 minutes after the procedure became pregnant, versus 20% of the women "whose embryo transfer was comedy-free" (para. 1). Even anticipating laughter, according to other research, can immediately lower stress hormones (Gayagoy, 2009). Laughing with coworkers, spouses, families, friends—even just laughing for no reason—has been linked with improved mood and improved health. Our attachment systems and the ways in which we learn to regulate affect have an impact on our health as well as the quality of our relationships.

Laughter as a Social Behavior

Almost all laughter researchers concur that it is a social behavior. In Provine's (2000) study people laughed "*30 times* more when they were around others than when they were alone" (p. 45). Most of the solitary laughing involved some form of media, which arguably is a form of distal social relating. At other times, solitary laughter may involve recalling instances of shared laughter after the fact. I do find myself doing that, successfully stretching the pleasure of the shared laugh beyond the moment. Even long-ago funny exchanges can bring a smile and a chuckle years later.

In studying the effect of humor on relationships Bazzini (as cited in Sanders, 2007) found, "When you reminisce about laughter, it makes you laugh again," thus enhancing closeness and creating a stronger bond (para. 4). In studying laughter among staff at a mental hospital, Coser (1960) found that humor served as "an invitation to those who are present to join in laughter, [that] highlights or creates group consensus" (p. 81).

Sociological research approaches laughter from a number of directions. Mulder and Nijholt (2002), for example, theorize that humor plays a role in maintaining and strengthening established social roles, whether within the family, a work group, or anywhere there is an "in-group and out-group" (p. 7). Humor is also seen by sociologists as an interactive event wherein the hearer determines whether or not a joke is funny based on the social and cultural context, thereby revealing insights about that culture—so-called "negotiation theories." In addition, sociologists look at humor from the standpoint of frame theories, a shift from a serious to a humorous frame. Jokes are seen as founded on the society and culture, but standing outside of normal discourse, thus allowing people to make comments and "breach taboos without causing offense" (Mulder & Nijholt, 2002, p. 7).

Laughter Research and Humor Research

Much of the research that purports to be about laughter, as noted earlier, is in fact about humor. When I used laughter as a search term on Google Scholar, it produced 79,600 hits, many of those in fact addressing humor. The term "humor," however, came up with 171,000 hits. Humor research, in general, tests the theories of humor mentioned in Chapter 3, including superiority, incongruity, and discharge/relief. Humor is the backdrop for laughter, as we described in the last chapter, and in that sense is of interest from an attachment standpoint and will be incorporated throughout the following chapters.

Humor researchers, as well as theorists, are multidisciplinary, approaching the topic through the lenses of psychology, philosophy, sociology, linguistics, and literature. Recently, computer science has been added to the list of humor scholarship as scientists in that field search for a humor-generating form of artificial intelligence. They are aiming to create and respond to humor in the interaction between machine and user, no mean feat. Artificial intelligence programs are now aiming to have "embodied conversational agents"—animated cartoon or human-like characters—who can also laugh at the right moment, making them "more believable to the user and to induce trust" (Mulder & Nijholt, 2002, p. 16). In other words, they are trying to facilitate the establishment of an attachment relationship between the computer and the user by artificially generating attachment behavior, which is either very scary or very funny or both. It would seem that the explicit and paradoxical process of "programming" implicit procedural knowledge into a software program is going to be very tough indeed. For computers to make us laugh, they would have to be able to appreciate and recognize our mood and our individual sense of humor, and many times we can barely do that with human exchanges online, even with the addition of emoticons ☺ to pass along clues. Still, the more we study, discuss, and make the implicit aspects of laughter conscious, as we are doing in this book, the more possible that might become.

Attempting to survey the body of laughter research is as daunting a task as surveying the theories of laughter. Here we have explored some of the relevant highlights of general laughter research in order to get a sense of how it might inform an attachment-based understanding of laughter. Laughter research, for the most part, has not addressed attachment issues, and attachment research has not addressed laughter. The research that comes the closest, however, is infant research about attachment and infant research about laughter, which we will explore in the next chapter. In the meantime, as a clinician, theoretician, and consumer of research, I can see much to be gained in both directions—attachment and laughter—if there were to be a body of attachment-based laughter research, and I would love to think that I might play some small part in inspiring it.

Part 2

Laughter in Infancy

5

THE DEVELOPMENT OF
LAUGHTER IN INFANCY

"Let's keep doing this; it's fun!" The message of infant laughter could not be clearer—and its infectiousness could hardly be more appreciated by adults. The "laughing baby" video on YouTube (mentioned in Chapter 1)—a simple, parent-generated video of a baby laughing in a high chair—has had a mind-boggling *80 million* hits! I regularly play it for my attachment and neurobiology classes when they need a little up-regulation. I even sneak a peek at it myself if I am having a bad day.

Infant laughter is a great big, happy, irresistible circle game. Adults feel good because the baby feels good, which makes everybody feel great simultaneously—that is to say, alive, positive, engaged, upbeat, loved, noticed, affirmed, and connected. Reddy (2008) an infant humor researcher, describes the circular process of baby laughter: "The more positive emotions the infant experiences, the more open to interpersonal engagement and knowing the infant becomes," and the greater the "infant's attractiveness to others, which further increases engagement" (p. 41).

In the early months and years of life, positive interpersonal engagement triggered by novelty is at the core of laughter. All it took for my 7-month-old grandson Leo to break out in giggles was for me to give a "singsongy" hello and lean forward and nuzzle his forehead. I ran out of energy for repetitions before he did. In experiences like this one, we see the bridge between attachment and exploration/play—between the baby's need for security and the baby's desire and need to learn more about the world. Human exploratory behavior is based in play, which by definition can only take place when there is no distress, when the child is feeling not only engaged, but also secure.

Smiling and Laughter: The Link Between Attachment and Exploration, Security, and Play

Granddaughter Aurelia first laughed when she was 3 months old, safely tucked into the crook of her father's arm while he was playing a slow-motion version of soccer in the back yard. The ball came to him, and, as he twirled around to kick it, she let out her first peal of laughter. Life was good for little Aurelia in that moment as she embraced something completely new and fun in the safety of her father's arms. "Hooray to this!" she seemed to be saying, and, "Let's do that again!"

Security is required for play, and shared play helps to enhance connection and create security. In that moment, Aurelia was secure enough to be open to the experience of something new and a little bit scary, to let her dad know she liked it, and to make him—and all of us in the back yard with her—feel part of her experience, and even more connected to her. That single laugh from a 3-month-old baby carried a lot of punch. It would have been a great occasion for the celebration of a "first laugh" party, if only we had known about the Navajo custom then.

Before the first, or any other laugh, however, the baby, like all of us, quickly appraises the stimulus, though it is of course an unconscious process for baby, as it usually is for adults, too. The arousal that follows is based on that appraisal: positive affect if the stimulus and person are deemed safe, or negative if they are deemed frightening. Smiles and laughs signal that the baby has determined that this person or thing is safe and doing a fun thing. Feeling secure is a necessary precondition for positive engagement, smiling, and, later, laughter. Positive affects such as delight, elation, and excitement are the gateway for exploration and play, which expand the baby's experience and learning. Play also impacts the development of the baby's nervous system as it "facilitates the processing of novel information and thereby improves learning capacity ... shaping developing brain networks" and increasing "neural interconnectivity" (Schore, 2003a, p. 13).

Oster (1978), who coded the muscle changes accompanying smiles in two infants during their first 11 weeks, was struck by the fact that almost half of the two infants' smiles were preceded by a knit brow. She speculated that the two expressions represent distinct processes: the knit brow reflects a concentrated attempt to make sense of the stimuli, whereas the smile reflects the infants' appraisal that the person and activity are engaging and safe. She also noted that these two babies stared at the caregiver's face before smiling, whereas their gaze was likely to be averted before crying. When feeling positive affect, babies seek more engagement, while with negative affect, they feel overwhelmed and in need of de-escalation and soothing from the caregiver before they can feel secure again.

Oster's observations provide a clear link between the exploratory system (experiencing the new or unexpected) and the attachment system (secure positive engagement). Babies, like adults, first appraise novel stimuli for interest and safety, and then, under the right playful social circumstances, embrace (explore) and share (attach) with accompanying expressions of delight.

Sroufe and Waters (1976) found further evidence of the appraisal phase in their measurements of infant heart rate. Upon being presented with a novel stimulus, an infant's heart rate was found to initially and briefly decelerate, followed by acceleration during crying (dangerous) or laughter (safe), depending on how that infant appraised the stimulus. These reliable heart rate patterns can be understood as reflecting the baby's attempt to first determine whether a given stimulus is safe (deceleration) to explore, share, and enjoy, in which case the heart rate accelerates and there is laughter, or, if not safe, there is a sober expression or crying.

Infants seem inherently drawn to finding pleasure in incongruity and challenges to their cognitive capacity. They are true partners in exploring the people and world around them, seeking new and increasingly exciting experiences as they mature and feel more secure. They become bored with too much "same old, same old" and if bored will stop smiling. Little Leo, at 7 months and newly crawling, is all about chasing after new toys, pieces of furniture, food—anything he does not recognize and yet finds attractive. I take that as good evidence that he has an active mind and that powering that active mind is a strong felt sense of security.

Smiling

Positive engagement starts out pretty low key with baby's first smiles at around four weeks. Smiling is a baby greeting, a sign of recognition, connection, and interest, most easily given to caregivers and familiar figures. The social smile is part of the inborn attachment system, drawing the infant and the caregiver into shared affective experiences just like crying and laughter. Unlike crying, which is triggered by separation, however, social smiles occur only when other people are around (Bowlby, 1969).

In the early weeks of life, a caregiver's little nods and gazes, gentle caresses, mellow silly sounds, or gentle movements are enough to bring a rewarding smile. In the beginning, babies take a long time to gear up to a smile and cannot sustain it very long. If parents push too hard or too long for the smile, it will overwhelm the baby and may lead to crying instead.

Parents told to "play" with their infants aged 3 months and under use a "rich array of animated facial, vocal, and gestural behaviors" (Oster, 1978, p. 51). They typically respond positively to their infant's early smiles, too, saying something like "Thaaat's a nice smile," or laughing, or exclaiming "'Oooooh!' with a rising voice pitch" (p. 56). Researchers in the Oster study said they loved doing it because watching these exchanges was so infectious. Family photo albums and online social networking sites are typically full of photos capturing the little one's first smiles. We are primed neurobiologically to key into our warmest, fuzziest selves in response to an infant smile. I watched several of the multitudes of first-smile videos on YouTube (one of the best of which was www.youtube.com/watch?v=tQOoVgJQDHg), and I quickly found myself feeling warm and fuzzy right along with their smiling parents.

The Neurobiological Significance of Smiling

Mothers and infants gaze intently at each other while absorbed in playful interactions, representing what Schore (2003b), a neurobiological attachment researcher and clinician, calls the "right-brain to right-brain" mother-infant connection. Shared gazes and smiles represent the mutual flow of affect "between the mother's mature and the infant's immature endocrine and nervous systems" (p. 14). The caregiver's joy is infectious and by sharing positive feelings, infants learn to recognize and manage their own and others' internal experiences. Infant affect, positive or negative, is "reciprocally related to the emotions of others" (p. 72).

The contagion during mutual gaze and smiling takes place neurochemically as well when the mother's face triggers high levels of endogenous opiates in the other's brain. These endorphins are biochemically responsible for the pleasurable qualities of social interaction. In other words, the observable pleasure in mother/child face-to-face engagement has an invisible, internal neurobiological component, as well. These positive, coordinated moments linking caregiver and infant are the neurological building blocks for the baby's sense of safety, security, and self-esteem—and additionally reward the caregiver with pleasure. They lay the foundation for a healthy sense of comfort with exploring the unfamiliar, and for regulating affect throughout life.

The Relationship Between Smiling and Laughter

By 3 months of age, when infants are mature enough to respond to more complex and intense stimuli such as patty cake and gentle bouncing, smiles begin to be accompanied by small prelaughter vocalizations. These sounds are described as high-pitched squeals, "close to a chortle" (Sroufe & Waters, 1976, p. 176), and when analyzed acoustically are similar in form to fully developed laughter sounds in older infants.

Smiling is a silent expression of positive arousal, whereas laughter includes distinctive vocalization patterns. Smiling is a gentle acknowledgment of pleasant friendliness and connection, a precursor to laughter that continues to serve a variety of functions throughout life. In infancy, the smile represents a different order of playfulness and engagement from laughter. Infant laughter is not a greeting or a "conversation" opener like a smile: it is a hearty thumbs-up response to a look, a sound, or a wiggle. Laughter endorses a mutual activity, and, when combined with gaze, is a bid for continuing it. It also represents the ability to explore and embrace novelty and increase learning.

One shared characteristic between genuine laughter and happy smiling is the appearance of a bright sparkle in the eyes, which first appears at about 4 months (by which time tear production is well established). When smiles and laughs are not accompanied by this brightness in the eyes, something seems off and may make the smiles and laughs seem fake or insincere. As mentioned earlier, the two types of smiles and laughs are termed "Duchenne," the term for bright-eyed, genuine, natural smiles and laughs, and "non-Duchenne," for controlled, socially produced smiles or laughs. Both types involve contraction of the muscles at the corners of the mouth, but only the Duchenne smiles and laughs also include contraction of the orbicularis oculi muscle, the one that raises the cheeks and forms crow's feet crinkles around the eyes. It is easy to make the mouth produce a smile or laughter expression, but infants, and similarly most adults, are not able to voluntarily contract the muscles around the eyes, nor create the sparkle and "brightness" in them.

Laughter

"Laughter is a remarkable development with profound implications," wrote Sroufe and Waters (1976, p. 179), and I agree. Its appearance marks a shift from the sleepy, mellow, smiley early months when babies are adjusting to life outside the womb to a readiness for energetic engagement with the world. Laughter represents increased physical maturity, including that of the nervous and muscular systems—increased comfort in the attachment bond, and increasing cognitive sophistication.

Laughter 3 to 6 Months

First laughs reliably occur between about 3 and 4 months of age. The father of 3-month-old Brian describes one of Brian's early laughter episodes (Field, 1982). The baby first gave a big smile in response to a smile from his mother who, encouraged by this, "made a funny face, tickled him on the tummy and he laughed" (p. 101). Now overaroused, Brian looked away from her, and she attuned to his need for a little breather and waited, "knowing he would come back for more" (p. 101). Brian's smile said, "I'm good with this" and encouraged his mother to engage further, though at this age, his ability to tolerate a higher level of stimulation was limited, as indicated by his averted gaze. Fortunately, his mother was attuned to his signals and knew to wait for the sign that he was ready for more instead of pursuing him when he turned away.

Washburn (1929/1972) has suggested that, since smiles and laughs represent the peak of positive arousal, young babies may almost always need to take frequent breaks to calm and regroup before embracing more of the same. Early laughter episodes last just fractions of a second, though they increase to nearly 1 second within the first year; frequency of laughter episodes also increases during this time (Nwokah, Hsu, Dobrowolska, & Fogel, 1994).

Hsu, Nwokah, and Fogel (1998) studied the characteristics of early infant laughter (4 to 24 weeks of age) by videotaping weekly 5-minute face-to-face interactions between infants and their mothers. They recorded 175 infant laughs among 13 infants and rated them for degree of intensity based on the number of vocal peaks (called waves of laughter in adults). The least intense laughs were designated "a comment," had one peak, and represented 38% of the laughs. The "chuckle," with two peaks, occurred in 19% of the laughs. "Rhythmical laughter," the most intense form, with more than two peaks, was the most common at 43% (p. 470). A distinguishing feature between the laughs was the amount of face-to-face engagement, with more direct face-to-face engagement associated with more intense laughter; this may have increased with age, though if so it was not noted in the report. Chuckle laughs were more likely when babies were playing tactile games while sitting (partially reclined) in infant seats, and rhythmical laughs were more likely when the babies were sitting up.

As might be expected, the variety and types of playful stimulation to which infants respond expands over the first year. Sroufe and Wunsch (1972) trained mothers to present 24 different face-to-face, laugh-inducing behaviors, all of them involving something novel or unexpected. The frequency of laughter at the various items increased remarkably over the first year of this longitudinal study, with 4- to 6-month-olds laughing at just 10% of the trials, while the slightly older 7- to 9-month-olds laughed at 37%, and the 10- to 12-month-olds at 43%. As the babies aged, they also got to be quicker on the uptake. At 4 months, there was a lag of 1–2 seconds between stimulation and laughter, but by 5–6 months, the laughter was immediate. By the end of their first year, the babies would either laugh immediately or even ahead of time in anticipation of the stimulus.

The favored comedic act also changed with maturity. At the age of 4–6 months, the top laugh-inducer was the familiar "gonna get you" game (50%), followed by stomach kissing at 33%. Most of the 11 items that produced laughter at that age involved auditory or tactile components—or both. The wilder antics preferred by the older infants such as silly walking, funny noises, peekaboo, and "coochy-coo," did not rouse even one laugh in the younger babies (Sroufe & Wunsch, 1972).

By 4 months, infants begin to show increased interest in the outside world. They gaze around the room rather than almost exclusively at the mother. At about this same time, Reddy (2008) observed the onset of what she calls parents' "desperation" for positive engagement. Caregivers "start performing more and more exaggerated actions" (p. 117), often involving the infant's body: bicycling feet (Aurelia's favorite), patty-caking the hands, or gently tickling. Infants indicate that they are ready for something new in the way of entertainment and exploration, and adults, who are eager for positive engagement, comply. As Reddy put it, "Infants seek more and adults do more" (p. 117).

Bowlby's (1969) suggestion that infant social smiles only occur when other people are around might equally apply to laughter, which in the first six months of life would rarely if ever be solitary. Early infant laughter takes place in the context of a face-to-face engagement, either with a caregiver or with another familiar person, clearly linking it to the attachment system. In observing laughter in a 12-week-old, Reddy (2008) found that "every smile, every chuckle, and every attempt to elicit an action or a laugh from the other was completely embedded within the other's response" (p. 201). The rare occasions for solitary laughter in these early months might include laughing at a mobile above the crib or at the antics of an animal, safe-enough novelties in the baby's environment that manage to engage without arousing distress. Little Leo, beginning at about 6 months, liked looking out the window at Dottie, his grandmother Tanga's dog. He would laugh at the dog, but then turn around to look at us to share in the fun.

Tickling is also about social interaction, a fact that becomes obvious as babies laugh, even at the approach of a caregiver's wiggling finger. A colleague's 13-month-old granddaughter Nora once did a little tickling experiment after watching her aunt play with Nora's 5-month-old cousin. After carefully observing her aunt's vocalizations and the way she tickled Oliver's tummy before he burst into great gales of laughter, Nora walked off by herself and began trying to re-create the game, repeating "ah, ah, ah" and trying to tickle her own tummy. She soon gave up, having discovered the age-old truth that tickling is an interactive experience—as is the laughter that results from it. Tickling must also take place in a safe-enough relationship, as quickly becomes obvious if a stranger tries to tickle a baby, or for that matter a person of any age.

A number of studies have noted that in the early months, smiles and laughter can quickly turn to distress and crying. In her detailed longitudinal study, Washburn (1929/1972) observed that the sounds of a baby's laughter would sometimes turn to those of crying without any rhythmic interruption. Overstimulation that is not reduced or regulated by the caregiver, even if it is intended as fun, can be responsible for this abrupt transition into distress. Some mothers, like my sister, note that another reason why laughter can turn to crying is because it may have occurred while a caregiver was attempting to soothe the baby's distress. If the affect regulation is not totally successful, the baby returns to distress after a laugh.

Laughter 7 to 12 Months

Life in the laughter lane starts to get more interesting in the second half of the first year. Babies sit up and become mobile and take a more active part in the fun. They laugh more and find more things funny. Variations on earlier entertainments continue to work, though visual and social items begin to gain more traction. More than half the babies in the Sroufe and Wunsch (1972) study laughed at visuals such as the mother covering her face or walking in a silly, slapstick manner. A whopping 86% laughed when the mother shook her hair, followed closely by 82% who laughed at the newly popular peekaboo. Leo at 7 months, for example, went into gales of laughter when his big sister jumped out from behind a chair and yelled, "Boo!" At a younger age, he would have startled and even cried if she had done that.

Babies at this age also start to laugh at things they do themselves: putting the peekaboo cloth over their mother's head, or reaching for their mother's tongue if she wiggles it at them. By 10 to 12 months, babies, especially those who are securely attached, are laughing in anticipation of "gonna get you," or the "There she is!" of peekaboo. After one 9-month-old sneezed, her mother followed with an exaggerated "aaaachoo!" making the baby laugh (Washburn, 1929/1972). On the second or third repetition, the mother only had to say "aaaah" and the baby would laugh.

It is important to note that the studies and developmental trajectories in this chapter all relate to American and European infants. As we know, caregiving patterns and goals differ from culture to culture. The "desperation" for smiles, laughter, and positive engagement with their infants that Reddy observed in parents in England, for example, may not be shared by caregivers in other cultures (Tronick, 2007). Therefore, the frequency and type and stimuli for laughter will differ accordingly, though the behavior itself is a constant in all cultures.

The need for safety as a necessary precondition for laughter and play may also be common to all human infants (Tronick, 2007). MacDonald and Silverman (1978) studied eight infants in the United States aged 10 to 14 months to see if they responded differently to peekaboo played with mothers and experimenters. All eight children smiled or laughed at their mothers, and at the experimenter, as long as the mother was standing by. All looked wary when the experimenter approached alone. Most eventually gave a slight smile, though three cried.

Tracing Aurelia's laughter through these months, a lot of new experiences just seemed to tickle (a lovely nonliteral word for laughter) her enormously. For example, she giggled with delight watching herself appear and disappear in the mirror while her dad held her in front of it and alternated standing up and bending down. Her mother's chicken dance, complete with flapping elbows and clucks, was a surefire "rhythmic" (multiple peaks) laugh-inducer, too.

The impact of "symbiotic entrainment," and "right-brain to right-brain" nervous system connections between positively aroused infants and their caregivers is becoming clear by this age. A study comparing the frequency of laughter between infants and their caregivers found that the more the mothers of 6- to 12-month-olds laughed, the more their infants laughed, and vice versa (Ziajka as cited in Nwokah et al., 1994).

From the time laughter first appears, "there is a bi-directionality of laughter responses" (Nwokah et al., 1994, pp. 32–33), meaning that laughter is a relationship behavior, rarely a solitary act. Of interest from a parenting standpoint, a longitudinal laboratory study of laughter in the first and second years found that mothers responded to their baby's laughter (198 instances in the first 12 months of the study) much more often than babies responded to their mother's laughter (only 45 times). Simultaneous onset of mother/baby laughs was rare (Nwokah et al., 1994).

The caregiver's engaged response to an infant's positive arousal is crucial in amplifying it over time. Babies who laugh a lot early on continue to be the most frequent laughers later (Washburn, 1929/1972). It is worrisome, though predictable based on the idea of symbiotic entrainment of the two nervous systems, that the absence of a response to a child's positive arousal—or alternatively a negative or overstimulated response to it—would lead to a similar effect: more distressed, negative arousal or silent withdrawal and, in cases of severe abuse, possibly dissociation. For better or worse, the child's nervous system is shaped by its relationship to the caregiver's nervous system and behavior, thereby establishing internal working models or attachment styles and patterns of regulating affect, as we will discuss further in Chapter 6.

Joining in the Laughter of Others

Beginning at 6 months, babies sometimes laugh simply to join the laughter of others, even, Reddy (2008) wrote, "when they cannot have a clue about its context" (p. 203). Aurelia certainly did this at 6 months, laughing along with us in the car. Leo a bit later, at 9 months, once crawled into an adjoining room to find his toys and when he heard us laughing in the next room turned around and laughed, too, even though our jocularity was at a distance and had nothing to do with him. Reddy noted this social laughter in 59% of 8-month-olds for certain, and possibly in another 23% as well. The mother of an 11-month-old in Reddy's study said that her daughter would join with others, even if the adults just pretended to laugh. "She'll sit there and chuckle with you and even if there's nothing funny about, you haven't done anything, even if you just sit there and laugh, then she'll laugh with you" (p. 203). Infant social laughter has a purity that affirms that attachment and connection are at laughter's core. The baby's wish to simply share in the fun is enough to evoke laughter, even in the absence of humor or comedy and the cognitive skills needed to comprehend them.

Clowning, Showing Off, and Teasing

Beginning at about 8 months, infants begin to realize they can evoke laughter in others. Reddy calls this "infant clowning," which she defines as an act that an infant repeats "deliberately in order to re-elicit laughter from others" (Reddy, 2001, p. 2). She observed that at 8 months, 87% of the babies in her study were clowning, and by 11 months it was a common everyday occurrence in 100% of them.

In an amazing leap, infants expand from reacting to something novel with laughter to creating something novel in order to evoke laughter. It can be something as simple as banging a spoon on the table, or as complex as imitating a snoring great-grandmother (as one youngster did in Reddy's study). Of course if the behavior is not one that parents wish to reinforce, parents may try to stifle their laughter—quite often unsuccessfully—in order to discourage repetition. Our family experienced this the time Aurelia repeatedly filled her mouth with milk and spewed it across the table. "Oops, that wasn't funny," we tried, unsuccessfully, to say with a straight face.

Reddy (2001) believes, as do I, that the developmental origins of humor appear, like laughter, to be "intrinsically social and emotional" (p. 6). Getting a response from another person is the whole point; the tricks one devises in order to do so are beside the point. Infants see humor in the context of social response, not in the act itself, which Reddy believes is also true of adult clowns. Having noticed the similarity, Reddy compiled a list of comedic acts common to both adult clowns and infant "clowns." The list is eerily similar: odd body movements, facial expressions or sounds, acting absurd, pretending profanity or hostility, violating norms or taboos, mocking and imitating others, adopting a grotesque appearance, and acting infantile or regressed. With each category she lists one or more examples from the infant repertoire. For example, an infant "acting absurd" might put a pacifier in his mother's mouth, kiss a sibling's knee, or bite someone's toes. Acting infantile seems like an oxymoron for an infant, but in fact immature "clowning around" is common to clowns of all ages.

At around 9 months, our little comedians also start violating social norms by playful teasing. They seem to find offering and withdrawing a cracker, or leaning forward to go into someone's arms and then pulling back quite funny, and seem to expect that others will, too. Aurelia liked to put the lid on the teapot after her mother filled it. Toward the end of her first year, she began to lean forward as if to do it and then withdraw her hand, smiling mischievously. Children also like to tease at being naughty or difficult. Tanner, my sister Marcia's grandson, at a similar age, reached for the soap and started to put it in his mouth. Marcia said, "Soap is for our hands, not our mouths." He repeated his original "error" for days, laughing each time she repeated her reality check.

To play teasing games you need at least two people: the provocateur and the respondent. Playful teasing (to be distinguished from malicious teasing later in childhood) brings the mischievous, engaged baby and the responsive, playful caregiver closer together. Teasing, Reddy believes, breaks mode of communication as usual, thereby creating incongruity that (like humor) leads to a higher level of engagement, prolonging and intensifying contact. Teasing intensifies novelty: what fun is it to routinely put a lid on a kettle or wash your hands day after day? Teasing makes the interaction a novel one, engaging both caregiver and child in extra ways, thereby making daily tasks more interesting and fun.

Duchenne and Non-Duchenne Laughter

By 8 months of age, caregivers are able to distinguish genuine laughs (Duchenne) from social laughs (non-Duchenne) in their children. Though people tend to find non-Duchenne laughs unconvincing, they do represent an attempt to engage with others. With Aurelia, it seemed to be her way of telling us that she was enjoying what we were doing. When she was an older infant, for example, I instituted the morning weather report, which consisted of holding her up at the front picture window to review the weather outside. I would comment on the sun, the clouds, the wind, and the flowers while she nodded seriously and pointed to each thing I mentioned. On occasion, out of the blue, she would give a forced-sounding non-Duchenne laugh. Was she being polite? Was she saying, "This is pretty good fun, so keep doing it"? I considered her forced laughter to be encouragement, and she seemed to agree by remaining engaged in our joint activity.

Malatesta, Culver, Tesman, and Shepard (1989) point out that expressive behavior and feeling states remain closely linked during early infancy, which is an argument against treating non-Duchenne laughter as "fake." Wired in congruence between external signals, such as movements, facial expressions, or vocalizations, and an internal state appear to be hardwired in infancy. This makes sense from a survival standpoint in that caregivers of infants need reliable signals so they can attune and give care appropriately. Not until the second year of life do infants begin to learn to neutralize or mask their feelings or cover one feeling with another (Malatesta et al., 1989). Before words, infants are short on communication skills, but have learned that laughter—and crying—communicate much. They may be "creating" laughter at younger ages, but it is to let their caregivers know they are truly playful and engaged, even if something is not necessarily "funny."

Laughter 12 to 18 Months

At about this age, infants reach the peak of their laughter cycle. These little toddlers are feeling their oats as they start to gain mobility and strength and as their left-hemisphere development gears up for expanding cognitive and explicit learning. It does not take much to get them going at this age, which is a delight to everyone.

Panksepp (2001) points out that while there is something "primitive" about the "stereotyped vocal pattern of laughter" and play, "emotional systems captivate cognitive process" (p. 154). Infant laughter builds toward adult humor, which he defines as "hard-wired emotional processes" (such as the attachment system) interacting with cognitive abilities (p. 154).

This calls to mind the time I described in Chapter 1 when Aurelia, then 13 months old, laughed at my silly word play asking her if the "chomp, chomp, chomp" of the cracker felt good on her "toofeys." She seemed to find humorous incongruity in the sound of "chomp, chomp, chomp" and the new word "toofeys." She appeared to in some way comprehend my reference and made a complex cognitive leap, finding humor in my words and tone of voice, in the absence of seeing me perform any physical comedy or even being able to see my facial expression as she was facing away from me.

Sroufe and Wunsch (1972) link laughter with cognitive development, pointing out that the baby has to be able to figure out whether or not something incongruent is funny or distressing—the knit brow phenomenon mentioned earlier. One interesting difference they noted is that when laughter occurs in response to a stimulus, such as an unfamiliar toy, the baby stays oriented toward the stimulus, reaches out and seems to want more. This seems to demonstrate the way in which an infant experiences pleasure while learning from exploring joyful, novel experiences. If the new toy presented to the baby creates distress and crying instead of laughter, the baby will pull back and turn away from it.

Both implicit and explicit learning have been linked with laughter. Panksepp (2001) emphasizes the importance, for example, of certain kinds of noncognitive play. He concludes that "all children need daily doses of rough and tumble (R&T) activities, for this may optimize brain organization" (p. 146). I began to notice how engaged Aurelia became when her "Nonna" (her Italian grandmother) got

down on the floor with her to play "doggie," complete with making noises, nuzzling, and raising one leg as if to pee. Aurelia laughed almost hysterically, too,
when her dad would run with her all through the house pretending to be various
animals: a frog, a bear, or a lion. Panksepp's ideas encouraged me to try rolling
around on a futon with her, and I discovered that I enjoyed it, too, even though
I confess greater proficiency at word games than roughhousing.

Laughter at Remembered Pleasure

Laughter also helps to mark important moments that are touch points for explicit memory and cognitive development. The desire to repeat a novel experience
helps it become something familiar that can be mastered. When Aurelia was 15
months old we were at a family gathering in Santa Fe. The next time I saw her,
about 2 months later, she asked me (with sign language as she could not talk yet)
to tell her stories about the visit. She prompted me with signs to talk about the
big ceramic frogs at the hotel, and playing ball with her cousin Tanner. Moving
on to greater complexity (she could sign in sentences, and later paragraphs, before
she could talk), she signed "bird" and "eating" and "more" to remind me to tell
her about walking around the plaza looking at the pigeons gobbling up food on
the ground. She listened intently as I recounted the narrative in words up to the
part where, all of a sudden, we could not see any pigeons. I ended the story with
flourish, "Finally, we looked high up on the statue in the middle of the plaza, and
there were all the pigeons!" At that point Aurelia burst out laughing just as she
had done in real time when we spotted the missing pigeons. Her response to the
retelling was as genuinely pleasurable as the original experience, reinforcing both
the cognitive and the affective parts of the experience.

Laughter at Success

As infancy progresses, laughter comes to include more than responding to novel
stimuli, teasing, and clowning. Linked with the exploration/curiosity system, it
also becomes an active process initiated by the child. When a new task is accomplished, laughter is frequently the result. For example, 13-month-old Douglas
was working on his block tower with great concentration. When he finally got
the fourth one to stay on top, he laughed out loud and clapped his hands (Lewis
& Rosenblum, 1978). His mother, attuning to and sharing his delight, called out,
"Good, Doug. It is a ta-l-l-l tower. Don't you feel good!" (p. 1). Douglas's mother
was right on target attuning to his positive arousal. Imagine the consequences to
his development if too many times she were feeling depressed, or overwhelmed
with other children, or distracted by checking her e-mails. Children, just like
adults, are geared to share their positive moments with another attuned person.
From birth onward, our nervous systems continue to be intertwined with the
nervous systems of those around us. Affect arousal, positive or negative, and affect regulation, are intrinsically mutual, and when the attunement is missing or

off-base, infants, children, and adults find positive feelings dampened and negative feelings intensified, resulting in disappointment and dysregulation.

Laughter 18 to 24 months

By this age, toddlers begin to find that their comic efforts may not always lead to laughter. For example, caregivers do not find it humorous when their young children tease them by performing provocative exploits such as trying to stand on a slide, or running away when called. Children may not always reciprocate adult laughter either, such as when they are mastering a new skill, or "mispronouncing a word but not understanding the mother's humorous response" (Nwokah et al., 1994, p. 33). Aurelia, for example, cried when she was experimenting with putting a sock on her head and her mother made a playful comment. She was serious about her experiment, not playing for a laugh.

Most caregiver-infant pairs by this age develop their own idiosyncratic laughter patterns. One mother would produce the facial expression of laughter and her toddler would jump in with the laughter vocalization, genuinely amused at the joint play. Another dyad would stare silently at each other smiling, and then "burst out with laughter almost simultaneously, in the absence of any apparent stimuli for laughter" (Nwokah et al., 1994, pp. 33–34). These "inside jokes" are mysterious to outsiders, but clearly build intimacy, attachment, and family closeness.

Somewhere in the second year of life, children learn to smile and laugh on request. I first tried asking Aurelia to smile at about 18 months when I was taking her picture. By 20 months, she was able to laugh on request from her laughter-researching grandmother, and at 22 months would produce a nice laugh on the telephone when asked—all non-Duchenne laughs, of course. At around this same time, she learned to "tell" a story about something she had done or seen in sign language. The story would include the affect as symbolized by the "sign" for laughter, which mimicked its sound, "ha, ha," or, if appropriate, the sign for crying, "eh-eh."

Laughter at Visual Jokes

Sight gags continue to go over big with children in this age group. A 20-month-old's dad put his child's pants on like a hat and got big laughs. At about 21 months, however, Aurelia had a different reaction to the similar attempt at humor. When her Nonna held up Aurelia's new little denim skirt as though Nonna were wearing it, Aurelia cried. All novelty is not funny, and individual differences in humor appreciation begin to assert themselves.

Laughter at Playful Substitutions

Deliberately contrived incongruencies, verbal, sung, or enacted, are a source of great amusement to many toddlers. For example, one mother was brushing her 22-month-old son's teeth. He looked up with a teasing sparkle in his eye and said,

"Brush nose?" And then, laughing at his own joke, continued with "Brush ear?" (McGhee, 2009).

Sometimes, however, the humor may be in the eye of the infant beholder. At 22 months, Aurelia was obsessed with drawing rabbits. One day she brought me a sketch book and crayons and sat in my lap on the bed to draw. I started looking for a blank space and found every square inch on every page already covered with rabbits. Finally, I exclaimed with mild consternation, "This book is full of rabbits!" and she burst out laughing. I was mystified—only she got the joke—though of course, I couldn't help laughing with delight at her delight, whatever caused it.

Smiling and Laughter in Children with Disabilities

The developmental trajectory for smiling and laughter may be different for children born with a variety of challenging physical and mental conditions. Their experiences, however, highlight the developmental needs of all children and the affect-regulating challenges of all caregivers.

One feels for the sighted parents in Fraiberg's (1979) study of blind babies. Deprived of the crucial and powerful face-to-face eye-gaze of early infancy and desperate to hear a laugh, the caregivers turned to "bouncing, juggling, tickling and nuzzling," to a degree that, to the research observers, seemed to extend well beyond the range of stimulation tolerable to an infant (p. 158). When faced with the "desperation" for positive engagement common to almost all parents, as mentioned earlier, these sighted caregivers struggled to compensate for their infants' absence of gaze and face-to-face engagement, the source of most infant laughter, by using exaggerated physical and verbal stimulation. Another researcher relates to any parents' disappointment at not getting a laugh from a baby when he wrote, "The sober regard of an infant is just as dashing to playfulness as that of an older person" (Washburn, 1929/1972, p. 482).

Children with other special needs may also show delayed, infrequent, or muted smiles and laughter. In her study of 4-month-old (corrected for gestational age) preterm infants, and "post-maturity syndrome" infants (babies delivered well after their due date who develop a variety of symptoms as a result), Field (1982) observed that both groups smiled and vocalized less than normal-term infants when their mothers played peekaboo or patty cake. They also frowned and cried more frequently. Based on their elevated heart rates, gaze aversion, and crying, it is also clear that these infants more easily reach overload. This means that "the caregiver is faced with a less adept social partner" (Malatesta et al., 1989, p. 24). The researchers found a similar elevated heart rate in the mothers, pointing to the stress the caregiver feels, as well.

These infants' under-responsiveness made their mothers more desperate for a response, as with the sighted caregivers of the blind babies. They talked more and worked harder to get a positive response, or tried to prolong the successful responses too long, causing the infants to overload and cry. Mothers of normal-term infants, on the other hand, were more comfortably able to recognize the importance of toning down the play, based on their infants' signals (Field, 1982).

Another study looked at "affect exchanges" between mothers and their infants ages 3 to 36 months. Some infants were typically developing while others had disabilities such as Down syndrome, or physical disabilities such as cerebral palsy or developmental delays in cognitive or physical spheres. Less smiling occurred overall in the special needs groups (Brooks-Gunn & Lewis, 1982). In fact, they found that one-third of the sample with special needs never smiled in the first two years. By the third year, 79% of these children were frequent smilers; however, the wear and tear on the caregivers would likely have been considerable by then.

Infants with Down syndrome also typically lag several months behind the 4-month mark in the development of laughter. Eventually, however, they do come to laugh at the same items in the same developmental sequence as non-Down babies, though their positive affect may be more muted. This early lack of smiling may partially be due to the "hypotonicity [or low muscle tone] of their facial muscles" (Denham, 1998, p. 191). This may also explain the findings that their social smiles at 3.5 months were "less intense and less engaging" (Emde, Katz, & Thorpe, 1978, p. 352). For example, Dawn, a baby with Down syndrome, was described by a researcher doing a home visit. He noted that Dawn would smile, but that there was something unusual about it. He also empathized with her caregivers and shared his own feelings about the interactive experience with her muted smile.

> There was bilateral upturning of the corners of the mouth, but the cheeks and eyes did not crinkle or participate; there was no brightening of the eyes.... and eye contact was poor.... Each of us who experienced this sequence felt a sense of being let down. We expected more. The smiling seemed to raise our expectation of a fun-filled social encounter, but its dampened nature seemed to discourage rather than encourage. Even more, the relative lack of eye contact seemed to "turn us off." (Emde et al., 1978, p. 356)

Infant physical therapist and mental health expert Karla Stromberger (personal communication, July 2009), who has worked with many parents of disabled infants, believes that the low muscle tone characteristic of Down syndrome and other developmentally disabled infants impacts their ability to smile and laugh. She said that it takes them a tremendous amount of energy to recruit the muscles necessary for smiling and laughing, not just in the face, but also in the rest of the body. She advises parents to be sure that their baby is well rested and held in a cradled position with head and trunk and limbs well supported before beginning gentle playful interactions. In this way, infants have the physical stability and energy to engage. "Then the babies can do several rounds of interaction and smiling," she said, "and later laughing, without wiping out, and their parents also feel rewarded by this play."

Laughter in infancy is a positive force field that keeps infants and caregivers motivated to keep each other's company. The input from caregivers and the input from infants are intertwined, setting the stage for patterns of connection and affect arousal and regulation throughout the infant's life. Positive arousal, attunement, and regulation contribute to the intergenerational transmission of internal working models of attachment, or attachment style, the topic of the following chapter.

6

AFFECT ATTUNEMENT AND MISATTUNEMENT AND THE FORMATION OF INTERNAL WORKING MODELS OF ATTACHMENT

Baby laughter is fun, but its cumulative impact lasts far beyond the moment's pleasure. Stable attachment bonds that "transmit high levels of positive affect are vitally important for the infant's continuing neurobiological development" (Schore, 2003a, p. 11). Repeated cycles of shared delight shape a neurobiological foundation for the child's emotional and social future. Tragically, so, too, do repeated experiences of misattunement, overstimulation, and neglect, not to mention prolonged periods of dysregulation.

Cycles of arousal (positive or negative), attunement/misattunement, and regulation/repair are the core ingredients in the formation of a child's internal working models of attachment, or attachment style, during the early months of life. Laughter fuels the process of secure attachment formation and is an important gauge of it, as well. Shared social/neurological moments in infant laughter are directly linked to the affective state "that underlies and motivates attachment behavior and...motivates attachment bond formation" (Schore, 2003a, p. 10).

Repeated cycles of positive (or negative) arousal, attunement, and regulation also set the template for the infant's patterns of affect arousal, appraisal, and regulation throughout life. Caregiver and infant nervous systems are intertwined in the early months of life so that, as Schore states, the caregiver is "down-loading programs from her brain into the infant's brain" (2003b, p. 13). In terms of affect arousal, experiences with laughter and crying provide the foundation for the expression of intense states of affect in childhood and throughout life (Nwokah, Hsu, Dobrowolska, & Fogel, 1994, p. 34). In addition, the caregiver's responses to infant laughter also lay the all-important neurobiological groundwork for affect regulation.

Neurobiological Aspects of Positive Engagement

Infants are particularly oriented toward the human face, especially that of the primary caregiver. What the infant sees in the caregiver's face is mirrored and felt by the infant. For example, when an infant watches a video of a woman crying (expressing negative affect), the baby's brain shows a similar pattern of negative affect (Davidson & Fox, 1982). Watching a laughing woman, on the other hand, results in a matching positive arousal in the babies.

"Intense states of elation," Schore writes (2003a), impact the nervous systems of both mothers and infants (p. 9). The mother's face is known to trigger the release of "high levels of endogenous opiates" in the child's brain which are responsible for "the pleasurable qualities of social interaction, social affect, and attachment (p. 10). The hormone oxytocin, for example, is released in response to tone of voice, touch, and warm facial expressions, providing the biochemical reinforcement for the baby to feel good and enjoy life.

The hormones, neurohormones, and enzymes that are released in states of elation impact not only the momentary feeling but also "influence the activation of gene-action systems that program the structural growth of brain regions that are essential to the future socio-emotional development of the child" (Schore, 2003a, p. 11). Facial expression is one important key to understanding the communication of joy or distress between caregiver and infant. The neurons that fire in response to another's facial expressions, especially the affect-laden face of the primary caregiver, are found in the orbitoinsular region of the prefrontal cortex. This is the region of the brain that enables the developing child to process subtle cues transmitted by facial expressions, especially those of the primary caregiver; this prepares the child for the later processing of all facial expressions. Being able to accurately tune into the meaning of subtle facial cues is necessary for interpreting and responding appropriately to social cues as well as for self-regulation of affect and body states.

As a student of both crying and laughter, I find it interesting that the anterior cingulate of the medial frontal cortex is active during both play *and* separation behaviors, during and laughing *and* crying vocalizations, and during the activation of facial expressions that are integral to both. Laughing and crying are both attachment behaviors that powerfully serve to initiate and maintain caregiver-infant contact, one in response to separation and distress, the other a bid for engagement and play. It is also the anterior cingulate of the caregiver's medial frontal cortex that responds to infant cry sounds reciprocally "tuning the infant's medial frontal cortex, thereby influencing the parcellation and final circuit wiring of the baby's developing anterior cingulate" (Schore, 2003a, p. 158). This describes in physiological terms the interpersonal process whereby the nervous systems of caregiver and infant are intertwined from birth. It is in this intersubjective field—what Trevarthan (1979) calls "primary intersubjectivity"—that the shared experience of caregiver and infant impacts the wiring of the infant's maturing brain.

Of primary importance in terms of the role of laughter in neurobiological development is the fact that the anterior cingulate regions develop in the second and third quarters of the first year, the ages when laughter first appears and peaks. These areas of the brain are conspicuously linked to the engagement of infant and caregiver during times of joy and times of stress, and to the ultimate wiring of the baby's anterior cingulate. This process points to the role of laughter in the eventual development of attachment styles and to the accompanying establishment of patterns of affect arousal and regulation.

Affect Attunement, Misattunement, and Regulation

As adults know and babies soon learn, life is not always fun and play. Mismatches between caregiver and infant affect are commonplace and result in many misattunements during the course of a day. Some researchers estimate that they occur in up to two-thirds of even the most attuned caregiver-infant transactions (Tronick, 2007). Attuning to infant's affect is no easy feat for caregivers. Malatesta (1982) videotaped 60 mothers and their 3- to 6-month-old infants during 16-minute play sessions in the lab. The very youngest infant changed expressions often—every 7 seconds, with the frequency of change decreasing to 9 seconds by 6 months. The most timely and effective maternal responses to the infant's expressions occurred within less than half a second after the expression change. The most successfully attuned responses matched the infant's affect without being an exact imitation: "One partner displays similar affect in a nonsimilar way" (Nwokah et al., 1994, p. 33). Caregiver misattunements can occur for a variety of reasons, including when caregivers meet infant affects with overly precise mirroring, too much dissimilarity of emotion, a neutral, blank face, or ignore the infant's arousal altogether (Schore, 2003a).

When a caregiver misattunes to negative arousal, infants respond by intensified crying, making the misattunement difficult to ignore. Misattunements to positive arousal, however, such as the failure to stimulate or respond in kind to an infant's smiles or laughter, or the failure to recognize, attune to and down-regulate or soothe positive overstimulation, are much subtler and therefore easier to miss. The infant may up the ante briefly in an effort to attain an attuned response, but if this does not work, the infant may quickly shut down, gaze avert, or withdraw, but only rarely, I suspect, will the infant become dysregulated enough to cry in protest. If under-response or overstimulation is chronic, the infant will in all likelihood abandon efforts to engage or remain in a withdrawn, dissociated state as a primitive means of self-regulation.

One of the most useful resources for understanding the immediacy of playful parental engagement with an infant is the well-known still-face experiment (Tronick, 2007). After playing with her infant for a few minutes, the mother (or caregiver) is instructed to still her own face and head in order to present the baby with a neutral, nonresponsive, mask-like face. Infants immediately begin to

increase their bids for engagement by smiling, pointing, reaching, gazing, or cooing. As the mother continues to present a still face, the child will begin to avert
gaze, squirm, and get increasingly unhappy and disorganized. Reddy (2008) tried
it with her daughter at the age of 6 weeks, which is considerably younger than the
usual 6-month-olds studied in the still-face experiment. At first, the little baby
sobered and looked away and then tried smiling and vocalizing to reengage her
mother, repeating that cycle a few times. Reddy (2008) writes,

> It must have lasted all of 30 seconds but felt much longer. I couldn't stand
> not responding any more and broke into a smile, spoke to her and leaned
> forward to hug her in apology. At this her face crumpled and she began to
> cry. I was shocked, dismayed, and immensely touched.... A lack of response
> is noticed by and matters to a 2-month-old. (pp. 73–74)

Attuned caregivers have a difficult time, as Reddy did, doing even a 30-second experiment. The infants quickly become dysregulated as they actively try to reengage
their mothers. The mothers in turn have a hard time keeping their own faces still
while ignoring their baby's bids for engagement and/or distress. A colleague said
she once saw a still-face video where the infant, after a few seconds of unsuccessfully
trying all kinds of bids to reengage the mother, burst out laughing. Research proto-
col aside, the mother involuntarily broke the still-face pose and laughed in response.

Successfully recognizing, attuning to, and regulating overstimulation can also
be challenging for caregivers. When the caregiver is unsuccessful, the prolonged
overstimulation can be dysregulating for their infants. I have seen a number of
videos where mothers who are instructed to "play" with their infants become vis-
ibly desperate, perhaps because of being on-camera and wishing to perform well.
It is painful to watch as the caregiver looms over a seated baby, talks too loudly, or
"chases" the baby, whose face is averted as a defense against too much stimulation
by their mother's imposing herself in the baby's field of vision. In one such video
the mother was frantically trying to entertain her baby and kept escalating her attempts to capture his attention with louder, more intense "playful" gestures. The
little guy could not handle it, squirmed, and turned away with increasing distress.
Occasionally, he would look at her and try a little smile, but he could not hold it
for long in the face of such intensity. Instead of an attuned experience of positive
engagement supporting exploration, there was too much novelty, noise, and intrusion so the baby had to shut down.

Ideally, play is mutual—both parties are up for it and both share in the delight
of the moment. Because of the infant's immature nervous system, however, the
responsibility for monitoring the baby's interest and tolerance levels for playful
exchanges belongs to the caregiver. Making that job more challenging is the fact
that not all infants or caregivers have the same threshold for positive stimulation
and positive affect. Thresholds may vary depending on factors such as hunger,
fatigue, or illness (Field, 1982). With moderate levels of stimulation, the healthy,

well-rested infant will engage comfortably in smiling and laughing. If it becomes too much, the infant will gaze avert, a signal easy to recognize once understood. If the threshold is exceeded for too long, negative arousal expressed in fussing or crying, or in extreme situations, vomiting, will occur. With age, the tolerance level for intense play seems to increase. Sensitive caregivers learn to observe and match their infant's cycles of engagement, retreat, and recovery, even when the changes occur within microseconds.

Caregivers, too, have a threshold for engagement that may or may not be coordinated with that of the infant. As a result, a caregiver who is lively and outgoing but has a baby who is more "reserved," or vice versa, a lively baby with a reserved caregiver, may face even greater challenges. It is in this experience of "primary intersubjectivity," attunement and misattunement, that the internal working models of attachment, what we call attachment styles, develop based on the neurobiological processes described in the previous section.

Depressed Caregivers

When caregivers are overworked, overwhelmed, depressed, or otherwise unavailable, the risk is that their infants will be understimulated, with too little playful engagement and exploration. If a child holds out a toy, laughing to share his pleasure, and is met with a moan, groan, or blank stare, or simply ignored, the child's joy quickly diminishes and dysregulation can result. The infant suffers from an absence of the mutuality necessary for joyful exploration. When mutually playful engagement is curtailed in this way, there is a physiological shift in the infant— into negative arousal and away from positive arousal.

One common symptom of depression, whether stemming from hormonal changes, a bipolar disorder, or family and life stressors, is the dampening of arousal. Referred to as flat affect, this is one of the features of caregiver depression that can create disturbances "in face-to-face interactions between depressed mothers and their infants" (Bettes, 1988, p. 1089). In the Bettes study, depressed mothers were shown to be "less responsive, less spontaneous, and more constrained" compared to mothers not suffering from depression (p. 1089).

Bettes recruited 36 mothers of 3- to 4-month-olds for a study of what infants and mothers "say" to each other when they play together. Interactions between infants and their mothers were audio-recorded in their home with researchers staying out of visual range. The mothers were also asked to complete the Beck Depression Inventory. Scores below 10 were considered in the normal range, and 10 and above, mild to severe depression. Approximately one-third of the mothers (10 of 36) were above 10, but only in the mild to mild-moderate range of depression. None of them had scores high enough to receive a moderate or severe depression rating.

Even the mild to moderately depressed mothers, however, showed significant differences from nondepressed mothers in interactions with their infants. One issue related to promptness of the mother's response to changes in infant facial expressions, optimally 1 second or less. Depressed mothers in the Bettes study did not seem to be able to fine-tune the timing of their responses as well as the nondepressed mothers. For example, they did not seem able to adjust the timing of their response slower or faster depending on what was happening with the infant's vocalizations or gaze. The length of time it took depressed mothers to respond to their infant was more than twice as long as that for nondepressed mothers. No nondepressed mothers waited longer than 1 second to respond to infant vocalizations, whereas 27.7% of the depressed mothers did. More than 13% waited longer than 3 seconds, an eternity for anyone poised and waiting for a response to a feeling just expressed to another. While 3 seconds may seem like an inconsequential time frame to adults, it has been established that the optimal response time to infant expression is 1 second or less. From an infant's perspective, "pauses of longer than 3 seconds indicate 'time-outs' or periods of disengagement" (p. 1095). The fact that the depressed mothers' average latency to respond to a bid averaged nearly 2 seconds in this study put their infants "at a disadvantage in their attempts to 'converse' or 'play' with their mothers" (p. 1095).

In addition to facial expressions, prosody, rhythm, and tone of voice also impact the infant's nervous system (Schore, 2003a). An attuned caregiver's voice is a wonderful tool for helping another, whether infant, child, or adult, soothe and regulate otherwise overwhelming feelings such as distress. An appropriately cheerful, modulated, or sympathetic tone of voice is crucial for attuning to an infant. Not only is experiencing comforting prosody important in the moment for its soothing effect, but it also lays down the neurobiological foundation for the infant to be able to read emotional cues from other people (Schore, 2003a). In Bettes's (1988) study, depression impacted mothers' vocal rhythms and tone of voice. The lengths of utterances and pauses between vocalizations were also inconsistent. Further, and more importantly, the depressed mothers were 6 times more likely to respond to their infants in a nonexaggerated (flat) tone or manner, thereby mismatching to the infant's affective signals. In many instances, depressed mothers lacked the exaggerated intonation contours of the sing-song, higher-pitched vocal pattern that is traditionally known as "motherese" (feminists prefer the nongenderized term "infant directed speech," or IDS, because it is common to caregivers of both genders), and that is typical of caregivers who are not depressed.

The findings of Bettes's study were based on 2-minute play segments between infants and their mothers who were only mildly depressed. It seems likely that if more seriously depressed mothers had been observed for longer periods, they might have uttered substantially fewer vocalizations and taken even longer to respond. Further, as Bettes studied audio recordings, facial and tactile behaviors demonstrated during the long pauses following infant vocalization were not available for analysis. In light of the still face experiments (Tronick, 2007), the caregiver's facial expressions and quality of touch, or lack thereof, would also presumably increase the infant's negative arousal—for example, if the mother were staring into space, looking blankly at the child rather than smiling and nodding, or playfully touching foreheads or noses.

Neglected and High-Risk Infants

Children raised in extremely neglectful situations without positive attachment figures consistently available show little to no laughter at all (Wolff, 1987). Wolff noted that institutionalized children's level of social responsiveness "depends critically on the level of social interaction to which they are exposed" (p. 138). The absence of positive interaction means that positive arousal either does not occur or the likelihood of it doing so is severely dampened.

Field (1982) worked with mothers and their high-risk infants. One group consisted of post-term, post-maturity infants who were hyperactive, easily aroused, and irritable. The second group was made up of preterm infants with Respiratory Distress Syndrome who were less attentive to stimulation and less alert. Field observed that both groups of high-risk infants spent less time looking at their mothers and appeared to "enjoy" these interactions less than typically developing infants. Their smiles and vocalizations were less frequent, and they frowned and cried more often. These patterns, she speculated, could be caused by emotional overload due to excessive stimulation. For example, when the mothers did make bids for positive engagement, they sometimes overdid it. "In their natural attempts to elicit positive affective responses, the mothers appeared to provide a level of stimulation that seemed to be counterproductive" (Field, 1982, p. 109).

With help and support, depressed mothers and mothers of high-risk infants can, however, come to understand the importance of attuned responses. Field observed that the mothers' "attentiveness and positive affect" were enhanced in both partners by even minimal work with the mothers. For example, even simply suggesting that the mothers try imitating their infant's behaviors resulted in the mothers toning down some of their misattuned overstimulation, which led to improved responsiveness in the infant.

Attachment Styles and Differences in Laughter Behavior

When I was writing my book on crying and attachment, it became apparent that different patterns of crying are related to different attachment styles. This led me to wonder if the same might be true of laughter. With crying, I was able to link certain characteristic arousal patterns with secure, insecure, and disorganized attachment styles using data gleaned from the separations and reunions in the Strange Situation studies (Ainsworth & Bell, 1970; George & Solomon, 2008), and other related research (Nelson, 2005).

The Strange Situation is a laboratory procedure for observing an infant in a series of separations from and reunions with his or her caregiver that are intended to slightly stress the infant's attachment system. The infant's behavior upon reunion is used to determine attachment style. Secure infants cry appropriately in response to separations from the caregiver. Because they are able to rely on the consistency and availability of their caregivers, their crying is an appeal to the caregiver to end the separation and to down-regulate the infant's negative arousal. Their negative arousal (crying) quiets almost immediately upon reunion with the caregiver, and, in general, their negative arousal is soothed with relative ease.

Of the two types of insecurely attached children (ambivalent/resistant and avoidant), those with an ambivalent/resistant style have attachment systems that are hyperactivated. Their behavior during the Strange Situation includes more crying, especially protest crying at separation and otherwise. Caregivers of these children are unpredictable, overprotective, anxious, and/or intrusive in their responses to negative arousal. As a result, the children have difficulties with affect regulation, both interactive and self-regulation. Their negative arousal is difficult to soothe upon reunion.

Avoidant infants, on the other hand, have learned not to display their attachment distress and so rarely cry. To do this, they overuse self-regulation as an adaptive defense, and rarely turn to their caregiver for affect regulation. Upon separation and reunion, they show little apparent interest in the return of the caregiver. However, when physiological measures of the infant's anxiety are monitored during the separations and reunions, the data show that avoidant infants remain anxious even though they do not express it openly.

Finally, infants who demonstrate disorganized attachment are those whose caregivers range from abusive or neglectful to psychotic, fearful, or depressed. The arousal of their attachment distress observed during stressful separations and reunions in the Strange Situation do not fit into organized patterns. Upon reunion, the infant may bang his head, run away from the caregiver, or strike out at her. The ability of the infant to interactively or self-regulate affect is ineffective. The infant may become silent and even dissociate, an extreme self-soothing measure used to regulate overwhelming distress, particularly stress that is generated by the caregiver.

Because attachment distress has been considered primary in rating the quality of attachment security, crying has been tracked and analyzed in those and related studies. This growing body of work was the foundation for my theories about the relationship between crying patterns and attachment style. There is, however, a paucity of direct research regarding the arousal and regulation of positive affect relative to attachment style. For that reason, I have taken a more indirect approach to answering the question about what infant laughter may tell us about attachment style, and what attachment style might tell us about infant laughter. I came at the question from odd angles: research on the contingency of caregiver responses to infant arousal linked with attachment style (C. Z. Malatesta, Culver, Tesman, & Shepard, 1989), a study (Washburn, 1929/1972) that includes a classification of types of infant laughter linked to information about the quality of caregiver-infant interactions now known to be relevant to attachment style, and finally, two "case examples" of infants highlighted in a study by Demos (1982). These studies, in combination with my thinking about crying and attachment style, provided a foundation for formulating hypotheses about the frequency and quality of laughter associated with each attachment style in infancy.

Caregiving Patterns, Positive Arousal, and Attachment Style

The only study I found that looks directly at infant affect expressions, including "joy," and their interface with maternal responsiveness and attachment style is by C. Z. Malatesta, Culver, Tesmand, and Shepard (1989). They regularly videotaped 58 preterm and full-term infants during 7 minutes of face-to-face play at home between the ages of 22 months and 2.5 years. When the children were 2 (meaning they were older infants), Malatesta et al. administered the Strange Situation procedure and found that 43, or 60.4%, were secure (similar to the percentage breakdown of secure children in most Strange Situation studies of nonclinical populations), while 23, or 39%, were insecure, though only 3 of those were ambivalent/resistant and the remainder avoidant.

While this study predates the explosion of interest in mutual affect regulation prompted by attachment and interpersonal neurobiology, it is definitely moving in that direction. As the researchers note, "The early interactive exchanges of caregivers and infants are more than merely a form of nonverbal communication; they are affective imperatives that elicit mutual accommodation" (C. Z. Malatesta et al., 1989, p. 76). In other words, the authors are aware that they are examining the powerful affective interconnection of the two nervous systems—mother and infant. Once attachment style was determined through the Strange Situation at age 2, they were able to note a number of interesting differences between the earlier affect exchanges of securely and insecurely attached children and their mothers.

Optimal caregiver responses—rapid and attuned with the infant's affect—are, as we have discussed, an important indicator of the mother's ability to regulate the infant's affect. Indeed, it was the mother's ability to match the child's affect within the first second following the infant's expression change that turned out to be associated with security of attachment in the Malatesta et al. study. The quality of maternal attunement not only predicted attachment style in 2-year-olds, but also patterns of expressive behavior, including positive arousal.

Misattunement in this study consisted of intrusive or anxious responses including overconcern to sad faces or overexcitement with happy ones, which are experienced by the infant as "unpleasant and aversive" (C. Z. Malatesta et al., 1989, p. 76). Misattuned responses such as these appeared to make the infants overstimulated and dysregulated rather than being soothing or fun. These caregivers were, as adults might put it, too "in-your-face." These impingements caused the infants to disengage by sobering, averting gaze, and sometimes crying. One complicating factor is that an infant's disengagement from too much positive arousal miscues some parents and leads them to redouble their efforts, thereby creating even more unwanted stimulation. When the caregiver increases the intensity of the engagement, the distressed infant is then forced to take even greater self-regulation measures in order to find safety, including dissociation when there is repeated exposure to unbearably intense caregiver arousal.

Difficulties with attunement occurred more often in this study among mothers of preterm infants, the group who were the least responsive and alert and overstimulated most easily. However, the mothers of the securely attached less responsive preterm infants were able to respond more gently to the muted positive arousal of their babies. Presumably, these mothers were also securely attached and thus were better able to coordinate with their infant's under-responsiveness. The greater adaptability of the mothers of the securely attached infants fits with what is known about the intergenerational transmission of attachment style. Here we see that primary caregivers of secure infants are more attuned to the child's affective arousal even when there are developmental challenges such as the premature infants with Respiratory Distress Syndrome and muted attention and arousal patterns.

Across the board in this study, the quality of maternal attunement—whether overmatching with too much anxiety and intensity, or well modulated and well matched—was strongly associated with the infants' patterns of positive arousal. Attuned maternal responses were associated with more smiling and laughter during the all-important reunion episodes of the Strange Situation, as well as when the children were at play. In fact, almost all of the infants whose smiling and laughter increased with age had attuned mothers (those with well-timed and well-matched affect responses). Those whose positive arousal decreased with age, on the other hand, had mothers who misattuned with too much, too little, or mismatched responses. All of the babies with the greatest decreases in smiling were likewise insecurely attached, though it is important to remember that in this study most of the insecurely attached children were classified as avoidant, a group that is characteristically less expressive. If there were a larger sample with more children whose attachment style was ambivalent/resistant, there might also have been examples of overexpressiveness, more crying and perhaps more forced laughter, because the attachment behaviors of ambivalent/resistant children are hyperactivated, whereas infants classified as avoidant would be expected to present, as here, less smiling and laughter and little crying.

The overall likelihood of the child being insecurely attached at two years was greatest for children whose mothers overreacted to positive arousal, or who denied, ignored, or minimized it. The children of the more attuned mothers were securely attached in 67% of the pairs, as compared with only 31% of the pairs in which the mothers were misattuned. This finding dovetails beautifully with what we know from interpersonal neurobiology, that the coordination of arousal, attunement, and repair between caregiver and infant is central to the development of attachment security.

In addition to the promptness of the mother's response to the infant's affect, the quality of the response also had an impact. In the Malatesta et al. (1989) study, for example, the more interest a mother showed in her infant's affect, the more positive affect the infant displayed. Mismatching by meeting the child's negative arousal with positive parental affect (interpreted by researchers as "nervous smiling and non authentic joy" [p. 51]), as many of the misattuned mothers did during the second reunion of the Strange Situation, was correlated with insecure, primarily avoidant attachment in their children. This type of mismatching suggests that the mothers themselves were avoidant and were defending against the pain of separation by defensively deactivating and suppressing expressions of attachment distress. Their behavior during the second reunion represents a part of the process of transmitting their deactivating, suppressing, avoidant defenses to the child. The mothers of the securely attached children, on the other hand, showed knit brows of concern and sometimes fear when faced with the attachment distress of their infants following separations. It was as if they, too, were sharing in the child's pain rather than defending against it.

The 2-year-old children of the misattuned mothers showed little interest, negative or positive, when reunited with their mothers following the second reunion, a pattern consistent with avoidant attachment (Malatesta et al., 1989). The authors speculate,

> Insecure infants [especially avoidant] appear to be exercising restraint or control over their emotions during reunion episodes. At home, however, they displayed some hostility on reunion or avoided their mothers during reunion showing signs of vigilance and suppressed anger. (p. 79)

Secure children with low-contingency mothers showed the most positive affect during the reunion. In a number of the Strange Situation videos I have seen, securely attached infants who are crying hard after the repeated separations smile through their tears almost instantly upon seeing their mother's face in the doorway during the second reunion. The different expressions of smiling and laughter in the securely attached and the insecure avoidant children in this study suggest that, with further study, we would continue to find distinct patterns of positive arousal in infants aligned with the different attachment styles, which are in turn linked to the quality of the caregivers' repeated affective interactions with the child.

Affect Patterns Linked to Family Differences

An infant laughter study conducted at the Yale Psycho-Clinic (Washburn, 1929/1972), prior to the existence of formal attachment theory and the Strange Situation, also observed striking individual differences in laughter and distress patterns linked to what they called "family circumstances." These observations, while old, remain relevant to efforts to link laughter and attachment style. Caregiving patterns change throughout history and differ by culture, but the inborn attachment behaviors—positive and negative—continue, true to form, to respond adaptively to the types of caregiving: acknowledging and nondefended (what we call secure), the defensive deactivation of attachment arousal, including distress and joy (what we call avoidant), or the hyperactivation of attachment arousal (what we call ambivalent/resistant).

The Yale study, thankfully for our purposes, made note of all instances of vocalized laughter in healthy "homogeneous" infants in the laboratory at 4-week intervals, beginning at 8 weeks up through 52 weeks of age. In the presence of the mother, an experimenter presented them with a series of potentially laugh-inducing situations, such as peekaboo, hand clapping, and what they called "threatening head" (shaking head and ducking into child's stomach while saying "ah-boo!" in a long drawn out vocalization).

In analyzing their findings, they identified three patterns of laughter, which they subsequently related to the infants' caregiving experiences. This data is particularly helpful in providing raw material for help in establishing the relationship between positive arousal patterns and attachment styles in infancy. They came up with a three-category classification of affect expression: *ambi-expressive* (positive or negative affect equally noticeable); *Risor-expressive* (more positive expressions), so named in honor of the risorius muscle that retracts the corners of the mouth in smiling and laughter; and *depressor-expressive* (more sober and crying expressions), so named for the two depressor muscles involved in distress expressions. With one or two exceptions, they found that the babies were easily classifiable into these groups, suggesting that identifiable patterns of expressive behavior are formed during the first two years of life, and that these may be related to particular caregiving experiences and attachment styles.

The ambi-expressive babies, those who showed both crying and laughter equally, fell into two subgroups based on differences in both the quantity and the quality of their expressive attachment behaviors. The first subgroup (the *parvi-expressive*) laughed and cried rarely, and when they did, it was less intense. The second subgroup (the *multi-expressive*) was the more excitable, emotionally labile group who laughed and cried frequently and with great intensity. A detailed record of one child per group was selected for analysis. Using these records, I will make my best guess about the attachment style of the child in question based on information about their affect arousal and regulation patterns and the caregiver responses.

Laughter and Avoidant Attachment

The boy selected to represent the parvi-expressive, or tranquil subgroup of ambi-expressive children (laughing and crying equally) was low-key and "serene," with few outbursts, positive or negative. At home, it was noted, he was kept to a well-regulated schedule, and his diet carefully watched. His mother spoke in a low voice, and rarely spontaneously. She always demonstrated what the researchers called a "smiling, unruffled good nature" (Washburn, 1929/1972, p. 511). She told the investigators that she did not believe her child laughed aloud even once a day, and showed little to no crying even when hungry, sick, or fatigued. When asked to try to stimulate laughter in her son with the research protocols, she was reluctant, but agreed to try. She succeeded on only three occasions throughout all of the play periods observed. The baby never laughed in response to the experimenter, either, though "no timidity was shown."

This child's deactivated attachment system and his mother's highly rigid and defended responses to affect arousal are classic patterns of avoidant attachment. Beebe (2003) has noted that "maternal difficulty in 'partnering' infant distress may result from denial of infant distress" and, by extension, denial of positive arousal, as well (p. 32).

There are several telling comments in the text, pointing to typical aspects of the transmission of an avoidant attachment style: "Independence was being cultivated. He was expected to amuse himself in a well-guarded place, and small accidents were wisely disregarded" (p. 511). As would be predicted by later attachment research on the intergenerational transmission of attachment style, these researchers noted a "resemblance in expressive type" to the mother (Washburn, 1929/1972, p. 514).

I also could not help noticing the cultural bias toward early independence, and hence avoidant attachment, in the researchers, who inserted the word "wisely" in front of the observation that the mother ignored small accidents. Early independence training and squelching of attachment affect have long been emphasized among European Americans, creating a small statistical bulge of avoidantly attached children, who are frequently described as "good (i.e., independent) babies." Nonetheless, in spite of their apparent cultural bias toward early independence, the researchers could see that the end result of overdoing independence training was a highly muted child with little enjoyment of play. What appeared to be "tranquility" and "serenity" came at the price of spontaneity and zest for life. We know now that such babies could continue to show the physiological markers of anxiety at separation even when they did not express separation distress openly.

Laughter and Ambivalent/Resistant Attachment

The child selected to represent the subgroup of children called multi-expressive, who showed excitable, exaggerated, and labile expressions of both crying and laughing, was a female. (It is interesting to note the gender affect-expression stereotype at work here as well, even though there are no gender differences found in attachment-style studies; the avoidant child was a boy, fitting stereotypical male affect patterns, and this one a girl, fitting stereotypical female affect patterns.) Her pattern represents the hyperactivation of the attachment system typical of the ambivalent/resistant attachment style, unlike the avoidant boy just described whose attachment system was deactivated. This little girl ranked second on the sheer number of laughing responses and first for crying. At ages 32 weeks and 36 weeks she laughed more readily than any other child in the group, but her crying behavior was also more intense. There were very few instances of "no reaction" to stimulation.

This child, unlike the understimulated parvi-expressive boy, was being raised in a busy household that included an older brother, two parents, and two grandparents. The researchers noted that "regularity and independence were hard to safeguard for the child" (again suggesting a bias toward independence) as her crib was in the middle of the household (Washburn, 1929/1972, p. 514). When asked to play with the child, the mother "wholeheartedly stimulated her and seemed to enjoy it as much as the child" (p. 514). The father was said to stimulate such hearty laughter that the baby could not sleep after playing with him.

Trouble was noted at age 24 weeks, when the little girl transitioned from laughter to crying without an appreciable interval between. "When she was taken from the crib…she was crying sharply, but when raised quickly into the air, she changed immediately and imperceptibly into a laugh" (p. 516). Subsequently, it was noted that she would laugh or cry but undergo complete affect reversals at slight changes. She smiled with little stimulation and cried without warning. At times, she screamed, though a moment before she had been laughing.

By age 40 weeks, "she seemed to be poised between laughter and crying and to topple with equal readiness in either direction" (Washburn, 1929/1972, p. 517), clearly showing signs of a hyperactivated attachment system. For example, the mother on occasion would help her with her walking, and the child would smile and vocalize. However, if she was interrupted, she would suddenly scream and stiffen her body, again a hallmark of anxious/ambivalent children who are easily aroused but difficult to soothe. She was highly reactive, screaming when her clothes were put on, or laughing when left alone with an experimenter. As would be predicted with the ambivalent/resistant attachment style, the researchers noted that her family stimulated expressive behavior, overstimulating and overreacting to the child, a pattern associated with what is presumed to be the parent's preoccupied attachment style.

Laughter and Secure Attachment

Reading that the infant boy selected to represent the Risor-expressive (or cheerful, laughing group) had achieved a developmental level ahead of the rest of the group first suggests that he might be securely attached. It was likewise confirming to note that our little Risor-expressive guy was the 4th most frequent laugher in the group, first in smiling, and 15th (last) in crying, recalling from Malatesta et al. (1989) that the securely attached children showed the greatest increases in laughter as they developed, whereas the insecure group decreased in frequency of positive arousal over time.

This boy, too, was from a large family and experienced a lot of stimulation, but there were also signs of good regulation in safeguarding his routine and sleep (as opposed to rigidly controlling them, like the mother of the parvi-expressive, "tranquil," boy, or overstimulating him as happened with the multi-expressive, "intense," little girl). Both of his parents played with the child and easily and comfortably produced laughter in him. There was not much crying, and by 29 weeks he would laugh "at anything or nothing" when first awake in the morning (Washburn, 1929/1972, p. 520). He smiled at everyone in the lab, though not when he was alone. At 44 weeks he was clowning by repeatedly making a face that earlier had made his family laugh, a wonderful example of playful attempts to engage his caregivers. Curiously, his parents were not especially expressive, and if anything were a bit on the sober side, though other babies in the Risor-expressive (high smile and laughter) group had at least one parent who was a hearty laugher, too.

There is too little information to support a designation of secure attachment for all of the Risor-expressive children; however, a comment about another of the children in this category suggests attuned, nonintrusive caregiver responsiveness. The researchers noted that the protest crying of that child was "reduced to a minimum by the excellence of the handling" (p. 521), suggesting well-attuned affect regulation by the caregivers. However, another child in the Risor group was noted to have "a hysterical quality about her laughter" (p. 521). I was struck by this comment, and wondered if this atypical, intense, eruptive laughter might represent some attachment disorganization, though there was no further family information to substantiate that. It does suggest that not only frequency of positive arousal (laughter), but also its quality must be considered when assessing for attachment style.

Laughter and Disorganized Attachment

The child selected to represent the depressor-expressive (sober, nonlaughing) group also suggested possible attachment disorganization. She is described as a tiny "doll-like" girl whose weight-height index was below average. Over the observation period, she showed increasing apprehension in the lab rather than acclimating like the other children. Her mother reported that the child laughed very little, and there was no social smiling at the experimenter, even when the girl was in her mother's lap and at her own home. She would always protest if the experimenter tried to touch her. Occasionally there was a smile or a brief "ha ha," but to the researchers it sounded more like conversational (non-Duchenne) laughter rather than genuine, playful amusement (Duchenne) laughter. Her habitual expression was round-eyed, mouth closed, with corners slightly drawn down, and the experimenters commented that something about her expressive style seemed unusual and disconnected, unlike the other children.

At 36 weeks there was no laughter and no social smiling at home or in the mother's lap, though there was some self-initiated smiling even when nobody was in the room, which is unusual for most children. This habit caused her mother to characterize her as having a "happy disposition" (Washburn, 1929/1972, p. 40), suggesting a definite lack of attunement to her daughter's generally depressive state. Involuntary smiling appeared "only when she was somewhat violently stimulated by her mother and never when stimulated by the experimenter" (p. 525).

The mother, oddly, described her unsmiling daughter as a "little clown" at home. She stated that the arrival of the child had changed the whole atmosphere in the home from gloom to cheer, suggesting the burden placed on the child in this depressive, unresponsive, and possibly neglectful household.

The researchers described the mother as serious with people, but that she "smiled constantly" at the daughter, almost in a frozen manner. The father was also noted to be serious and tense, and his play a bit rough and frightening to the child. When the experimenter did the "threatening head, 'ah, boo'" game at 28 weeks, "there was a convulsive contraction of the child's body and grabbing at the experimenter's hair with wide-opened eyes and startled appearance," so much so that he withdrew. Even after repeated trials, the whimpering continued. When trying to play patty cake with her, the child's arms were so tense that the experimenter couldn't bring the hands together to clap, though at the end she completely "relaxed," appearing to "give up" the struggle (Washburn, 1929/1972, p. 523).

The elements in the description that point to possible disorganized attachment in this child include the marked inconsistency between the child's behavior and the mother's description of her, the lack of social responsiveness typical for a child her age, the smiling when alone instead of with familiar caregivers, and the signs of excessive fear in response to play. It is also possible, however, that there were undiagnosed or unrecognized developmental issues that could mute smiling, laughter, and the ability to play, and leave the mother and father "at sea" in their attempts to connect with the girl, consistent with the experimenter's experience.

The relationship between patterns of laughter and disorganization is speculative as there has been so little research in this area. However, one interesting clue may be found in a study of the relationship between infant disorganization at 18 months and the mother's attachment state of mind as measured by the AAI (Lyons-Ruth, Yellin, Melnick, & Atwood, 2003). A subcategory of disorganized/disoriented state of mind, known as "hostile-helpless," is used for adults who hold contradictory or devaluing feelings toward their early attachment figures.

This particular subgroup of disorganized mothers, it was noted, would often laugh when they related painful anecdotes about psychological or physical distress. While Lyons-Ruth et al. understood laughter at pain to be a form of "affective numbing" (p. 334) that serves as a "defensive behavior to communicate toughness and deny the impact of childhood experiences of vulnerability" (p. 339), it raises interesting questions about the impact of such a defense on their infants and children.

Lyons-Ruth and Jacobvitz (2008) describe the types of parental affective communication errors that appear to relate to attachment disorganization. They include such mismatches as negative-intrusive behaviors, withdrawal, affective communication errors such as being contradictory or nonresponsive to infant cues, and having disorienting exchanges with the infant such as using odd tones of voice or changes in pitch.

Laughing at an infant's distress would definitely represent an affective communication error, as well as being negative-intrusive to the infant. In Beebe's (2003) assessment checklist of mother–infant interaction, observers are to note whether or not the mother mismatches her infant's distress by laughing, giggling, or saying something like "this is sort of fun," as the infant cries, or if she mocks the infant's distress. All these responses have the potential for contributing to the infant's disorganized attachment.

Billy and Ben: Case Examples of the Intergenerational Transmission of Attachment Style and Positive Arousal

Two little boys called "Billy" and "Ben" were chosen to represent strikingly different styles of affect expression in children between the ages of 19 and 24 months (Demos, 1982). Demos believed that the differences between the children in their expressions of laughter/positive affect reflected different "transactional styles of the mothers" (p. 152), suggesting the intergenerational transmission of both patterns of affective expression and attachment styles.

Billy produced 71 smiles during the study period, but almost half of these were blends that included a clenched jaw and other signs of tension. At times, he also had a forced laugh that was in contrast to the spontaneous smiles and laughter that occurred on occasion with peers or his mother, though never with his father. Many of his smiles and laughs seemed uncertain and distancing rather than engaging.

Sometimes, after a particularly intense smile, Billy would bite his lower lip, producing what appeared to be an opened-mouth smile mixed with elements of anger and disgust. On one notable occasion, Billy was being filmed as his mother helped him to successfully perform several somersaults while his father watched. He first smiled, then screamed, and then began hitting the cameraman, quickly moving from positive arousal to anger to hitting. The combination of fake-sounding laughter and scream seemed to the observers to indicate a blend of anger, disgust, and enjoyment—a series of intense and unexpected emotions in a child under two after completing somersaults before an audience. This hyperactivation of both positive and negative attachment affect along with being difficult to soothe points toward an ambivalent/resistant attachment style, whereas the extreme shifts and combinations under minor stress seem to indicate periods of disorganization, as well.

Billy's mother was described as seeming "most certain and decisive when expressing disapproval, and when structuring the child's interests with commands" (Demos, 1982, p.152). There were few examples of shared enjoyment, and Billy's expressions of interest were responded to minimally, ignored, or interrupted with a negative comment. Here we see evidence of the kind of overstimulated, mismatched caregiving that is associated with the anxious/ambivalent attachment style. There are also suggestions of the type of affect communication errors that Lyons-Ruth and Jacobvitz (2008) implicate in disorganized attachment: negative-intrusive behaviors (disapproval and giving commands), withdrawal (minimal responses to expressions of interest), affective communication errors, such as being contradictory (interrupting him with a negative suggestion), or nonresponsiveness to cues (ignoring).

All of Ben's smiles were relaxed, smooth, and straightforward, all qualities of positive arousal that point toward secure attachment—quite in contrast to Billy's. There were wonderful blends of affects as well, including enjoyment mixed with excitement when he was laughing at a spinning top, a blend consistent with a well-balanced attachment/exploratory experience in a securely attached child. Another time he showed a combination of enjoyment and surprise when he was sitting in his mother's lap and started to fall over backward. He recovered and quickly repeated the experience using playful exaggeration. He concluded by smiling and mugging for the cameraman.

Ben's mother matched his affects in quality and intensity. She focused on maintaining mutuality and allowing Ben to pursue his interests. She invited his response by getting involved and participating in his fun. She comfortably and appropriately expressed her enjoyment of his playfulness, and communicated it with positive arousal of her own.

There are typical patterns of positive and negative affect arousal associated with each attachment style (Mikulincer & Shaver, 2007). Knowing this can aid in our assessment of a child's laughter patterns and attachment style. Further, knowing a child's attachment style suggests the type of early caregiving experiences that were formative for her. Knowing, or making, an informed assessment of the attachment style of the child also suggests certain patterns of positive and negative arousal. With a securely attached child, we would expect predominantly positive arousal accompanied by the ability to self-regulate overstimulation, along with the occasional expression of appropriate separation distress. With an avoidant child, we would look for the suppression or deactivation of the attachment system, and a low level of arousal, positive or negative affect. Hyperactivation of attachment affect, including much crying and laughter (most of it non-Duchenne laughter that is nervous, hostile, appeasing, or seductive), would point to an ambivalent/resistant style, and eruptive, chaotic, or dissociated arousal would point to disorganized attachment.

Caregivers may also vary in their attunement to and regulation of positive arousal according to attachment style. Parents with securely attached infants in one study would help to regulate positive affect by stepping in to help tone it down for the infant before the balance tipped away from positive affect into distress (Grossmann, Scheuerer-Englisch, & Loher as cited in Grossmann, Grossmann, Kindler, & Zimmermann, 2008). Avoidant parents also noticed the child's overstimulation, but reacted differently. They would join with the child while they explored and played, but when they became frustrated or stopped playing, would "more often than not withdraw and wait for the infants to overcome their distress alone" (p. 864).

Children have also been found to demonstrate different types of attitudes and emotions during play based on attachment security (Grossmann et al., 2008). Securely attached children are noted to have longer attention spans, greater curiosity, less frustration, and more enthusiasm and positive affect during free play. Insecure children, on the other hand, are more negative and frustrated, less eager and less concentrated.

Infant Laughter and Culture

Tronick (2007) points out that patterns of affect expression differ from culture to culture depending on "cultural belief systems, ecological factors, caregiver and infant strategies, and the interplay among them" (p. 101). Smiling and laughter, as part of our inborn human attachment systems, suggest, according to Tronick, "an underlying universal form" (p. 149) that is modified by cultural norms and caregiving practices.

Tronick studied infant-mother interactions around play among the Gusii, a southwestern Kenyan, Bantu-speaking tribe. Gusii parent-child relationships are characterized by avoidance of eye contact and restraint in play. Eye contact is considered dangerous and to be avoided at all ages. As Tronick points out, the early caregiver-child relationships among the Gusii "are characterized by avoidance of eye-to-eye contact and restraint in playful interactions" (p. 137).

Though the infant is in almost constant physical contact with the mother and there is great attentiveness to crying, the infant is usually carried on the mother's back with little opportunity for face-to-face social engagement. If the Gusii infants would initiate positive interaction, the mother's response would be to diffuse or dampen it.

Tronick set up a field lab and placed mothers and infants in a face-to-face position, instructing them to talk to and play with the babies for 2.5 minutes. The mothers agreed, though they were reluctant and thought it was a "pleasant waste of time" (p. 147). When the mothers did interact as instructed, however, their infants would pay close attention and sometimes smile. The mothers returned the gaze, but with what appeared to be a "grossly distracted quality" (p. 143). They frequently gazed away or directed their gaze to some part of the baby's body other than the face.

In spite of their mother's discomfort, all of the Gusii babies showed positive affect under the experimental conditions. Some of them laughed out loud, which produced mixed responses in mothers, who would either giggle nervously, respond with a neutral mask, or avert their gaze (p. 143). The mother's responses would diminish the infant's positive affect, but did not completely dampen it. Confirming that the attachment behavior is universal, though the caregiving behavior obviously is not, Tronick noted that positive affect was uniformly present in the infants and that some of them "laughed out loud" (p. 143). The mothers had mixed reactions to the positive arousal in their child. "Some giggled nervously; others' faces became devoid of expression and turned away" (p. 143).

Adult Gusii typically have little face-to-face contact, even during conversation. Adults avert their gaze so much that they typically talk to each other at a 90-degree angle or greater. The Gusii live in a very close, interpersonal situation where extremes of affect could cause disruptions and conflicts. Even strong positive affect could set up jealousies or expose individual vulnerabilities. In addition to socializing the children to the social mores of their culture, Tronick speculates that the child-rearing practices may also be protective for mothers in a culture with high infant mortality rates, dampening their attachment to the infants who may die.

Infant laughter has much to teach us about attachment formation, and attachment theory and research have much to teach us about infant laughter. When laughter goes well in infancy, when it is part of a comfortable, growth-enhancing, security-building network of caregiving relationships and experiences, it lays a solid foundation for close relationships throughout life, and contributes to the security and resiliency that help to cushion some of the stresses and blows that are an inevitable part of life. When a child's attempts at playful engagement are rebuffed or ignored or met with hostility, the wounds can run deep. More than just the ability to join in and "get" the jokes will suffer. Insecurity may rob an infant of the ability to laugh and play with ease, or it may corrupt laughter so that it appears primarily in its non-Duchenne, sometimes corrupted, detaching, and distancing forms. In the following chapters on laughter in childhood, we will examine the ways in which the security or insecurity of attachment established in infancy may impact laughter in older children.

Part 3

Laughter in Childhood and Adolescence

7

THE DEVELOPMENT OF
LAUGHTER IN CHILDHOOD

Children are great laughers, outdoing adults in both frequency and enthusiasm. Some estimates claim that kids laugh up to 400 times a day versus the paltry adult sum of 15 times a day, though there is, in fact, little research documenting frequency (Krysstel, 2009; Martin, 2010). What little data there are, in combination with simple observations of kids, however, suggest that chuckles, giggles, and loud guffaws are, for many children, a common occurrence, and one that far outdistances the frequency of their crying (Brackett, 1933).

Childhood laughter is also familiar in cultures around the world, judging from the many engaging examples documented in a video study recording one full day in the lives of "sturdy" (resilient and thriving as culturally defined) 2.5-year-olds in five countries (E. L. Cameron, Kennedy, & C.A. Cameron, 2008). A little girl in the United States laughed, or tried to get her parents to laugh, 22 times during a half-hour lunch. Four other "thriving" little girls—Peruvian, Italian, English, and Thai—were also frequent laughers and used humor in surprisingly sophisticated ways. When the same naturalistic video technique was used to focus on a weekend day in the life of at-risk 13- to 15-year-olds identified as resilient, laughter and humor were ubiquitous, serving both to help them negotiate tricky social situations and to bond with peers and family (E. L. Cameron, Fox, Anderson, & C.A. Cameron, 2010).

Individual and Developmental Differences

Individual differences in laughter frequency and patterns, similar to those discussed earlier among infants, are also found in older children. Consistent with the speculation that laughter frequency and quality are related to attachment style, the few longitudinal studies of childhood laughter have found consistency in a particular child's frequency of laughter over time. The children who are frequent laughers at one age continue to be so when they are older (Brackett, 1933). Another study found that the biggest laughers (among 7-year-olds) are also the most frequent smilers and make more eye contact, as well (Chapman, 1975). If we consider eye contact one measure of the comfort and ease a child feels in making social connections, this association also supports the idea that frequent use of laughter, at least genuine spontaneous Duchenne laughter, and security of attachment are related.

Laughing With Others Versus Laughing Alone

The most consistent finding about childhood laughter, documented in more studies than any other, is that it takes place almost exclusively, 95% of the time or more, when other people are around: parents, familiar adults, siblings, and peers (Martin, 2010). The presence of familiar people enhances both the amount of laughter and its contagion: young school children laugh more when the other children around them also laugh (Foot & Chapman, 1996), no surprise to us former children.

Even in childhood, perhaps especially in childhood, being in the presence of a safe adult or another child, especially one who is also laughing, is almost a necessary precondition for laughter. Occasional bouts of apparently solitary laughter may occur during a video, book, or playing with a pet, but some sort of "relationship" can be inferred, whether it be virtual (video, book) or with a nonhuman animal. Some children with lively imaginations regularly relate to internal or fantasy playmates, stuffed animals, or dolls, and may laugh in the context of those "relationships," as well. It seems more likely that these examples of solitary laughter in the context of imaginary friends or inanimate toys would be non-Duchenne laughter rather than genuine, spontaneous Duchenne laughter, however.

While children do laugh primarily in the presence of others, it does make a difference in whose presence they find themselves, as two researchers following identical protocols with groups of children discovered (Foot & Chapman, 1996). Pairs of 7-year-old school children in Cardiff, Wales, watched cartoons with one or the other of the male researchers, who had made a conscious plan to act exactly the same in the presence of the children. It soon became apparent, however, that with one of the men the children laughed more than they did with his colleague. As the two compared notes afterward, they realized that "the attempt to standardize our behavior and mode of interaction was not successful" (p. 208). In particular, there were consistent differences in the frequency and intensity of each of the researcher's smiles and laughter (and, we might speculate, their attachment styles). Children, their implicit procedural antennae on full alert, sensed a different feeling in the air with each and looked at and laughed more with the more expressive researcher than with the quieter one.

Childhood Laughter: Infectious and Contagious

Laughter at any age is contagious, but at no time more so than in childhood. It is delightful to watch and experience, even from an adult vantage point. At times, however, laughter does get out of hand, a situation familiar to all of us who have ever "lost it" while laughing with friends somewhere inappropriate, such as school or church. When Andrea Lee (2008) was an elementary school student at a multicultural Friends school in Pennsylvania, the classes took turns reciting from the Bible at the meetinghouse. When it was her fifth grade class's turn to recite a Psalm, things quickly deteriorated. The first child stumbled and blushed, and Lee, who came next, froze until her teacher prompted her. The next section, which was to be spoken in unison, contained an unfortunate reference to "errors" and "secret faults" (Psalms 19:12). Those words, under these circumstances, were what Lee called a "tripwire: somebody's helpless giggle becomes a rout. We double over, choking with uncontrollable laughter" (p. 40).

An attachment-oriented observer notices several things in this scene: the contagion of the laughter shared among classmates, the futile attempts at controlling it for the sake of social propriety, and the bond the laughter created among the children. Humor researchers would be more inclined to focus on the incongruities that made the children laugh, which are also of interest: the fact that their "errors and secret faults" were suddenly not so secret. Instead of being hidden, they were on display before the entire assembled community in the form of stumbled-over words, not to mention inappropriate giggling.

What Makes Children Laugh? Types of Childhood Humor

Most childhood "laughter" research focuses on what provokes the laughter response: the incongruities, jokes, nonsense, games, tickling, toys, cartoons, books, and songs. The real deal, however, the laughter spontaneously created by children in the course of their everyday lives, is frequently overlooked. With children, as with adults, it is most often the silly incongruities of life that make them laugh. For example, a child might laugh at seeing an adult do something clumsy or a dog dressed in a sweater, or hearing a strange and unexpected noise from another child, a bathroom word uttered out of the blue or an off-the-wall comment from a young friend. These seemingly inconsequential laughter triggers differ little from the kinds of events and comments that are hilarious to adults, as well.

As with adults, children's spontaneous laughter taken out of context seems distinctly "unhumorous" when looked at from a more formal perspective. Ben, now close to three, for example, began laughing when he was standing on a stool helping his grandmother cut corn off the cob to make soup. A messy cook, she soon had scattered kernels all over the kitchen counter and said, in mock exasperation at herself, "Ben, we've got corn all *over* the place!" He laughed heartily and, thrilled by his response, she repeated it several more times with the same effect. What did

Ben find so funny about a silly little comment from his grandma? Not much to analyze in the way of cognitive dissonance or intellectual challenge other than an adult messing up and making fun of herself for doing so and perhaps exaggerating a bit in the process. Yet those insignificant-seeming words connected them in laughter in a precious and meaningful way.

Cameron et al. (2008), the "Day-in-the-Life" researchers mentioned above, identified four categories of childhood humor: clowning, teasing, jokes, and physical play. The multiple humorous exchanges of Katy, the child who clocked 22 humorous exchanges in one half-hour lunch, included (counting examples that overlapped categories) 55% clowning, 27% teasing, 86% jokes, and 36% physical play.

In one example, Katy combined deliberate clowning and joking when she repeated her inadvertent mispronunciation of the car name Mini Cooper as "mini pooper" simply to reexperience the laughter of her mother and older brother. She presumably did not understand the joke, but she certainly wanted more of the laughter. Teasing took the form, on another occasion, of Katy affectionately and laughingly taunting her mother, a Canadian, by reciting the pledge to the American flag. On another occasion going for the laughs, Katy combined physical play, teasing, and clowning by spitting out a piece of pineapple at the lunch table, at which no one laughed except Katy. She kept trying anyway, pronouncing it a "trick," until her father remarked that he didn't like that trick.

Overall, Cameron et al. (2008) note that Katy's humor "seems largely to serve a familial attachment function between Katy and her relatives, and especially with her mother" (p. 14). The early "linguistic and emotional synchrony" between Katy and her mother, they point out, serves to establish a secure base from which Katy moves to learn more about and experience more of her environment, including relationships with other people. The use of laughter and humor to playfully connect with others grows exponentially with age as the attachment and friendship circle widens to include fathers, siblings, grandparents, and childcare providers, and then teachers, peers, and even safe strangers.

The meanings behind what children find funny are complex and multilayered, just as they are for adults. Getting to the core of childhood humor is also equally difficult, because to understand a particular child you have to know his or her family culture extremely well. Addressing the need to understand the impact of family context, Johnson and Mervis (1997) used a family diary, case-study method to trace one child's development of verbal humor. They correctly point out that the "family language" and codes of communicating can be mystifying to an outsider. The unique playful context of each family and the multiple "inside" jokes shared among family members speak to the primacy of the attachment process, and the link between humor and the laughter/attachment and play/exploration systems in the child's particular caregiving environment.

Ari, the subject of the Johnson and Mervis study, was not yet 3 years old and just developing language. Still, he would laugh at incongruent labels, incongruent attributes, and other forms of word play. For example, he deliberately misused one of his first words, "duck," when pointing to other birds—once a little hummingbird—that he clearly knew were not ducks. On one occasion, after saying the wrong name, he looked at his mother and laughed. When his mother did not laugh with him, he corrected himself and said "birdie" and smiled. Another time, reading with both parents, he pointed to a hedgehog and said "chipmunk," laughing hysterically. This time his parents played along, misnaming other animals, at which the little boy again laughed with obvious enjoyment.

To appreciate incongruity, a child must be able to comprehend it. Ari had to know the difference between a duck and a hummingbird. To recognize, acknowledge, and enjoy an incongruity, it must appear in a context in which the child feels secure. Social cues from trusted caregivers, such as a wink, facial expression, or tone of voice tip the child off as to the fact that what is coming is playful. If a child does not feel comfortable, no matter the signal, her response will most likely be curiosity, astonishment, or even fear. If a child does not understand incongruities, he may be heard to ask adults he trusts, why are you laughing? or, why is that funny?

Humor and Cognitive Development

As cognitive development proceeds with age, the ability to appreciate more sophisticated types of humor follows suit. On the other side of the equation, incongruities and the pleasure they bring help children to expand their cognitive capacities, as well. White (as cited in Sroufe & Wunsch, 1972) suggests that stretching to appreciate incongruity is part of the appeal of humor to children, as they "most enjoy that which lies at the growing edge of their capacities" (p. 335). Most interesting to them are the things they are just able to understand—linking incongruity with exploration, playfulness, and mastery.

Children's abilities to appreciate humor move through stages that parallel their cognitive abilities. McGhee (1979) traced four stages of humor development beginning with pretend play (peekaboo or "horsey") and moving with verbal development to incongruous labeling of objects (hummingbird and duck) and events (mother with a silly hat). Next comes level 3, the ability to perceive conceptual incongruity, followed by level 4, the ability to understand incongruity imbedded in ambiguity or multiple meanings. Most children are not able to appreciate ambiguity and double meanings until early in their school years, but once they are able to do so, it opens the way for them to appreciate riddles and jokes, as well as irony, sarcasm, and satire.

Children, by about five years of age, are just beginning to appreciate what makes pictorial humor funny (Loizou, 2006). My sister's granddaughter at just that age looked at a cartoon drawing of a quiche with broccoli and an elephant baked inside. She asked her grandmother what it was and when it was explained to her, she thought it was incredibly hilarious and kept coming back to it repeatedly, as if she were delighted with her newfound ability to understand this type of humor. When Loizou asked children that age to describe a picture and say whether they found it funny and if so why, most were able to do. They could recognize the incongruities (such as a man taking a bath with his clothes on; flowers in a trash can) and attribute the funniness to the incongruity.

Jokes and Riddles

Jokes help children to explore their world. Riddles and word play (What is black and white and red/read all over? A newspaper.) expand their knowledge, and help stave off fears of ignorance (How does the little clown warm his feet? On the "toe-ster."). Jokes and riddles also help children to deal with mistakes, failures, and judgments that can otherwise be painful. Confusing or anxiety-producing feelings may be mastered by sexual jokes or comments. Anger and hostility, too, can find expression in jokes. Jokes can also serve an affect-regulating function and help children to master the anxiety-producing aspects of being a child, and of "not knowing" so many answers about the complicated ways of the world.

Perhaps most importantly from an attachment/affiliative perspective, jokes are shared. They travel around grade school classrooms like wildfire. The pleasure of "getting the joke" is only part of the fun; the rest of it comes from sharing it with friends, from being part of an "in group" that knows and appreciates the joke. Even the corny childhood jokes that make grownups groan bind the little peers closer together. Perhaps the little ones take some small satisfaction in taking control and irritating the adults in their lives by repeating their cornier jokes endlessly.

Irony and Sarcasm

The comprehension and appreciation of irony and sarcasm requires even more complex cognitive abilities. For example, in the story about a fireman who smoked in bed and burned down the fire station, the child must be able to comprehend the multiple layers of meaning (Creusere, 1999). When irony or sarcasm takes place in social situations, a child is also called upon to factor in the speaker's intention behind the comment, including sorting out whether it is intended as affectionate teasing or hostile bullying, which can sometimes be confusing, as well. Demorest, Meyer, Phelps, Garner, and Winner (as cited in Creusere, 1999) found that by age 6 children were able to distinguish sincere from insincere statements, but did not successfully distinguish between deceptive and sarcastic ones. The children would err on the side of identifying satire as a lie, and they also misidentified lies as sincere. The older children, 9- to 13-year-olds, understood that satirical utterances could be deceptions. This study, however, was based on audio-taped examples alone, so the children were missing the all-important visual and contextual clues that could guide their interpretation of the words so as to help them better make such distinctions.

Nonsense and Procedural Knowledge

Kids love nonsense, which makes me wonder if it is giving an early boost to their developing implicit procedural ways of knowing and relating to others by helping them learn to "get" subtly communicated unspoken messages behind humor. Nonsense, humor, and silliness in general are nonlinear, musical, non-conscious, pictorial, and responsive to surprises. As such, it likely resonates with the nonconscious part of ourselves that enables us to negotiate in our social relationships without thinking every response through consciously. It may be that the pleasurable appeal of nonsense—the mystery behind the joke and what makes it funny—helps children learn what they most need to know as they grow into maturity: how to function in relationships. It entices them into developing a theory of mind that is useful in understanding all kinds of otherwise confusing communication.

The Multiple Functions of Childhood Laughter

A Bridge Between Developmental Worlds

Grotjahn (1957) writes that children's humor provides a way for them to turn the tables on adults—a way to express and claim their own immaturity. By late childhood, he suggests, word play, puns, and bathroom and sexual humor represent a regression to a more primitive view of the world that is a way to both experience it and master it. By the same token, the regressive aspects of adult humor allow us to turn the tables on ourselves—a way to reclaim our own immaturity. The playfulness of laughter helps us connect the inner and outer worlds. When we say incongruent things, do silly things, or share a moment of private language that tickles our fancy, we are bridging developmental stages. The pull of the immature and regressive aspects of childhood humor and laughter also allows—and even encourages—adult caregivers to be drawn into the fun of mutual positive arousal with their children, and to share the special feeling of closeness: "We both get this and think it is funny."

Humor helps children to negotiate some of the trickier aspects of their own development. A study comparing the humor of 10- to 11-year-olds in rural and urban schools in Denmark found that their humor content reflected the developmental challenges of their age group (Führ, 2001). Both rural and urban boys and girls liked sex jokes, though boys preferred them more. When asked to write down some good jokes, both genders included sexual ones. Anxieties of prepubertal children are high relative to sexuality. Being able to connect with each other over their sexual anxieties continues to serve an attachment function, by providing a secure base among peers that encourages and promotes exploration and growth through the regulated and modulated positive arousal created by jokes. Of course, some sexual humor can become harassment and bullying, as we will discuss further in the next chapter.

Reading Other People and Rules of Social Discourse

A large part of what is challenging about humor for children is knowing how to read the actions and reactions of their peers as well as adults. As Schore (2003a) writes, appropriate interactions between peers depend on the ability to engage in affect synchrony with other children.

> This capacity involves the abilities to nonconsciously yet efficiently read faces and tones and therefore the intentionalities of peers and teachers, to empathically resonate with the states of others, to communicate emotional states and regulate interpersonal affects, and thus to cope with the novel ambient interpersonal stressors of early childhood. (p. 173)

Watching the four little age-mate cousins in our family play together at our last family reunion gave me a wonderful opportunity to observe the intricate ups and downs of "age appropriate interactions with peers." Within a short period of time, there were repeated instances of shared laughter, hurt feelings, connections and disconnections, empathic caring, and disinterested apathy. At one point, all four of them were in great form, giggling hysterically while they rolled marbles back and forth underneath the playroom door. They took turns supplying and retrieving requested marbles in order to keep the fun going and at a fever pitch. Transition to a new activity, however, served as a stress point. One cousin, tiring of the marble game, initiated a different game. Another cousin rushed to join the new activity with shrieks of laughter, whereas the other two clearly wanted to continue with the marbles. Kids' signals to each other can be subtle and unspoken, or direct and obvious, as it was for the cousins. Either way, it can be tricky to negotiate as feelings change, alliances shift, affect needs regulating, boredom and fatigue set in for one while withdrawal from an activity can mean hurt feelings for another.

Laughter is contagious, but it is also sensitive and particular. The negotiations needed to maintain affect synchrony are complex and multilayered. The early experiences of attunements and misattunements with primary caregivers lay the groundwork for the management of interactive communication. There is much, however, to be learned as peer relationships stretch children's relational capacities.

Seven-year-olds in Wales listened to humor on headphones in two different pair situations. In one, they listened with a companion listening to the same thing they were, and in the other with a companion who was not listening (Chapman, 1975). As might be expected, the children listening in pairs laughed far more than those listening alone. Those who laughed the most also sat closer together and engaged in more eye contact, which was not particularly easy because they were seated side-by-side. The association between physical closeness and gaze also points to the interpersonal synchrony taking place between the nervous systems of two companions sharing a laugh, and suggests that the tendency to laugh more is "augmented by eye contact and close proximity" (p. 145).

On a parenthetical note related to gender differences, both boys and girls in this study laughed more with a companion than when alone. Factoring in the gender of the companion turned out to make a difference, however, but only for the girls. They laughed more when their companion was a boy than when it was another girl, anticipating similar gender-based findings in adult laughter research.

In addition to the mostly implicit ways that children learn to pick up cues about laughter from other people, parents and teachers also consciously and explicitly coach their children about social etiquette relative to laughter. For example, a teacher might reassure a child who is timid about answering a question wrong for fear others will laugh at him. The same teacher may also coach the other children on how to be supportive of others who are experiencing performance anxiety. Parents, my own included, can be quite explicit about the many rules governing appropriate laughter, instructing their children not to laugh in church, or when they win a game, or when someone else does something clumsy and embarrassing. Parents may also try to help children sort out the difference between affectionate teasing and bullying, and making fun of others.

All in all, learning to recognize and verbalize one's own subtle inner workings and to "read," empathize with, and respond to those of others around us is a complex affair. It is, however, made much more appealing by the presence and desire for positive arousal common to children and adults alike.

Affect Regulation and Scaffolding

As Cameron et al. (2008) write, "There is a rich socio-emotional web created by humor, and the cognitive and linguistic advances made by the child appear enhanced by this contextually affective scaffolding" (p. 13). The arousal, attunement, and regulation of positive affect all contribute to the neurobiological scaffolding so important for the child's growing ability to negotiate complex interpersonal terrain and to self-regulate over- and underarousal when it occurs.

Jasmine, a 3-year-old, for example, opened a holiday gift at a family gift exchange during the holidays. It was a book by Art Spiegelman called *Open Me—I'm a Dog*. An early reader, she glanced through the book enough to take in the idea that the title referred to a dog who turned himself into a book in order to hide from danger. On the page where the dog protests against his book-ness by repeating the refrain, "I am a Dog!" printed in increasingly large print on the page, Jasmine correspondingly read in a louder and louder voice until she was screaming, "I AM A DOG!" The whole circle of family adults seated around her, of course, laughed loudly each time.

Eventually, Jasmine's "I AM A DOG!" reached a fever pitch. The positive arousal and attunement of the group of adults was so intense that Jasmine was becoming overstimulated. At this point, her mother intervened to help her to calm down before she got further into a frenzy of hyperarousal. Timely intervention like this aimed at soothing and down-regulating hyperarousal is extremely important, even when it is positive. Helping children to stay within their tolerable limits of arousal helps to form the important scaffolding needed to develop their ability to self-regulate affect, both positive and negative.

Jasmine's experience of gentle interactive regulation with her attuned mother stands in contrast to my friend Neal's experience as a child. Neal recalls being at a theater watching a movie satirizing war and death starring a comedian by the name of "Joe E. Brown" (Neal does not recall the name of the film) and "laughing his head off" at an irreverent line that ended with something like, "just bury me now." At that point, his mother sternly admonished him to "shut up!" Whether it was her sense that he was laughing at sensitive subject matter (war and death) or laughing too loud and long in public that led her to regulate his affect so sternly, he was never sure. This example demonstrates how and why a child may misunderstand a parental message and hear only stern negative judgment for his humor appreciation.

A member of my family, Russ, similarly recalls falling into hysterical fits of laughter watching an animated turtle trying to go down stairs in *Snow White,* one of the first movies he ever watched. His mother repeated the story of his laughter fit with a mixture of awe, judgment, and admiration, which was a bit confusing for him. He was left not knowing for sure whether she was telling him that vigorous laughter in public should be reigned in, or whether she was a bit envious of his abandon and thought it was cute.

Using positive humor rather than humiliation to coach youngsters on how to behave can also help to scaffold a child's affect arousal and regulation, as well as his behavior. In an article on Los Angeles schools, McGray (2009) describes an encounter among the assistant principal and two "skinny Latino boys" skateboarding in the school breezeway. Zeus Cubias, the school official, said to the boys, "What did I tell you? Don't act the fool." As they stooped to pick up their skateboards, he said to the taller boy, "Especially when you're wearing a Guns N' Roses shirt. Don't embarrass the shirt." The boy laughed, appearing to acknowledge the caring, humorous, unexpected admonition, even though Cubias ended with a threat: "Next time I'm taking the boards" (p. 69).

Scaffolding the Regulation of Positive and Negative Arousal

There is a German saying, *Lachen und Weinen kommt aus diese selbe Koptf,* which means "laughter and crying come out of the same pot." I recall my partner's young nephews roughhousing as young boys. Jordan, the younger by 5 years, loved to engage his revered older brother Derek in physical play, giggling and asking for more until a line would be crossed and Jordan would get hurt and start to cry. Ten minutes later, affect soothed and the temporary pain forgotten, he would be back for more. The thin line between laughing and crying is familiar to all parents and caregivers of children. It often requires adult intervention to help regulate an overstimulated child and restore the balance. This is the stuff whereby successful empathizing with others is learned, self-regulation acquired, self-esteem enhanced, and relationship security established.

Regulation of Overarousal in Groups of Children

Sherman (1975) studied the phenomenon of what he called "glee" appearing during lessons given to small groups of preschoolers 2.5 to 5.5 years of age. He defined glee as "joyful screaming, laughing, and intense physical acts" that occurred either "in simultaneous bursts" or "spread in a contagious fashion from one child to another" (p. 53). The group was made up of Caucasian and African American children, equally split by race and gender and representing a wide socioeconomic range.

More than 40% of the 596 lessons videotaped had at least one incident of group glee that involved close to half or more of the group. Gender also made some difference here, with mixed gender groups having more episodes of glee. The kinds of things that set the kids off sound remarkably similar to those that trigger adult audiences: funny words or incongruities, nonsense songs, breaking taboos, and using "bad words." Sometimes, as when the teacher was resolving suspense or making a transition point or coming to an ending, the children's glee seemed almost like applause. The least frequent trigger for glee was derision at a teacher's predicament or a (fictional) child's misfortune, which indicates high levels of empathy and perhaps security in these children.

The 30% of gleeful incidents that were disruptive combined laughter, screaming, and intense physical movement and were usually confined to a few children. The 70% of incidents that were nondisruptive mostly occurred as a "simultaneous burst" (p. 60), like the audience response to a punch line. Often the teachers would join in the fun and laugh along with the children. Alternatively, they would ignore the giggles and proceed ahead with the lesson.

The disruptive incidents tended to be confined to a few children and to contain physical acts, which the teachers felt a need to suppress. When they stepped in to soothe the overstimulated kids, they sometimes tried to terminate the behavior by reprimanding, telling the children to calm down, or using touch to calm them. The other method of regulation was more indirect, channeling them back into the activity at hand without directly instructing them to calm down.

Cultural norms vary regarding how to soothe gleeful children. The Quaker adults who responded to the glee that spread among the Bible-reading fifth-graders at a Quaker meeting suggest one effective example of indirect affect regulation. Unlike the severe looks and reprimands I might have received for such an outburst in church, these elders, "the Friends," are described by Lee (2008) as

> not severe and condemning, nor yet smiling with the kind of amused indulgence with which grownups greet endearing childish mishaps. Nor do they display any desire to make this a character-building experience. Those

old faces are simply present: alert, regarding us ... with a boundless, patient comprehension that raises us to their own dignified level. We let the silence flow back. And, gradually, something becomes clear: a kind of radiant indifference to words, mistaken or correct. What the elders, the Friends, pass on to us this morning is an inkling of how strong silence is. (p. 40)

Humor as Affect Regulation

In addition to attuning to and down-regulating children's levels of positive hyperarousal, children and their caregivers also use laughter and humor as a means to soothe too much negative arousal. Sensitive adults, siblings, and playmates are often successfully able to use laughter, humor, or comedy to soothe a negatively aroused child, enabling children to learn to use it themselves or in relationships with other negatively aroused adults or children.

Adult-to-Child Affect Regulation

A great deal of caregiving skill and sensitivity are required to titrate and time humor so that it does not feel like a shaming or mean misattunement to a child. Also, its overuse or exclusive use as a regulator misses the mark of both attunement and regulation, delivering instead the message that the caregiver must be "humored" at all times, even when the child is negatively aroused. I once saw an adult woman who smiled so continuously that it made my jaws ache. As I got to know her history, I learned that her father had died when she was 5 and that her job became that of keeping her mother from tipping irrevocably into a grief-laden depression.

Contrast this with the gentle "humoring" of a child who has suffered a mild but scary injury. For example, several times my granddaughter Aurelia has tripped over the sidewalk or her own feet while running enthusiastically. She will start to cry, but once I have her in my arms and have hugged and comforted her, I often say, "Did you go bumpity bump?" For some reason this always makes her chuckle and helps to soothe her.

By contrast, imagine being a young child who hits a bump and is thrown over the handlebars of her bicycle badly scraping her chin. Years later, this now adult woman recalled the occasion: "When I looked up, I saw my shirtless father standing by the hedge, shears at his side, staring at me. And then he laughed." He eventually caught himself, she said, and then told her to go inside for help, but he never tried to console or help her himself. Years later in therapy, when asked to share a painful memory, she said, "It was this one that popped into my head: of my father laughing at me when I was down" (C., 2003, p. 36).

My own mother, on the other hand, was masterful at providing just the right amount of light humor in tense situations of all kinds. She always responded with empathy and soothing during the rough moments, but was quick to inject a little lightness when that moment had passed. She even used affectionate teasing to give us gentle redirection when we misbehaved. If we were caught sneaking into the kitchen to get a forbidden treat just out of the oven, she would laugh and say, "You little monkey, are you trying to run off with one of those cookies?" I can't capture her tone of voice on the page, but it was lighthearted, cute, and warm, not accusatory, harsh, or mean-spirited in any way. We knew we had been caught in the act, "busted," kids would say nowadays, but we did not feel harshly judged for trying. We would put the cookie back with a guilty chuckle, still feeling loved and understood. She had regulated our behavior in a lighthearted, attuned manner, not shaming us in the process.

Child-to-Child Affect Regulation

Another way that children use laughter is to help engage an unavailable or negatively aroused peer whose attention is important to them. Being around someone who is feeling down is no more fun for children than it is for adults. One of the tools in a child's affect regulation bag is to create comedic situations that may help improve the mood for both. If her companion becomes more responsive and positively engaged, the child, too, feels better.

The little Peruvian girl profiled in the "Day-in-the-Life" video studies, for example, spent 10 minutes trying to engage her sick cousin (we might say upregulate to a more positive affective state) by doing a lighthearted, comedic performance with her aunt's toothpaste and toothbrush (E. L. Cameron, Gamannossi, Gillen, & C.A. Cameron, 2010). She didn't appear to be going for a laugh from her cousin, necessarily, but she did start laughing herself right away. She appeared to just want her cousin to feel better so they could play.

Laughter also serves as a form of interactive affect regulation, as when children and adolescents use it to diffuse awkward, embarrassing, or tense social situations with peers. The two subjects of the resilient youth "Day-in-the-Life" studies, 15-year-old Lorraine and 14-year-old Neil, for example, were masters at using laughter and humor—joking around, sarcasm, irony, and teasing—as a way to avoid or deescalate negative arousal generated in their social networks (E. L. Cameron et al., 2010).

Both of the young adolescents, from an impoverished urban area in eastern Canada, came from what was termed "high risk" backgrounds. Lorraine had been removed from her substance-abusing parents' custody and was living with a 28-year-old aunt. Neil's parents were divorced, and he had recently moved in with his father, because of conflict with a younger brother at his mother's home. In spite of significant stressors, both of these young people were identified as resilient by community advocates. Both skillfully used laughter to negotiate the complex relationships in their lives, using it to interactively regulate negative arousal—their own and that of peers and family.

Lorraine, for example, was out for a walk on the day she was being filmed and ran into a group of rowdy boys who started questioning her in a teasing/harassing way as to why her "sexy ass" was being filmed by the camera crew. In a light, teasing tone she said, "Shut up, Jerry," to the offending kid, and then laughed off subsequent questions. When the boys asked what the movie was about, for example, she laughed again and said, "Me" (p. 12). At another point, she laughingly pretended to be offended when one of the boys called her by the wrong name. The researchers observe that her laughter is a "signal of her intention to keep the tone of the interaction light" (p. 12). Throughout the exchange, her laughter and humor help to regulate her own and the boys' affect—as she laughs off their teasing and tosses back some of her own. Even the common English-language usage of the phrase "to laugh it off" points to the affect-regulating properties of laughter in diffusing a tense situation.

Neil, the other resilient teen, was also able to effectively make use of humor and teasing to interactively regulate affect. When his friend Brad arrived for a visit at his home, he greeted Neil, with "Hey, Fatty!" Neil turned the teasing right back on him, making fun of the way the boy ran down the street. His friend quipped back, "Who, me?" and Neil replied, "No, the Michelin Man," using a "lighthearted sarcastic tone," eliciting laughter from both boys. The teasing tone of voice, the bantering quality of the conversation, and ultimately the shared common ground of laughter all served as effective affect-regulating tools that kept the negative jabs from disintegrating into overt conflict and hurt feelings.

Cartoons were used in one study to measure humor comprehension and affect expression in response to humor (indexed by a mirth score) in an ethnically mixed group of 10- to 14-year-old school children (Masten, 1986). The children with better humor production, comprehension, and greater mirth were described by teachers as

> more effectively engaged in the classroom and more attentive, cooperative, responsive and productive. Their peers viewed them as more popular, gregarious, and happy and as leaders with good ideas for things to do. (p. 469)

I remember kids like that from elementary school, and with the hindsight of attachment theory, I see them as having been securely attached youngsters who could make even geography fun, helping us regulate the negative arousal of boredom or fatigue with a joke that even the teacher would find funny. Some class clowns get it titrated just right, and the whole class is the better for it. In the next chapter, we will discuss the negatively aroused children who, coming from a place of insecurity, adopt the role of class clown with a much different outcome.

Using humor as a strategy to connect with classmates and become "popular" is apparently a solid one. A study in Denmark found that the person with the highest status in a mixed-gender class of 11- to 12-year-olds was a boy who was the person in class that most frequently made jokes, funny quips, and even remarks with implicit sexual references (as cited in Führ, 2001).

The Danish 10- to 11-year-olds were asked if they had ever done something when they were really unhappy to get a laugh (Führ, 2001) and 85% answered yes. A follow-up questions asked them how they felt afterward and 32 of the 40 children said they felt positive. The 8 who said it was a negative experience said either that it made them feel "stupid," or made them feel simultaneously better and worse. This kind of confused ambivalence about humor may be related to their attachment style, as we will discuss in the next chapter.

Child-to-Adult Affect Regulation

Children also learn to use laughter and humor, through clowning, to draw a distracted or irritated parent or other adult into positive engagement. Writer and humorist Shalom Auslander (2007) gives a moving example of himself as an 8-year-old using comedy to diminish family tension, regulating the negative arousal of the whole family, and thereby his own.

> As the clouds over our dining room grew heavy with bile, and the winds of bickering blew across the table—*Keep it up,* my father would growl at my brother, fists clenched beside his dinner plate, *see what it gets you*—I would jump down from my chair and make my way to the foot of the table. Showtime. (p. 36)

Auslander's most successful standup routine, reflecting the times, was a Richard Nixon imitation he had learned from watching Dan Aykroyd on television. The 8-year-old would declaim dramatically, "I am not a thief, I am not a thief," in his version of the Aykroyd/Nixon character, thereby disarming his father and brother and up-regulating everyone's negative mood:

> My father would try his best to remain angry, but a few more Nixons up and down the table and he would smile, and the storm would pass and the sky would start to clear. Soon, everyone at the table was laughing, and no one could remember why my father and brother had almost killed each other. (p. 36)

Affectionate Teasing

Keltner (2008), a smile, laughter, and happiness researcher, extols the virtues of a type of friendly childhood teasing that is marked by "affectionate banter" among friends or the "repartee" between siblings. He rightly points out that teasing in general has gained a bad reputation because of its link with bullying and harassment. Affectionate, nonhostile teasing, however, is mostly lighthearted and good-natured, though it may at times be pointed. When friendly intent is recognized, it can be both funny and fun. It is a mode of play that stands in contrast to mean-spirited taunting with its demeaning, repetitive insults; hostile bullying that is detached and has violent undertones; and sexual harassment with its crude, demeaning, and often threatening implications.

Teasing, on the other hand, is a behavior that incorporates attachment and play, linking them with the conflict/appeasement system of behavior. Teasing, Keltner says, gives us a way to "negotiate life's ambiguities and conflicts," even if it is play that sometimes has "a sharp edge" (para. 5). He points out that even monkeys tease—pulling each other's tails—and dogs jump all over each other—not unlike roughhousing little kids.

Though infants under a year have been noted to effectively and "knowingly" tease (Reddy, 2008), it is not until ages 11 or 12 that children are fully able to understand and use the complexities of teasing. Keltner writes that this is also the age when children add irony and sarcasm to their repertoire—and, interestingly, it is the age that there is also a big drop in reported incidences of bullying. Teasing rises and bullying drops off, which Keltner (2008) sees as a developmental step forward.

> In teasing, we learn to use our voices, bodies and faces, to read those of others—the raw materials of emotional intelligence and moral imagination. We learn the wisdom of laughing at ourselves and not taking the self too seriously. We learn boundaries between danger and safety, right and wrong, friend and foe, male and female, what is serious and what is not. We transform the many conflicts of social living into entertaining dramas. No kidding. (para. 28)

The tricky thing about affectionate teasing, as Keltner points out, is that it has to have communication markers that suggest the words should not be taken literally. For example, with affectionate teasing we use exaggeration or a slightly humorous tone, a twinkling eye or bemused expression, along with a smile or shrug or chuckle. A good example above is when Neil's friend greets him as "Fatty" and Neil responds by making fun of Brad's running style. When everybody gets the affectionate tease and its hidden intent (and obviously that does not always happen), spontaneous laughter usually ensues. As Keltner (2008) writes, the "shared laughter becomes a collective experience, one of coordinated action, cooperative physiology and the establishing of common ground" (para. 19). In other words, affectionate teasing, when it goes well, contributes to attachment and affiliation.

Affectionate teasing may link attachment and play systems with the conflict/appeasement system. Sometimes there is play hostility in response, as when my friend's granddaughter would call her "Graham Gracker" instead of "Grammie," and Grammie would play-growl or play-glare back at her. The link between teasing and appeasement shows up in the ways some victims of teasing show embarrassment by averting their gaze, blushing, or giving a slight smile. These behaviors are gestures that are, according to Keltner (2008), "ancient signs of appeasement that trigger a reconciliation response in most mammals" (para. 20). In a study by Keltner, Young, Heerey, Oemig, and Monarch (1998) of teasing among college fraternity brothers, these appeasement behaviors were amply demonstrated.

Adult-to-Child Teasing

Occasionally, even roughhouse teasing that to an outsider may seem cruel seems to effectively engage a child in positive arousal and play. Reddy (2008), for example, describes a grandfather repeatedly poking a 2-year-old with his walking stick until the child finally falls over. Eventually, the boy "playfully attacked his grandfather—both of them laughing, and now both started playing together" (p. 212). Here is a case of a teaser with affectionate intent who is able to correctly gauge the amount and type of aggravation and frustration he dishes out to the child and does so in combination with just the right amount of invitation-to-play and lighthearted affect. The attachment, clearly a positive one, carried the day, and the affectionate teasing accomplished its goal.

Duchenne and Non-Duchenne Laughter in Children

The type of laughter discussed throughout this chapter and in most of the childhood laughter research is presumed to be spontaneously erupting Duchenne or genuine, sincere laughter. While even babies in their first year learn to insert conversational non-Duchenne laughter into their communication, there has, until recently, been little focus on the distinction in childhood.

Relying on observations of my granddaughter, however, I see multiple examples of conversational laughter inserted in her daily life. It is a way she has of joining the fun or letting others know that she is happy with the proceedings. On telephone calls to her during a recent trip away, she would insert loud, fake-sounding peals of laughter at almost every statement we made, even those without funny intent or content. There was a hint of distress in her laughter, presumably at the separation, mixed in with her pleasure at hearing from us. A potential area for fruitful research would be to look at how children learn procedurally to use laughter as a signal in conversation even in the absence of humor, and, in the case of the telephone, to communicate in the absence of facial expressions. A colleague who is an attachment researcher recently told me that in a study of telephone communication between children and caregivers, she noticed that the children seemed to laugh out loud at times when they would be smiling if in face-to-face contact (C. A. Cameron, personal communication, December 15, 2011).

Child Laughter from a Global Perspective

Laughter Yoga for Kids

The international Laughter Yoga movement established by Dr. Madan Kataria has expanded to include Laughter Yoga for children. In *The Laughter Yoga Deck* children's pack, there are instructions for leading a laughter session with young children. The instructions advise keeping things playful, encouraging eye contact, motion, and deep breathing. The goal is not to be funny, but simply to laugh. One exercise, for example, that seems to exemplify the goals is called "Jumping Frog Laughter." The children squat down with their hands on the floor between their knees. Then they jump once saying "ha," and a second time saying "ha ha," and a third time increasing to three "ha's," and ending with fast jumping and continual laughter. It makes me smile just imagining the fun! Promoting laughter in groups such as these is a way to use its universal appeal and its natural association with children in the realms of health, group cohesion, and connection.

Clowns Without Borders

An Internet posting about children and laughter caught my eye. It described an inspiring group of people, Clowns Without Borders, who travel to scenes of natural disasters, wars, and violent traumas to bring laughter to children there. The group was founded in Barcelona in 1993 and now has active chapters in nine countries, including the United States. While much of the group's work has been with children in war-torn countries, Clowns Without Borders was quick to travel to Haiti and bring laughter to the traumatized children in refugee camps in the aftermath of the devastating earthquake. Watching the videos and even the still photos of the group's work around the world, we see that the children are able to connect through laughter in spite of the wide variety of language and cultural differences. Helping to "arouse" positive affect in the midst of trauma is a tricky affair, but done with sensitivity and a warm heart, it goes a long way to bringing the healing that can only come through human connection.

Most of the childhood laughter described in this chapter is of the optimal, attuned, securely attached type. Looking at laughter from this perspective is designed to create a prototype for use as a point of reference during the next chapter, where we discuss the less optimal variants of childhood laughter. Such optimal experiences of connected laughter represent affect arousal and regulation in the service of attachment security and play.

All of these elements could be seen and heard in the laughter I observed on the street in Berkeley. A little girl about three was holding the hands of both her parents as they walked. She said to them, "Let's run." They glanced at each other, shrugged as if to say, "Why not, even though we are in our fancy dress clothes." They took off, high heels, suits, and all, with their daughter propelled along between them. The little girl looked extremely happy for a moment and then began to laugh with delight. Playful laughter shared with responsive parental caregivers would seem to be the best of all possible kid worlds. Her laughter signaled them of her delight and could not help but draw them into sharing her elation. It certainly captured me, a casual onlooker who felt blessed to witness this intimate attachment circle, experiencing their mutual delight. In the next chapter, we will look at what can happen to laughter in children whose affect arousal, caregiver attunement, and interactive regulation have been met with painful and repeated misattunements of all kinds.

8

CHILDHOOD LAUGHTER IN A CLINICAL CONTEXT

While child therapists probably laugh all the time with their young patients, it is little discussed in the clinical literature. My search turned up only a few book chapters and journal articles on the topic, and most of those are about humor—with laughter seen as a by-product of humor rather than as a clinical experience to be reflected upon and understood in and of itself. Perhaps laughter with children is not discussed in the literature because it does not stir up controversies about neutrality as it does in work with adults.

Another reason that laughter flies under the radar in the clinical literature may be because it is a nonverbal attachment behavior that is difficult to analyze. Laughter, like crying, arises spontaneously in relational contexts and is part of our implicit, procedural nonconscious way of relating. This makes putting the complexities behind laughter into words more difficult as it occurs outside of explicit awareness and consciousness. An attachment viewpoint gives us a way to consciously explore and understand laughter and to see why and when it is helpful clinically and why and when it gets in the way of growth and the working through process in the context of the therapeutic relationship with children.

Positive affect in general has only recently begun to receive much attention in the clinical literature. The predominant focus of clinical work traditionally has been on trauma and negative arousal, and working through loss and grief. As a result, therapists may seldom think about the importance of positive arousal in treatment, even in work with children. Affect regulation, as Schore (2003a) points out, is

> not just the reduction of affective intensity, the dampening of negative emotion. It also involves an amplification, an intensification of positive emotion, a condition necessary for more complex self-organization. Attachment is

not just the reestablishment of security after a dysregulating experience and a stressful negative state; it is also the interactive amplification of positive affects, as in play states. (p. 78)

A consultee, working with an 8-year-old foster child, for example, focused on and struggled with how to access the painful affects related to multiple traumas that she knew were lurking beneath the little girl's chirpy exterior. She wondered how she could support the child in accessing her negative arousal so that the little girl could get in touch with her anger and pain and begin to work through them. I suggested that she set that agenda aside for a time and focus instead on what the child liked and what was fun for her, as a way to establish a secure-enough therapeutic attachment bond. With that in mind, the consultee recalled the child saying that she loved to look at pictures of baby animals on the Internet, which, we agreed, clearly represented the child's solo attempts to cope with and regulate her attachment distress and her mood. The consultee reported that with her enthusiastic participation, the little girl had quickly engaged over their talking about the baby animals and finding pictures on the Internet for them to share. Only after trust and a secure base had been established through positive engagement could the child open up and speak of her anger, fear, and loss.

Children, like adults, need to feel safe and connected before they can explore their pain. Exploration—in therapy as elsewhere—is best accomplished in the context of a safe haven and secure base. These can be established as much from the therapist/caregiver attuning to the child's positive affect as it can be by soothing the negative. From positive affect to laughter is a short step with children. If children are happy and having a good time, they laugh, in therapy, just as in the rest of their lives. Laughter and positive connection help develop the therapeutic attachment bond. A secure base is what enables the child to tolerate negative arousal as she explores experiences, including trauma, that are frightening and painful.

Laughter as Sign or Symptom

Sometimes, though perhaps not often, children are referred to therapy because of "inappropriate laughter." Teachers, parents, or other concerned health professionals may, often correctly (though sometimes not), recognize that the child's laughter is a defense against pain, or a symptom of some deeper underlying difficulties. Inappropriate laughter may take place alone, only in a particular relationship under particular circumstances, or be part of a pattern of targeting another child or person for belittling laughter.

Hostile Teasing and Bullying

From a clinical perspective, it is important to clarify the distinctions between what in the previous chapter was called "affectionate teasing" and hostile teasing and bullying. To clarify the distinctions, teasing will be divided into three subcategories suggested by Jade (personal communication, December 30, 2011), each considered from the standpoint of the instigator of the laughter. While these types typically appear in childhood, they may continue in adult life, as well. The categories are nonhostile teasing with positive results; nonhostile teasing with negative results; and hostile teasing/bullying.

Nonhostile Teasing with Positive Results

In this type of teasing, the child's intention is nonhostile and playful and the recipient does not get irritated or angry. Recipients either take it in good fun, or are adept at walking away, firing back a nonhostile retort, or otherwise setting boundaries that the child can comprehend and respect. This type of behavior, also referred to as friendly or affectionate teasing, would rarely result in a referral.

Nonhostile Teasing with Negative Results

When things go wrong and "negative results" ensue from nonhostile teasing, it rarely results in a referral for the instigator, because adults are able—or believe they are able—to judge that the instigator's intention is nonhostile. The target child, however, might be singled out for therapeutic help for being unable to "take a joke" or for being "too sensitive." Looking at this issue from the "sensitive" child's perspective, such a negative reaction to affectionate teasing may be a sign or symptom of difficulties with correctly reading the intent of another person or with affect arousal and regulation. On the other hand, it is also possible that the instigator of the teasing is not as benevolent as the adults may think. In that instance, the targeted child may be picking up on subtle cues of hostility or meanness missed by the adults.

Hostile Teasing with Negative Results

Hostile teasing and bullying are usually identified as symptomatic of the instigator's difficulties with "controlling" his or her aggression. The laughter that accompanies them, though mean-spirited, can nonetheless be viewed through an attachment-system lens. Hostile teasing and bullying are often accompanied by patterns of affect arousal that suggest insecure and disorganized attachment. Hostile teasing, for example, may represent an attempt by the instigator to regulate his or her attachment-related distress over familial or relational wounds or trauma. By creating another victim and laughing at that victim, he or she is able to defensively create positive arousal in themselves instead of feeling the pain and distress of their own victimization.

Child-to-Child Bullying "Gleeful taunting," a form of hostile teasing, is defined by Miller and Olson (2000) as "an intense display of inappropriate positive affect" (p. 347). These researchers use the term to describe hostile behavior in the high-risk preschoolers they studied, such as taking toys away from another child and laughing, or "other forms of relational aggression" (p. 347). The children who engaged in gleeful taunting were the ones consistently rated lowest in appropriate social behavior by both teachers and peers. It turned out, in fact, that "intense positive but no intense negative affect displays during conflicts were associated with negative outcomes" (p. 348). Hostile taunting laughter such as this may represent the need for connection, defense against vulnerability, and strong aggression that may likely be associated with or fueled by an insecure or disorganized attachment history. Instead of "laughing with" in the service of positive connection, the child ends up "laughing at" and cruelly victimizing others, and ultimately driving adults, peers, and even sometimes pets away.

An element of some hostile teasing or bullying is when the instigator uses it as a means of connecting by excluding one or more "outsiders." Laughing at someone outside the group is a way to solidify the group bond. Though dysfunctional, it can increase affiliation and attachment in the insider (and sometimes the outsider) groups. It is one means of bolstering a sense of belonging for children who lack a safe haven and secure base with primary caregivers or who are themselves victims of some form of abuse. Children who are insecurely attached—especially those with disorganized attachment related to abuse or neglect—may be especially prone to engaging in hostile teasing and bullying. The Sroufe (2005) longitudinal studies of the relationship between attachment style and later development, for example, found that insecurely attached children were more hostile and less empathic with their playmates, even those who were injured or struggling.

Conscious efforts have been made in many schools to help teach children and parents how to recognize hostile teasing, to understand what drives it and the dangers posed by it, and to coach them in how to eradicate it. I was moved recently by a high school graduation video of a young man with Asperger's syndrome. Rather than being the target of merciless hostile teasing as is so often the case, he was shown in the film surrounded by adoring classmates who hugged him and smiled with obvious pride at his accomplishments. The soccer team he helped to manage created a special trophy to acknowledge his hard work. The boy's mother told me that a superintendent in their Tennessee school system some years before had made a concerted effort to introduce a sensitivity program into all of their schools, and here was the heartening result.

Adult-to-Child Insensitivity and Bullying
Children may experience the pain of being laughed "at" rather than "with" by caregivers, as well as other children. Too many such misattunements may result in a child feeling confusion, shame, fear, rage, and even trauma. A YouTube video, "Bloody Baby" (markgarza22, 2006), for example, plainly shows a child's confusion when his distress about his baby brother's bleeding lip is met with laughter from his videotaping father. The little boy, with increasing frustration, ends by screaming, "It's not funny!" His

father, making an effort at control, repeats, "It's not funny," while simultaneously bursting into more laughter. Even though there is clearly some affection in the father's voice, and the baby is attended to appropriately by the mother, the child's understandable and palpable distress (negative arousal) is nonetheless an apparent source of laughter, not only to the parents, but to the vast majority of the millions of people who have commented online after watching it. While the father's response does not seem intended to be hostile or to put the child down, it is an example where the father's laughter was definitely misattuned to the child's appropriate distress over his sibling's injury.

Once, in an advice column, I saw an item sent in by a grandmother who was dismayed because of the cruel teasing instigated by the adults at her 5-year-old granddaughter's birthday party. For some reason, the child's mother thought it would be funny to push the child's face into the birthday cake after the candles and song. The little girl burst into tears while everyone else, children and adults, roared with laughter. From the frightened child's point of view, this was a sudden hostile interaction by her trusted caregivers, causing her confusion and shame at an important moment during her birthday party. Adult laughter is confusing enough to children without adding the contradictory messages implied in this kind of teasing. The role modeling is not lost on children who eventually learn that it is all right to make jokes at someone's expense, if you are doing it for a laugh. When adults use amusement at a child's expense to up-regulate their own positive arousal or down-regulate their negative arousal, there is the risk that the child will be hurt in the moment and in the long run may develop ambivalent, nonempathic internal working models for future relationships.

Class Clowns

Some class clowns thrive in their role, the securely attached ones, perhaps. Not all class clowns are secure, however. There are those who are, as the saying goes, "laughing on the outside, crying on the inside." They manage to annoy their teachers, and sometimes their classmates also end up feeling irritated or having a difficult time with the disruptions. Even if other children laugh and respond positively, it may be hard for a class clown who is insecurely attached to internalize a sense of connection. An adult patient once told me that she remembered consciously adopting the role of class clown in school in order to get people to like her. In her own insecure self-appraisal, she said, "I was the class clown so people would like me. I had nothing else; why would anybody like me? I had to be funny, it was the only way." She added, "I was always in trouble at school for talking."

Author Wes Moore (2010) writes of his experience feeling out of place as a poor, African American student at an all-white prep school in New York. Smart and capable, he nonetheless felt so isolated and uncomfortable that he refused to perform academically. He was looking for a way out of the school and back to the neighborhood kids with whom he felt comfortable. He consciously used his humor to annoy the teacher. Finally, she tacitly agreed to not report his absences from class, since "class ran smoother when I wasn't there" (p. 77). The grating humor that played on the teacher's nerves was a sign that this particular child was in pain. For unknown reasons, the teacher misattuned to his affect and took the clowning interruptions as a reason to support his skipping class rather than reaching out and trying to help him find a way to connect and stay in school.

I was interested to read some online advice for teachers (Snider, 2010) at Edutopia, the George Lucas–supported educational foundation. The advice for dealing with class clowns is not to ignore or attempt to squelch the behavior, but to "go with your gut: laugh," especially if the child is really funny. The idea is to forge a sense of understanding, to attune to the attempt at positive connection, even knowing that there are "social insecurities or academic shortcomings" or a "troubled home life" underneath. "Kids are always evaluating themselves through other's eyes, looking for positive feedback, and if they don't get it, they compensate" (para. 3). Another suggestion is to use hand signals or silence to alert the students that they need to calm and self-regulate. Of course, this approach is only possible if the class clown's attempts at humor are relatively benign and not hostile or victimizing of the teacher or the other children.

Uncontrollable Laughter

A laughter "fit" is not by definition symptomatic per se, as most children know from experience. It would seem rare for a child to be referred to therapy for uncontrollable laughter, though "giggling in school" (to the point of disrupting lessons and disturbing the class) was the precipitant for one 13-year-old girl's referral for a psychiatric consultation (Sachs, 1973).

When talking with the analyst, the young girl quickly confessed that she and her friend had a running joke about the teacher. They decided that whenever he hooked two fingers onto the button on his sweater, it was a signal to his wife that he wanted to have sex, which must happen often, she reported, because he has six children. When he would make that gesture, she said, "Sometimes we laugh so much that we cannot stop, and everything hurts from so much laughing. . . . Once we laughed for a whole hour" (p. 482).

The young girls' "out of control" laughing fits, Sachs proposed, might represent a defense against uncomfortable adolescent feelings about sexuality. However, this "private joke" was shared with an age-mate and friend and thus would also seem to represent an attempt to master the anxiety about sex through connection with someone close who shares the "secret." While this child's laughter may have been disruptive, it seems more an enactment around mastery and growth than symptomatic.

At other times, however, out-of-control laughter can occur in response to trauma, representing heightened negative arousal in a situation where crying or screaming would be dangerous or socially unacceptable. I found myself suffering in empathy as I read another example by Sachs (1973), which came to her attention at a resort hotel where she was a guest. Also staying there was a family with two teenage daughters. One day at the pool, Sachs observed, the daughters were joined by a young man who quickly began making advances to one of them in full view of her sister and other guests. He began by touching her foot, then her legs, and in short order her breasts. The young woman did not pull away, but began "giggling louder and louder, until it became uncontrolled laughter, with a strident, gasping sound on inhaling" (p. 482). Her gasps for air dislodged the young man's hands, but he persisted. "Her laughter got louder, less controlled, and obviously painful to her" until tears ran down her cheeks (p. 482). "Suddenly, still convulsed with laughter, she got out of her beach chair and jumped into the pool, leaving a trail of urine behind her" (p. 482). By that time, her convulsions of "laughter" were clearly painful, uncontrolled contortions. She was finally pulled from the pool and rescued.

"Peggy," as Sachs called this young woman, appears to have been completely unprepared for being sexually assaulted, let alone by a man her parents had invited to visit. No one tried to stop him or help her initially, perhaps due to his brazenness and her "laughter." Peggy understandably was in shock, terrified and totally confused by all the circumstances. She was caught between thinking it must be all right if the young man thought so (her parents had invited him to visit) and if he was doing it in public. She had nowhere to turn with her discomfort. The laughter, initially an attachment appeal for connection and help, failed. Eventually, when her panic and distress were painfully obvious to all, she was finally removed from the situation.

"Giggle Incontinence" or Enuresis Risoria

Uncontrollable laughter can at times cause what is called "giggle incontinence" (technical term: *enuresis risoria*), which is uncontrollable voiding and urgency caused by hyperarousal accompanied by laughter. These laughter fits are not necessarily trauma-induced, as was the case in the above example. Sometimes the humor is just too funny and the physical response to it too persistent, a situation familiar to many of us from childhood.

Psuedobulbar Affect (PBA)

Involuntary laughing or crying can also represent a neurological disorder called variously pseudobulbar affect (PBA), emotional lability, emotional incontinence, or involuntary emotional expression disorder (IEED). PBA is a symptom of a variety of neurological disorders, including gelastic epilepsy (a form of temporal lobe epilepsy with fits of mirthless laughter), juvenile ALS, a brain tumor, or a brain injury. This type of laughter may erupt in response to something mildly funny, or even when something is not humorous at all. While this is not a common symptom, clinicians should take note of it so that underlying physiological conditions can be ruled out in cases of uncontrollable laughter in children.

On a blog called Autismcrisis (Kulp, 2009), in a discussion about autism and laughter, a person who identified himself as "Roger" wrote about his own experience of seizures that included uncontrollable laughter.

> When I am physically very sick, either from an acute infection, or in the case of a severe stroke-like episode, seizure, or whatever the hell these are, my autism always gets worse. . . . In the case of the latter, . . . the severe phase lasts a day or a day and a half or so, and as I recover, my autism gets worse. I am unable to talk other than weird vocal noises. I headbang. I flap my arms a lot, and I laugh, titter and giggle a lot. There is no cause for this, it is entirely reflexive. (Comments section)

Contagious Laughter

Contagious laughter can be another type of symptomatic uncontrollable laughter in children. One of the most extreme cases occurred in 1962 in Tanganyika (now Tanzania). It started at a boarding school among young girls 12 to 18 with attacks lasting from a few minutes to a few hours. Beginning with 3 girls, it spread to 95, forcing the school to close. Eventually, the epidemic spread to other schools and to the girls' communities when they were sent home. School children and young adults of both sexes were affected. Though the best speculation was that this was true emotional contagion and not the result of a toxic syndrome or encephalitis, some doubt remained because some victims had symptoms such as fever, rash, pain, and headache (Cardosa, 2001). Eventually affecting 1,000 people, the outbreak lasted for 18 months and required a quarantine to end its spread.

Absence of Laughter and Atypical Laughter as Symptom

Research on laughter by children on the autistic spectrum, though there isn't a great deal of it, has shown that such children laugh with the same frequency as neuro-typical children (Hudenko, Stone, & Bachorowski, 2009). Sometimes the laughter parallels the playful responses of any child to physical or verbal incongruities. At other times, it seems more idiosyncratic. Reddy (2008) writes of one 5-year-old autistic child who would laugh every time someone said a certain word, for example, the word "black." The same child's parents also said he would laugh alone in bed at night. Another little girl would stand in the corner staring at her mother's huge pile of ironing and "go into mass hysteria," according to her mother (p. 196).

Many individuals on the autistic spectrum report having a hard time figuring out what humor is, and when and when not to laugh. They describe the difficulties as related to their propensity for being literal and communicating with unfiltered honesty. Not being able to laugh along with others or being the target of teasing laughter about their social difficulties can be painful. The fictional "Jacob," in *House Rules* (Picoult, 2010), a teenage boy diagnosed with Asperger's, gives an example: "When a classmate asks, 'You play baseball? What position? Left out?' and gets a big laugh from the rest of the class," Jacob says that he cheers himself up by calculating this one kid's relative importance as 1 of 6,792 billion humans on the planet, which is just "one-eighth of the solar system, whose sun is one of two billion stars in the Milky Way galaxy" (p. 145). He was able to turn his literal, factual capabilities into a coping mechanism to help him deal with the pain of hostile teasing and bullying.

Another struggle children on the autistic spectrum have is "getting" run-of-the-mill conversational humor. This difficulty is believed to be related to their struggles with attuning to the inner experiences of others and accurately reading facial expressions (Grandin, Barron, & Zysk, 2005). Understanding jokes, especially subtle quips, and getting the timing right, are implicit procedural skills that are almost impossible to teach, though, of course, charts, graphs, descriptions, and other tools can be helpful in making the implicit explicit.

In their book, *Unwritten Rules of Social Relationships,* Grandin and Barron, both of whom are adults on the autistic spectrum, discuss their struggles to figure out how to understand humor and learn to be funny. Barron recalls noticing that funny kids were more popular with his peers. "And in my case, an ability to get my middle school classmates laughing harder and longer would go a long way toward reversing a self-history fraught and littered with despair and suicidal ideations" (Grandin, Barron, & Zysk, 2005, p. 331).

He describes a plan he designed to elicit laughter in his family and friends: copying funny lines (those with laugh tracks) from *Gilligan's Island* and from the Kool-Aid and Sugar Crisp cereal commercials. He even tried to imitate the respective characters' movements and tones of voice in an effort to teach himself these foreign implicit skills. Sadly, the efforts backfired, making him the object of more ridicule. The other kids would, he said,

> mock me by repeating snips from the commercials or other sayings I came up with on my own before I opened my mouth. And I had no idea how to be funny or where to go with it when I was in the position of having to respond to what someone else said....I couldn't understand how someone else could view something that was hilarious to me in any other way than how I saw it. (Grandin, Barron, & Zysk, 2005, pp. 332–333)

Perhaps the most compelling insight, one he did not learn until well past childhood, is the idea "that spontaneity is humor's lifeblood" (p. 334).

Another implicit procedural truism that took Barron a long time to figure out is that humor depends completely on context, and that when uttered in the wrong context, something meant to be humorous may be "insulting, hurtful or inappropriate" (p. 333). It did not help that many peers violated these rules when teasing

Grandin and Barron. Both report difficulties learning the "unwritten social rules" about not laughing *at* or embarrassing other people. However, both were taught these rules consciously by their parents, as are most children. It was easier to master something so explicit than the unwritten rules about how to be funny and when to laugh in the flow of conversation. Imitation was another coping mechanism. They both learned to recognize a group's prevailing positive mood and to just join in and laugh along with everybody else, even though nothing in particular struck them as especially funny.

Hudenko, Stone, and Bachorowski (2009) have studied different types of laughter in autistic children. They have identified two types of laughter based on acoustical differences: voiced and unvoiced. Voiced laughter has a "tonal, song-like quality," whereas unvoiced laughter is atonal and "noisier," sometimes almost "grunt-like" (p. 1398). Evidence suggests that these two types of laughs serve distinct functions (similar to the distinction referred to elsewhere as Duchenne and non-Duchenne laughter). Voiced laughter is most strongly associated with positive arousal, whereas unvoiced laughter is believed to represent a lower arousal state, and functions to affirm others during conversation or to reinforce social interactions.

In most young adults, the two types of laughter occur about equally. Comparing the responses of groups of 15 8- to 10-year-old children with and without autism to humorous games in the lab (popping bubbles, knocking over towers, chasing a deflating balloon), Hudenko et al. found significant differences, not in the number of laughs, but in the types. When the children with autism laughed, 97% of the time it was voiced. On the other hand, in typically developing children matched for age-equivalency, only 63% of the laughter was voiced, and in typically developing children matched for chronological age, just 52% of the laughter was voiced.

Children on the autistic spectrum do indeed experience positive arousal, and their voiced (or Duchenne) laughter seems to signal that they find something genuinely funny. What they appear far less able to do, however, is to produce unvoiced (non-Duchenne) laughter. This is the type of laughter that is inserted into all kinds of communications to "grease the wheels" of conversation and relationship, again part of the "unwritten" social rules children on the autistic spectrum find so difficult to master. About half of such children had no unvoiced laughter in this study.

Laughter and Attachment Styles

In Sroufe's (2005) longitudinal studies of the relationship between attachment style and the various developmental functions and challenges, he notes,

> We were able to document the greater frequency of positive affective expression of those with secure histories when they initiated a contact with a peer or responded to a peer initiation, and the way they used positive affect

to sustain and build interactions, all in stark contrast to those with anxious attachment histories. They also were significantly higher on specific indicators such as "shows exuberance, lights up" and "has a lot of fun." (p. 357)

Without referring specifically to attachment styles, Denham (1998) also noted that children differ in the expression of emotions, each presenting with their own unique balance of positive versus negative emotion.

Based on the attachment style distinctions between the frequency and quality of infant laughter, we would expect to find a preponderance of genuine (Duchenne) positive arousal in securely attached children along with occasional, appropriate expressions of crying in distress. As Schore (2003a) writes, attachment security "allows for the interactive generation of high levels of positive affect in shared play states" (p. 281). Denham (1998) describes one such child, Juan, for example: "He grins broadly the minute he sees a friend; when his teacher reads a funny passage of a book, he is delighted" (p. 19).

A child with an avoidant attachment style develops defenses that suppress the need for connection and cover over the expression of attachment affects, positive or negative, a process known as deactivation of the attachment system (Mikulincer & Shaver, 2007). Denham's (1998) description of a child named Colin, for example, seems to fit the avoidant pattern of affect arousal and regulation: He "rarely shows positive emotions; he exhibits negative emotions or none at all...everyone just tries to stay out of his way, and might not even notice a flicker of positivity from him" (pp. 19–20). The last comment is particularly telling in light of the fact that research consistently shows that there may be small physiological indicators of negative arousal in avoidant children that are equally easy to miss.

A British study showed that "more aggressive, disruptive, assertive, controlling, and attention-seeking behaviors, and significantly fewer positive behaviors" were observed in insecurely attached compared to securely attached boys (Turner as cited in Grossmann, Grossmann, Kindler, & Zimmermann, 2008, p. 867). It was also observed that, presumably as a result, these insecurely attached boys also received "less guidance, instruction, or help, but elicited the most discipline and were least compliant with teachers' discipline" (p. 867).

Zachary, another child described by Denham, exhibited a pattern consistent with hyperactivation (the expression of high levels of attachment anxiety and distress) of the attachment system, which is typically associated with the ambivalent/resistant attachment style (Mikulincer & Shaver, 2007). Zachary's affect appeared to be hyperactivated in both positive and negative attachment affects, similar to the pattern described for the multi-expressive infants mentioned earlier. "He laughs uproariously on the playground when involved in rough-and-tumble play, but roars with anger when someone thwarts his building in the block corner. He keeps peers and adults alike on their toes" (Denham, 1998, p. 20). The note in the last sentence points to the difficulties that children with ambivalent/resistant attachment styles have with regulating affect on their own or with the help of others. Another child described by Denham also sounds ambivalent/resistant in attachment style, due to having quick reversals from positive to negative affect and back again, making it "hard to predict how interacting with her will turn out" (p. 20). A third, Roberto, manifested a slightly different anxious/ambivalent pattern. He had long periods of being quite neutral, but when someone did something funny, he retained the humorous response a long time. On the other hand, he also would stay angry for a long time when someone did something mean or upsetting. Here we see the pattern of high affect arousal combined with difficulty in being soothed. All three of these children show hyperactivation of positive and negative arousal and difficulties with affect regulation that are consistent with the ambivalent/resistant style of attachment.

Disorganized attachment represents a collapse of attachment strategy often stemming from abuse, severe neglect, psychotic parenting, exposure to violence, trauma, or fearful caregivers. Disorganization also impacts the child's ability to experience and display positive affect. For example, Denham (1998) reported that it was only the "maltreated children" who resisted their peers' "affectively positive overtures during play" (p. 196). She speculated that exposure to "high intensity negative emotion may spark the postulated process of children's inattention to that emotion" (p. 94). In other words, playful childhood affect dims—or dies—in the harsh light of negative overstimulation. Furthermore, the fact that dissociation is a common defensive feature in disorganized children may mean that their attachment and affiliative affects are blocked from consciousness for self-protective purposes.

Laughter researcher Panksepp (2001) points to the individual differences in the capacity for fun and laughter, but says, "We presently know next to nothing about the underlying psychobiological causes" (p. 155). He is correct in observing that little direct research has focused on the links between attachment style and positive arousal. However, our knowledge of the wide-ranging effects that internal working models have on all affect arousal and regulation enables us to build a bridge between the related attachment research and individual differences related to laughter. Once we have established a child's patterns of expressing positive affect, including the frequency and propensity of laughter, we will know something about his ability to use humor and laughter as a coping strategy and/or a defensive one. We will also be able to speculate about how different types of laughter, both Duchenne and non-Duchenne, are utilized. We may also be able to ascertain how a child's laughter links her attachment system with the exploratory, caregiving, and/or conflict systems of behavior. Further, knowing the child's attachment style will suggest something of the caregiving experiences he has had earlier in life and the possible traumas to which he may have been exposed.

Frequency and type of laughter can help predict attachment style, and attachment style can help predict frequency and types of laughter. Attachment style differences also point to certain characteristic early caregiving experiences. Typically, children whose internal working models are secure have experienced caregivers who are reliable, attuned, and consistent. Children with ambivalent/resistant internal working models of attachment are more likely to have experienced caregiving that was unpredictable, intrusive, or mismatched. The caregivers of children whose attachment style is avoidant, on the other hand, tend to be unavailable or neglectful and encouraging of early independence, self-regulation, and self-control. When a child's attachment affect, positive or negative, is eruptive or dissociated, it points toward attachment disorganization resulting from abuse, severe neglect, fearful, helpless-hostile, or psychotic caregiving.

Laughter in Children with Secure Attachment

To illustrate the link between laughter, humor, positive affect, and attachment style in children, consider the following observation of a boy named Joey.

> Four-year-olds Joey and Mike are pretending to be pirates.... They are having a lot of fun. Joey finds the buried treasure—hurray! But then things get complicated.... Mike suddenly decides to be the Queen's Navy, and Joey has to 'sword-fight' him. Then Jimmy, who has been nearby, tries to join in. No way! Joey wants Jimmy to leave. At almost the same minute, Mike steps on a Lego and starts to cry. And Rodney, the class bully, approaches, laughing at Joey and Mike for making believe and at Mike for crying. Joey deals with all of them: He comforts Mike appropriately, manages to tell Jimmy to stay out of the game without alienating him, and does his best to ignore Rodney's teasing. When their teacher calls them to have a snack, everybody is satisfied with the morning. (Denham, 1998, p. 1)

Based on what we know about the relational skills of securely attached children, it would be easy to guess that Joey is a securely attached child. He is a good laugher, a good friend and caregiver, and a good regulator of affect—his own and that of his peers. He can also read, understand, and help to regulate the feelings of others, even when they are a bit over-the-top and complicated.

Mikulincer and Shaver (2007) point to what they call a "cascade of mental and behavioral events," which accrue from the securely attached child's consistent experience of an available and responsive primary caregiver (p. 38). Consistent, attuned, and supportive caregiving can "impart a sense of safety, assuage distress, and arouse positive emotions." Securely attached people "can therefore remain relatively unperturbed under stress and experience longer periods of positive affectivity" (p. 38).

Laughter in Children with Ambivalent/Resistant Attachment

Contrast the anecdote about Joey with a story from the memoir of a woman who is the oldest in a family of nine children (H. Moore, 2008). She writes about the great sense of loss she felt at the erosion of her mother's availability to her upon the arrival of each successive sibling. She recalls a childhood lunch at their summer lake home. Though the family typically did not tell jokes as such, she remembers her mother laughing that day at a remark made by one of her sisters or brothers. "We had all competed for that laugh and now someone has won it, and she has thrown her head back." The young Moore immediately chimed in with her own effort to connect with her mother.

> "Mom," I hear myself say, "When you smile, it lights up the room." There is silence. I remember reflection from the lake dappling the walls. "Why, thank you, sweetie," she says, awkward. No, on second thought I don't remember her saying anything. I remember silence, just pure silence, though I can't swear the room was really silent. A space opens between us, a path as straight as a chute, the path I lost when my first sibling was born, the path whose entrance receded further every time my mother and I fought, every time another child pushed out of her and she brought it home. But now it was opening again, that true path from me to her.
>
> And then someone broke the spell. "I'll bet you never thought of yourself as a light bulb, Mom."
>
> I can't promise that was the sentence that actually began the ridicule, nor do I remember who said it, but a chorus of teasing, a sequence of that sort of remark, burst like pandemonium and obliterated the light, the chute, the path, the momentary view of heaven I had cleared through our history. (pp. 238–239)

The premature independence forced on Moore apparently took its toll on the other children, as well. There is not enough of their mother's positive engagement to go around. They competed for her laughter, for her recognition. When someone won it, someone else lost. Laughter slipped from the attachment system (someone had won the laugh) to the caregiving system (Moore tried to connect with her mother through attuning to her laughter) and then to the conflict system (the ridicule of her siblings who were reduced to trying to undo her attempt at connection by shaming and teasing).

This pattern of laughter speaks more of the ambivalent/resistant attachment style found in children whose parents are at times available and responsive—even over-responsive—and at other times are unavailable or nonresponsive. This inconsistency results in a child having a hyperactivated attachment system, with increased arousal of attachment distress and feelings of greater dependence on the caregiver. The goal of hyperactivation, as with Moore, is that by sending out a lot of high intensity attachment signals, it will maximize the chances of gleaning some positive caregiving attunement and regulation. While exploration and play punctuated with laughter usually present opportunities to connect, the end result is unpredictable and often disappointing. Often these children become caregivers to their parents, as with Moore, trying to bolster the caregiver's sagging energy and availability.

Anxious joke-telling, nervous giggles, too-ready laughter at another's comments can all represent a hyperactive need for connection. So, too, can laughter that is used to engage or soothe a disengaged or dysregulated caregiver. Ambivalent/resistant insecure attachment leaves a child desperate for a secure base and therefore less adventuresome in exploration and less open to novel experiences. As a result, one would expect less Duchenne laughter and possibly more non-Duchenne laughter.

Laughter in Children with Avoidant Attachment

Mark, a man I once worked with, had a father who was a serious, well-respected mathematician. Mark's mother was a homemaker, a soft-spoken and nonassertive woman. The parents were never particularly animated, nor was emotional expression of any kind their strong suit. Depression was the prevailing mood, especially after Mark's mother became ill with polio and was confined to a wheelchair. To counteract the depressive atmosphere, Mark became an appealing little comedian, regulating his own and his parent's affect by making them laugh. Laughter was his primary coping mechanism for affect arousal, attunement, and regulation. If that did not work, Mark had no backup. It was only after Mark reached adulthood and gained some distance and ability to reflect, that the extent of his buried anxiety and insecurity became clear to him. His attempts at evoking laughter expressed his one hope of connecting with his chronically unavailable caregivers.

Mark's comedy served as an attempt to animate and up-regulate the mood of his avoidant and depressed parents and thereby increase their availability to him. It was also a defense against his own negative and unwanted attachment distress: sadness, protest, grief, and loss. Sounding upbeat and humorous was a way of deactivating his attachment system and shutting down his own need for closeness, the hallmark of the avoidant child. It was a way of adapting to caregivers who were chronically unavailable and unresponsive. Other avoidant children such as Colin, the young boy described by Denham who rarely showed either positive or negative arousal, represent a different manifestation of this internal working model.

Laughter in Children with Disorganized Attachment

Laughter in disorganized children may present as bizarre and inappropriate to the circumstances. For example, a disorganized child may laugh when another child hurts himself, or when a caregiver or teacher loses patience and gets angry at her. Disorganized children are, I suspect, also highly represented among bullies and hostile teasers who initiate cruel laughter at people and animals. Their dissociative defenses in response to trauma make it difficult, if not impossible, to feel their own vulnerabilities or empathize with those of others. Bearing the brunt of cruel teasing at the hand of abusive caregivers or the desperation of trying to get a response from severely neglectful ones can establish a pattern for hostile bullying disguised as humor.

Laughter in the Clinical Hour

Maya was a 9-year-old girl in therapy with a former student of mine. Despite her young age, Maya had experienced numerous traumas, including sexual abuse and being removed from her mother's care and placed in a foster home. The therapist noted that Maya did not laugh easily, though she did smile. One of Maya's more painful symptoms was that she could not recognize or respond to the intent of other children who would seek her out to play. She was, as Denham pointed out, resistive to, and frequently misinterpreted their playful overtures. Likewise, she could not figure out why they would withdraw from her or resist her invitations to play. She could not explain her feelings or theirs or what had gone wrong. Insecure attachment, especially disorganized attachment, isolates children and brings them more shame and censure, just the opposite of what they need.

Maya's therapist and foster family worked hard to create a safe haven of caregiving and affect regulation to help establish the safety of a secure base for her to explore some of her experiences and struggles. According to her therapist, Maya came in to one therapy session very excited about having seen a movie about Ray Charles and his music. Her positive arousal seemed appropriate and infectious as she repeatedly sang "Hit the Road Jack" using a variety of inflections. After more than a half hour of the same song, however, the therapist became increasingly uncomfortable and felt a need to interrupt Maya in order to prevent her from cycling into overstimulation. Maya did stop singing and played a game with the therapist for a few minutes. Soon, however, she switched to another song, "Georgia On My Mind." At that point, the therapist looked at her, and with a twinkle in her eye said, "Another song, oh no!" To affirm that this was teasing and mock consternation, the therapist laughed out loud and Maya instantly joined with her in spontaneous genuine laughter. The therapist writes, "We laughed convulsively as each of us tried to verbalize what had happened and what was so funny. I took the chance to let Maya know that her singing was affecting me in an irritating way and she recognized that she was hooked on Ray Charles's songs and unable to help herself."

Not only was this the first time that Maya had been able to laugh at her own behavior, it was also a step in the direction of recognizing her effect on another person. The teasing and the laughter were what Stern (1998) has called a "now moment," a nodal point in the therapeutic process. The therapist writes:

> The laughter became a point of reference in future sessions when Maya wanted to make sure that what she thought was funny was also funny to the therapist. She would say, "Remember 'Hit the Road Jack?'" and the two of us would laugh together.

The laughter was a shared experience in the therapeutic attachment bond and represented an important shift—Maya's beginning ability to understand her own internal experience and that of others. Of course, one cannot overlook the humorous content, either. Instead of the command, "Hit the road," as with Jack and as in her own experiences of multiple traumatic separations from loved ones, Maya was being invited into a sustained relationship with her therapist and foster parents. She was being offered security and connection. No wonder she was laughing.

Zall (1994), in his article about humor in therapy with children ages 5 to 11, writes that play therapy relies on fantasy and, at times, silliness, and frequently includes humor initiated by the child or by the therapist. Laughter in therapy with children can be a way to mutually intensify positive feelings, or a way to avoid or defend against negative ones. Laughter can be self-soothing or an interactive regulator of interpersonal stress. It can also be, as with Maya, a way of connecting.

From an attachment viewpoint, humor and laughter reveal something about the state of the therapeutic attachment bond and its potential to serve as a safe haven and secure base for the child patient. When Maya was able to accept the affectionate teasing ("Oh no, another song!") from her therapist, it was an indication that the therapeutic attachment bond was moving toward the attachment style known as "earned secure," when security is achieved after a traumatic early childhood. Maya understood and trusted the motivation behind her therapist's words and was able to share in a lighthearted moment without dissociation, dysregulation, or shame. The secure base and the safe haven of the therapeutic attachment bond made that possible.

Laughter and the Therapist as "Safe Haven"

Zall (1994) describes the treatment of a 7-year-old boy referred for anxiety triggered by separation and loss, depression, and ADD. The boy began each session with the same practical joke. When the therapist opened the door to invite him in, the child would be hiding behind it. He would jump out, and say, "Boo!" followed by a chuckle and the words, "Gotcha this time!" (pp. 27–28). Zall felt that the ritual helped to reduce the child's anxiety about meeting with the potentially scary and upsetting therapist. I would also point out that the "gotcha" translates on another level to, "I've got you!" which carries an attachment message. The attachment interpretation, "I've got you," reaffirms his connection with his therapist, who will serve as his safe haven to help him regulate the affect related to his anxiety and depression, and as his secure base for exploring the pain behind them. The chuckle is his appeal for the therapist to be connected with him even though the therapist might also be "scared a little" by the "joke" as the boy is a little scared by the therapist. Underneath the practical joke is a powerful attachment appeal.

Another of Zall's young patients ended his session routinely with, "Goodbye, Mr. Pooh-Pooh Head!" There are many ways that this comment might be understood, but Zall points to the relationship and attachment significance, saying that this ambivalent comment was made with "obvious hostility, affection, and delight" (Zall, 1994, p. 29). Zall took the tone of voice and the child's implicit communication into account rather than buying into the hostile, rejecting words. Zall understood the child's ambivalence because of his understanding that a therapist is a person who simultaneously arouses negative affect (by asking questions, talking about forbidden topics, encouraging sad and scary feelings to emerge) and soothes it by way of acceptance, reassurance, explanations, or other means.

Laughter as Defense and Affect Regulation

When working with another 7-year-old boy, Zall made a comment about the ongoing tension between the child's parents. Immediately afterward, the boy "playfully" covered the therapist's eyes with a pillow and burst out laughing so hard he fell off the couch. The therapist concluded that this "joke" was a diversion, and that covering the therapist's eyes seemed to mean, "Let's not look at this right now." He suggested as much to the child, who giggled, nodded his head, and brought out a game. The child's "joke" was a way for him to regulate the anxiety triggered by talking about his parents' troubled marriage. It was his attempt to derail the conversation and send it off in a different affective direction. At this point in time, the therapist chose to acknowledge the child's defense out loud while at the same time respecting it. Another choice, once the relationship is firmly established with its secure base function in place, would be to redirect the conversation back to the topic at hand and help the child work through the scary feelings more directly.

Brooks (1994) sensitively describes the use of humor and the effects of laughter in his treatment of an adolescent girl he called "Ann." She was experiencing great despair and depression and spent most of her therapy hours crying. Eventually, Brooks came to see that the crying, while genuine, also served as a barrier between them. Well into the treatment, after trust had been established, he interrupted a crying spell saying, "Excuse me, Ann, I have something important to say." She stopped crying and asked what it was that he wanted to say. Brooks responded, "I hate to bring this up, but I am afraid that I'll have to raise my fee." When she asked why, he said it was because of the cost of all the tissues she was using, supplementing his words with a tone and facial expression of perhaps exaggerated respect and caring. Brooks realized that he was taking a calculated risk and so was relieved when Ann laughed warmly. Her laughter underscored their therapeutic connection. She laughed "because she understood that I cared and that I had faith in her capacity to deal with her distress" (p. 70).

Laughter and "Now Moments"

Stern's (1998) concept of "now moments" in therapy builds on the idea that moments of implicit connection involving heightened, often positive, affect between an infant and a caregiver also occur in the therapeutic relationship. These now moments, when affect spontaneously jumps to another level, are unpredictable, surprising, and nonlinear. They get the attention of both partners in the therapeutic relationship and are, by definition, mutually engaging. These are moments when something shifts and the flavor of the relationship is transformed to something new.

Some instances of laughter shared by therapist and child represent such now moments. Carlberg (1997) was interested in what constitutes significant "turning points" (which resonate with the idea of now moments) in psychotherapy with children. He interviewed child therapists immediately after a turning-point session, and 1 and 2 years later. The title of the paper describing his study is "Laughter opens the door," referring to a child therapist who identified mutual laughter as a turning point in her work with a 10-year-old girl.

The therapist had been working with the child for about 8 months when the little girl brought in some candy with a funny name and they both started laughing. The therapist said, "I have never laughed like that during a therapy session" (p. 332). The next session confirmed that this experience both made and marked a transformation in their relationship. Previously wary of the therapist, the little girl now drew a picture of two people holding hands and walking toward an open door, indicating that she could now accept the therapist as a secure base. Something had shifted in that moment of shared laughter, a transformation toward greater security in their connection that was deeply felt by both of them. The source of the laughter—the name of a candy—seems beside the point in this instance. Rather, it is the fact that they both found the silly name amusing and started to laugh in the same moment. "This," the little girl must have felt, "is a person who is on my wave-length." The therapist felt it, too.

Sharing a laugh is a precious and intimate experience based on a subtle, shared common inner experience—a "tie" between two people. For this to happen, as Zall (1994) notes, "Both the child and the therapist must know each other well, and have confidence in the relationship (p. 37). Shared laughter both creates the closeness and helps to solidify and maintain it.

Jokes and Jabs: Laughter and the Therapeutic Attachment Bond

Zall (1994) lists a number of other functions that jokes serve for children: mastery, managing fears and conflicts, challenging cognitive capacities, self-soothing, and self-esteem—I would add caregiving to the list. Jokes in therapy may also serve some of these functions.

Children may also sometimes introduce jokes as a test of the therapeutic relationship. The therapist's reaction to the jokes becomes part of the process of establishing that the therapist is reliable, available, and attuned to the child. Another child may play practical jokes on the therapist, or insult his clothing or accent, also as a test of how safe he is with the therapist. After the joke or jab, the child may retreat with a laugh by saying, "I was only joking!" Of course, the therapist must be extremely careful not to respond in kind with a jab at the child.

Later in the relationship, one might share the experience of feeling hurt or saddened by certain jokes made by the child at the therapist's expense. Such an intervention is more in keeping with the later phase of treatment and is aimed at helping the child to understand the impact of his actions on others, as we saw with Maya's therapist expressing irritation at Maya's seemingly interminable repetitions of a song.

Understanding the content of jokes and riddles brought to the therapist, on the other hand, is not unlike the usual clinical task of looking at layers of meaning in words and narratives. Following in the tradition of Freud's exploration of the unconscious meaning in jokes and wit, the content of children's jokes may also carry symbolic meaning.

Grotjahn (1957), for example, points to the disguised aggression in the jokes popular among children in that era. They included the use of a then marginally acceptable but now demeaning term for people with intellectual challenges, which I will here render as "clown." For example, "Why did the little clown jump from the Empire State building? Because he wanted to make a hit on Broadway." Or, alternatively, "Because he wanted to show that he had guts" (p. 77). I agree that the violent content and the groaner punch lines might represent hostility directed toward the therapist or others in the child's life. However, if a child told that particular riddle in therapy with me, I would be thinking more about the hint of suicide in the story and be concerned about the child's level of self-loathing in identifying both with the "clown" and with the violent death to "show others" he could be a "hit" or "have guts."

Zall (1994) describes the following series of riddles told to him by a bright 10-year-old patient. To him it seemed that the riddles were a way for the child to engage him in an "intellectual challenge" by means of the use of words, multiple meanings, and complex ideas.

R[iddle]:   There's a man in a room with no windows and a locked door. The only thing in the room is a piano. How did the man get out of the room?

A[nswer]:   He kept playing the piano until he found the right key.

R[iddle]:   There's a man in a room with no windows and no doors. The only other thing in the room is a bureau with a mirror on it. How did the man get out?

A[nswer]:   He looked in the mirror to see what he saw. He took the saw and cut the bureau in half. Two halves make a (w)hole and he climbed out the (w)hole." (p. 29)

These riddles, however, are also rich in symbolic content related to the therapeutic attachment bond and the therapeutic process. The man in the room with no windows might be the therapist and/or the child patient. There appears to be no way out. In the first version, the man must persist until he finds the right "key," and, in the second, until he deconstructs the materials at hand and makes an escape by reconstructing those same materials. I find these images compelling and hopeful, a way of describing what goes on in the dark, apparently scary therapy office that can seem entrapping until further experience deems it liberating instead. The "key" might be the therapist (secure base) who will "play" (explore) with the child and help him to find a way out of the place where he is stuck (safe haven affect regulation). Alternatively, the mirror might be seen as a reflection of the self, the bureau as the contents of the psyche and/or the past, and the saw the tool for escaping the "prison" and being restored to whole-ness: "Two halves make a whole."

Group Treatment

Dana (1994) describes peer groups of children as having "theater, tempo, and imagery that is a rich breeding ground for role playing, risk taking, action and reaction" (p. 41). Within his therapy groups, he has found that the give-and-take of quips, jokes, and one-liners helps children to regulate affect and develop the capacity to "tease and be teased" in a playful manner that is "nonmalicious." Inevitably, of course, some of this teasing is also aimed at the therapist in a playful or "quasi-aggressive" manner, allowing him to model appropriate responses.

One of the techniques he uses with adolescent groups, for example, is to create a fictional patient and ask the group for help in coming up with solutions to that person's problems. After one such vignette, one of the boys looked at him and said, "If you're going to try to get us to do your work for you, you're going to have to pay us," at which the whole group burst into laughter. The therapist agreed, saying, "You're right. Would you guys be my consultants?" thus modeling how to "roll with the punches" even when humor expresses conflicted feelings (p. 43).

The group's spontaneous laugh at the therapist's expense cocreated new experiences, new meaning, and perhaps new neurological pathways for the group members. Children with attachment insecurity often have a difficult time handling, much less enjoying, the spontaneous, playful, and at times, "aggressive climate of teasing and confrontation" (Dana, 1994, p. 41). Children who have been verbally abused, perhaps through cruel, demeaning adult "teasing," will have an especially difficult time "rolling with the punches." To the degree that the therapist is able to serve as a safe haven, comfortably regulating his own responses to jokes and jabs made at his expense, he can help to render such surprises "safe" (Bromberg, 2011) by modeling how to handle them.

Sometimes, Dana points out, children suffer from learning disabilities that lead them to be much more literal and/or concrete in their thinking and therefore prone to "not getting" or else misunderstanding jokes and humor. Jokes involving irony, paradox, or satire, for example, may tax their current level of development. Some children in groups may also suffer in social situations from being overly serious (those with avoidant attachment styles, for example). They may have a difficult time publicly negotiating and/or privately integrating the complex inter-personal experience of teasing, humor, and laughter. Attachment style differences and the absence of the ability to fully empathize with others may also render some children more vulnerable to teasing or being teased (children with ambivalent/resistant attachment styles, for example). The key to being able to frame teasing as humor is in being able to recognize and appreciate the affection and caring, or lack thereof, behind humorous comments or ribbing.

The therapist, in providing a truly secure base in a group, must also help to regulate any cruel or demeaning "humor" or bullying that might creep into the group dynamic, either toward another group member or toward the therapist. This modeling, too, may be helpful in increasing group members' capacity to empathize with and understand others while helping them to feel protected and safe. Humorous teasing is meant to dilute and/or conceal hostil-ity, not to brutalize or verbally abuse or otherwise victimize another person, what has been called "coating the pill" rather than "salting the wound" (Dewes & Winner, 1995).

Humor and the Child Therapist

In assessing the role of humor in working with children, a therapist is challenged to understand its role in his or her own affect regulation and attachment style. Furthermore, the therapist must assess the child's developmental level and cogni-tive skills so that any humor used is matched to the child's level of comprehension and appreciation. It is, of course, impossible to do this moment to moment on an explicit level. For that assessment, we must depend on our right brain implicit procedural knowledge and the information gleaned from our on-the-spot obser-vations and empathy with the child.

Zall (1994), for example, describes a 7-year-old who was anxious about a sec-ond appointment. He attuned empathically to the child's anxiety but found lit-tle evidence of it abating. Next, he recalled out loud that in the first session the patient had relaxed after the therapist told a joke, and said the boy was probably waiting for him to tell another one. The little boy's head remained down and his face covered. The therapist said, "I'm trying to think of a joke, but please don't smile and say anything until I can think of one." When the boy showed a small smile behind his cover, the therapist said with mock exasperation, "I told you not to smile yet!" at which point the boy began to laugh (p. 35). Such a complex act of affectionate teasing—dosed out exactly right with perfect timing and prosody—would be nearly impossible to do solely by conscious planning and intent. Each step of the way, the therapist must attune procedurally to a wide range of affective signals. If other therapists are like me, they will sometimes briefly tinker internally with a response before saying it, and yet at other times blurt out something that seems to be "out of the blue." Such an implicit, intuitive, unplanned interpersonal communication may pull the therapist out of a more cognitive, verbal comfort zone, especially if the therapist normally sees herself as relying on logic and insight to achieve results (Fischer & Fisher, 1987).

Similarly, if the therapist is going to use humor as a way to make an interpretation, he or she must call upon right brain procedural knowledge to guide the delivery. One child repeatedly taunted Zall (1994) each time the child won a game, once with a joke about crowds applauding his win. When the therapist won, the boy told him that the crowd had gone out for food, and they both laughed. Zall had come to understand that the boy's desire to win was so that people (the crowd) would respect him and not think badly of him. Based on that understanding, the therapist said something like, "I know you aren't perfect and that is perfectly OK with me."

Countertransference is always an issue in the use of humor, as children often easily and accurately home in on areas that are sensitive to an adult. They can "poke" the adult therapist in an aggressive or otherwise annoying manner. Another countertransference issue may arise when a therapist has a hard time tolerating depression and negative arousal in a patient. He may be tempted to cut short attuning to and staying present with the child's negative affect, and instead try to "joke the child out of it." Doing so would deny the child a safe haven and additionally risk triggering the child to act as if he were feeling better solely in order to please or take care of the therapist.

Another countertransference risk, pointed out by Fisher and Fisher (1987), might occur in the treatment of a gifted comedic child who may become a source of entertainment to the therapist. Many such children do learn to use their gifts to up-regulate depressed or overburdened caregivers. If such a child senses any level of need or vulnerability in the therapist, the child's caregiving may be even more pronounced.

Fisher and Fisher also point out that testing the therapist is a common tactic of comic children. They may provocatively zero in on the therapist's vulnerabilities or, alternatively, be "seductively self-deprecatory" (p. 113). In such an instance, the therapist may benefit from seeking consultation to help get the sessions back on track.

Laughter may be fun, but it is not exempt from having a dark, aggressive, and painful side. This possibility needs to be kept in the therapist's consciousness at all times in order to avoid harmful or destructive or unhelpful dynamics. Enactments are ever-present in laughter as they are in other affective interchanges in the therapeutic encounter.

Bromberg (2011) points out that enactments within the therapeutic relationship offer a chance for a child (or adult) to experience a person who can be "self-reflective, involved, and caring... who will not indefinitely protect his own truth by holding it to be self evident" (p. 105). Positive enactments—as when Dana acknowledged the layer of "truth" behind the joke the kids in the group made about them doing his work for him—impact the brains of everyone involved and can strengthen the therapeutic attachment bond. "At the brain level, new groups of neurons fire and wire together within old communities, allowing new information to become part of a neurosynaptic network that had been relatively unable to evolve previously" (p. 105). This process depends upon what Bromberg calls "safe surprises" that lead to new cocreated "self-other meanings" (p. 105). These new meanings grow out of "shared events that are infused with an energy of their own because spontaneity and safety can coexist" (p. 105). Interestingly, the phrase "safe surprise" seems to also capture the essence of spontaneous jokes, quips, nonhostile teasing, and Duchenne laughter (Jade, personal communication, December 15, 2011).

The attachment prototypes for laughter in infancy and childhood prepared us for the clinical discussion about laughter-gone-awry during these early developmental phases. It also offered us perspective on how laughter plays a role in the therapeutic attachment bond, similar to the role it plays in the infant/child/caregiver relationship. As we turn now to a discussion of adult laughter, this developmental exploration and understanding will serve as a foundation for understanding the complexities of adult laughter (Chapter 9), including laughter in the clinical hour (Chapter 10).

Part 4

Laughter in Adulthood

9

ADULT LAUGHTER IN EVERYDAY LIFE

We know adult laughter to be a healthy, affect-regulating, and resilience-building form of human connection. On the other hand, laughter can sometimes be off key, off base, and off-putting. Looking at laughter from an attachment perspective makes it possible for us to unravel some of these contradictory and confusing experiences. It gives us words for describing this spontaneous, implicit behavior that so often defies linear explanation. Doing so can help us as family members, friends, and romantic partners to understand the dynamics of mutual affect arousal and interpersonal affect regulation, and the reasons why laughter can sometimes solidify closeness while at other times, it creates distance. It also helps us as parents give growing children a narrative about appropriate and inappropriate laughter that can prove useful in negotiating the tricky terrain of interpersonal relationships.

I recently had an experience that made me feel grateful for such words of explanation when a close friend told me of an accounting error she had made at work. Without thinking, I let out a giggle, to which she replied, "Don't laugh. It wasn't funny." I quickly launched into an explanation of everything my laughter meant, beginning with the fact that it had nothing to do with her error being funny. Rather, I said, that was an "oops" laugh, meaning to imply empathy with an honest mistake and that she should not be so hard on herself about it. By the time I finished my explanation, she no longer felt wounded by the mismatch and rupture she had initially felt. Being able to put the nuances of meaning into words without being defensive served to repair the temporary misattunement she experienced and to convince her that the intention was to express my feeling of solidarity with her, not glee at her error.

Understanding different types of adult laughter and patterns of laughing also offers the clinician valuable clues about the patient's attachment style and history, as we will see in Chapter 10. It further helps the therapist to determine when laughing with a patient is an appropriate, growth-producing, affect-regulating behavior contributing to the development and consolidation of an earned-secure attachment, and when it is a mutual enactment that may replicate old, or even create new, attachment wounds.

Types of Laughter in Adult Life

In the opening chapters of this book, laughter was positioned as one of the early-occurring attachment behaviors designed to positively engage caregiver and infant, thereby helping to lay the groundwork for the arousal and regulation of affect throughout life. Building on this laughter-as-attachment-behavior prototype, we then discussed the different types of laughter that occur as, over time, it is linked to other systems of behavior. Further, we distinguished between the genuine, spontaneous laughter outbursts known as Duchenne laughter and conversationally inserted non-Duchenne laughter. Both are based in the attachment system, but the latter serves a variety of implicit communicative functions, such as the non-Duchenne laugh described above aimed at making my friend feel less guilty about her error.

Continuing with the analysis of the meaning and development of laughter throughout the life span, we will now look at how the various types of laughter manifest themselves in adult life. We will first focus on Duchenne and non-Duchenne laughter, and then proceed to look at types of adult laughter linked to other systems of behavior: exploration/play, sociability/affiliative, caregiving, sexual/mating, conflict/aggression/appeasement, and fear/wariness.

Duchenne and Non-Duchenne Laughter

Several laughter researchers (Gervais & Wilson, 2005; Hudenko, Stone, & Bachorowski, 2009; Keltner & Bonanno, 1997) have pointed out that much laughter research is hampered by not making a distinction between Duchenne and non-Duchenne laughter. From an attachment viewpoint, there can be some confusion as well. Duchenne laughter, the capacity for which is inborn, is an attachment behavior that serves as the prototype. Duchenne laughter can, however, be imitated and a facsimile of it created voluntarily, though seldom with conscious forethought.

Duchenne laughter at its core functions as a medium for attachment and play, a way to connect during times of safety and security, bringing people into almost instant connection. Non-Duchenne laughter, though it sounds and feels different, can also be connecting, attachment-based, affiliative, and even playful. It can grease the wheels of social interactions between loved ones, friends, and acquaintances, and give us clues about how to "take" certain comments and communications. On the other hand, it can also be annoying, misunderstood, and used to humiliate, distance, and dissociate rather than connect and coach.

Why There Are Two Kinds of Laughter

Laughter is "arguably the most potent stimulus" in our Environment of Evolutionary Adaptiveness (EEA). It is used for signaling safety, eliciting playful affect, and regulating lingering stress and negative arousal. As such, it is believed to have conferred important survival and reproductive advantages for our human ancestors (Gervais & Wilson, 2005, p. 415). The fact that laughter is contagious is one of the features that makes it especially potent, as the listener/audience resonates physiologically with the laugher. The contagion of laughter is believed to result from the fact that both the action and the perception of laughter share neural bases in a process that bypasses cognitive mediation, what Rizzolatti et al. (as cited in Gervais & Wilson, 2005) call "automatic resonance behavior" (p. 416) and Gervais and Wilson refer to as "biobehavioral coupling" (p. 401).

Individuals in our EEA who are able to restore positive affect most easily are in the best position to "broaden and build" (Fredrickson, 1998) their base of security, while maximizing their skills at adapting to novelty and change. They can also help to regulate the affect of close loved ones and other members of their community who are not quick to recognize the safety of a given situation because of lingering insecurities and stressors. Remaining stuck in a stress-fear mode after danger has passed not only dampens one's mood, but also discourages the exploration necessary for learning something new. Contagious laughter is a powerful tool, serving to entice others "into playing through the elicitation of positive affect" (Gervais & Wilson, 2005, p. 413).

Speaking from an evolutionary perspective, Gervais and Wilson suggest that Duchenne laughter may have been "co-opted" to serve other ends. It has been suggested, they write, that this became possible when humans developed the ability to have some conscious control over their mouths, faces, and voices (Deacon as cited in Gervais & Wilson, 2005, p. 418). The qualifier "some" is important, however. Darwin (1872/1965) pointed out that the muscles around the eyes are the least subject to voluntary control, and it is interesting to note that it is these muscles that distinguish Duchenne and non-Duchenne smiles (Frank, Ekman, & Friesen, 1993; Keltner & Bonanno, 1997), meaning that this "control," as Darwin noted, is not complete with smiling and presumably with laughter as well. Another distinguishing feature of a face engaged in Duchenne smiles and laughter is the "twinkle" (or brightness) in the eyes, which is also impossible for most people to control voluntarily. Interestingly, it has been noted, however, that positive facial expressions such smiling or laughter, even feigned ones, may "foster positive self-regulation and lead to relevant physiological and affective changes" (Krumhuber & Manstead, 2009, p. 808).

Examples and Discussion of Duchenne Laughter

As part of my research for this book, I arranged for a Laughter Yoga instructor to give a demonstration to some faculty colleagues and their partners, many of whom I did not know. The instructor taught us laughter exercises that seemed much like vocalized yoga breathing. One I recall was repeating "mango la-ha-ha-ha-asse" over and over, louder and louder. The hitch was that, instead of sitting on our individual yoga mats facing forward, we were instructed to circulate from person to person, making eye contact with each other. As I walked around feeling like a fool manufacturing laughter among strangers, I occasionally met up with a colleague I knew well. In the blink of an eye, my laughter went from "fake" to real. I could feel the shift instantly throughout my body. The two laughs seemed distinct—one a form of warm connection with friends, the other a form of awkward embarrassment among strangers—one predominantly physiological, the other predominantly social.

My Duchenne laughter experiences, like this one, are unambiguous as I am aware of a profound physiological change moving deeply through my body and brain, what has been called the "rewarding neurochemical cocktail" (Gervais & Wilson, 2005, p. 401) of laughter. Keltner (2009) describes the "cocktail" that accompanies shared Duchenne smiles as being when both parties experience "reciprocally coordinated surges of dopamine and the opiates. Stress-related cardiovascular response reduces. A sense of trust and social well-being rises" (pp. 112–113). That also sounds remarkably like what a good belly laugh does to the body.

In the online, reader-written Urban Dictionary (2011), one person coined a term that seems a perfect description of the experience of Duchenne laughter. The term is "laughterglow," and it is defined as: "The amazing feeling you have after sharing a good laugh, akin to postcoital glow." I like it because, unlike "neurochemical cocktail," it incorporates the interpersonal concept of "shared" laughter and the relationship connection that is central to the experience. Using the word in a sentence, the contributor further emphasizes the potent relationship/ attachment ingredients: "After a long laugh, she caught her breath and giggled, 'Wow, it felt so amazing to laugh with you. ... I am basking in the laughterglow!'" (para. 1).

Duchenne laughter is perhaps most at home in the context of an intimate attachment relationship. I made note of the following experience one night as I was thinking about how laughter represents and reinforces intimacy with our attachment figures. My partner and I were eating dinner in front of the BBC mystery/ comedy show *Rosemary and Thyme*. The two female detective-gardeners had been called in to inventory an Edwardian botanist's collection of seeds, around which an entire murder investigation was focusing.

We were having red snapper for dinner that night, and as I was finishing my last bite, I said to Lori, "How many 'seeds' did you find?" After a moment, she quizzically asked, "How many seeds?" I drew a blank, and said, "Did I say something?" She responded with, "You asked how many seeds did I find?" I was puzzled for a moment, looked at my plate, saw the fish bones on the side and realized what had happened. "Did I say 'seeds,' I meant 'bones.' How many *bones* did you find in your fish?" We looked at each other in a split second of shocked recognition of my unconscious error and then simultaneously burst into audible, digestion-altering, stress-relieving belly laughs. She thought it was hilarious; I thought it was funny and embarrassing all at the same time. Her affectionate laughter regulated my embarrassment, turning it to positive affect to match hers. In the security of our relationship, it was a moment of beautiful, comfortable, joyous closeness. Our laughter reconnected—and mutually up-regulated us—a welcome change after the stress, overload, and fatigue of our respective workdays.

As an attachment behavior that supports positive, playful engagement in adulthood as it does in infancy and childhood, Duchenne laughter has powerful potential, not only for solidifying connections, but also for helping us to regulate affect interactively. Tony Taccone, artistic director of the Berkeley Repertory Theater, and playwright Tony Kushner are good friends and collaborators who, according to an interview with Taccone (Oldham, 2009), love to laugh together. Their favorite rib-ticklers are takeoffs on old Borscht Belt vaudeville sketches that end by breaking into song. In the interview Taccone says,

> I mean, we really like to laugh. I think we both feel that the world is in such dire shape, the only way to survive is to laugh our butts off. And so I think that there's a kind of "survivor's laugh" that we have in common. I mean, real belly laughs, falling down off your chair in rehearsal, that kind of thing. It's fun. (p. 19)

Their Duchenne laughter represents positive arousal, bringing them closer together, and mutually up-regulating their existential despair.

Robin Williams, recounting a trip to Iraq with two other comedians, also gives an example of Duchenne laughter supporting attachment/affiliative connections and serving a mutual affect-regulating function (Ross, 2011). A troop of eight entertainers and partners, including Williams, were caught in a sandstorm and had to hunker down together overnight. He described the scene: "Eight of us, in one room. So much blinding, blowing heavy sand." During the night, Williams added, Lewis Black, one of the comedians, made a crack that if it rained enough, "it would turn the whole country into pottery" (p. 23). My hearty Duchenne laughter, even though I was not there feeling the tension, made me feel connected with the whole group. I could participate in their sense of camaraderie under stress, even without being there, and understand their gratitude to Lewis Black for regulating their affect under these difficult circumstances.

Examples and Discussion of Non-Duchenne Laughter

The attachment/affiliative features of non-Duchenne laughter are often readily apparent as well. It helps to fill in pauses, punctuate conversations, maintain the interest and attention of a partner, disguise embarrassment, offer an apology, and bolster cohesion in families, among friends, and even strangers (Foot & Chapman, 1996). Chuckles, giggles, and guffaws used as affectionate teasing, joking around, or conversational inserts are signals that help to facilitate closeness and friendliness and to regulate affect. Non-Duchenne laughter can also appeal to others for solicitation and understanding, and help to avoid misunderstandings and conflict. In doing so, non-Duchenne laughter serves one of the core functions of the attachment bond: the interactive regulation of affect.

Non-Duchenne laughter, like its Duchenne prototype, is almost exclusively limited to interpersonal contexts. There are solitary moments when we give out a playful non-Duchenne chuckle, or a private "evil" cackle, thinking about somebody or something, but that is rare compared to its frequent occurrence in pairs or groups of people. It signals our intent in conversation and gives nonconscious, implicit, procedural cues to recipients of our signals.

Though Gervais and Wilson (2005) define non-Duchenne laughter as "spontaneous conversational laughter that occurs in the absence of attempts at humor" (p. 401), there does seem to be a rather large borderline area where certain conversational inserts, almost like sitcom laugh tracks, are feeble attempts at humor. These give rise to appreciative, amused chuckles or short laughter bursts, without rising to the level of a full-on, "losing-it" laughter episode.

I was listening to some friends in the beginning stages of forming a rock band. As they were discussing their musical influences, somebody commented that a certain female drummer was "the best drummer on the planet." One of the other band members, a beginner, said in obvious jest, "But has she heard me yet?" which got a good giggle out of everyone. This laughter, like much I hear and observe, would seem to be on the borderline between mild amusement and take-over-your-body laughter. The speaker did have humorous intent, playing for a little laugh by making fun of herself. Perhaps it makes sense logically to think of this type of laughter as being on a continuum of intensity with Duchenne laughter. On the other hand, it has been suggested that the two types of laughter, Duchenne and non-Duchenne, have different neurological pathways (Gervais & Wilson, 2005; Wild, Rodden, Grodd, & Ruch, 2003) and different acoustic properties (Hudenko et al., 2009) and therefore may be distinct expressive behaviors.

Non-Duchenne laughter also occurs with close loved ones, though it also happens among strangers, acquaintances, colleagues, and friends. It is a less intimate form of laughter, one that helps us negotiate the complexities of daily social discourse. Non-Duchenne laughter also has its roots in the attachment system, and can nudge, or sometimes propel, us into a state of positive arousal—or negative if it is felt as a criticism, barb, or jab.

Recently in a restaurant, I overheard an example of a meant-to-be humorous, non-Duchenne "punch line" that served both as affect regulation, as "coaching" about behavior and attitudes, and as conflict avoidance. The first person said, "I won't do that because I would get shot. You [addressing a companion at the table] might get shot, too, but you would deserve it." The whole table burst out in hearty laughter. A strong implicit message about conflict avoidance and differences between the styles of the two people in that regard was delivered in a humorous package. The laughter affirmed that it was received in that vein, whereas a nonhumorous admonition might have led to irritation, annoyance, or conflict.

Bachorowski and Owren (2001) suggest that people use laughter "in a nonconscious yet strategic fashion" to "shape listeners' affect" (p. 252). It is a great nonverbal way to provide shadings of color, intensity, and intent without doing so directly or thinking about it consciously. For example, I might not want to tell someone I've just met that I find them attractive, but a little extra energy in my laugh might do it for me. I also might hesitate to chastise a friend arriving late for dinner, but a little well-placed chuckle as I tease him about needing an earlier-than-everybody-else start time might give me an opportunity to say it "in fun." If all went well, he might join in and laugh right along with me.

There are so many examples of non-Duchenne laughter in the course of a day that they flow by with hardly a notice. At the best of times, there is mild amusement, sometimes a cover for discomfort or awkwardness, sometimes a plea for latitude or understanding. At other times, non-Duchenne laughter signals attunement. At still other times, it issues a polite invitation to connect socially, quickly helping to establish kinship, even among strangers.

When I was checking in at a large medical clinic recently, the receptionist asked me the languages spoken in the home. When I replied, "English only, unfortunately," she laughed, and said, "You got that right," and I laughed back in agreement. We didn't even know each other's names, and I'm sure neither of us found my comment funny. What we did find to laugh about, however, was the pleasure at our shared common ground. As I walked into a large common waiting room a moment later, I overheard three people, apparently strangers to each other, trying to figure out which door to use, and all three were laughing. It may have been slightly comical to them, but clearly their laughter was much more about the pleasure and relief they felt about sharing their embarrassing mutual predicament.

For all its powerful positive uses in human interaction, non-Duchenne laughter can also be turned upside down, transforming it from an attachment/affiliative behavior to a distancing one. It can be used (or heard) in the name of conflict, aggression, manipulation, or domination, leading to negative arousal and hurt feelings rather than positive arousal and closeness. The hostile, bullying, victimizing uses of laughter will be discussed in the following chapter. It is worth noting also, however, that hostile laughter can help to solidify the closeness of an in-group as they join in laughing at the expense of a scapegoated individual or out-group. Depending on the context and intent, that kind of laughter can build positive group solidarity and/or devolve into victimizing others. One distinguishing feature would, of course, be whether the "victim" was an absent target or present and listening to the hostile jokes and laughter.

An example of targeting people who were not present occurred in a study of laughter in a focus group of women discussing work place barriers in Information

Technology (IT) jobs (Allen, Reid, & Riemenschneider, 2004). It turned out that the women laughed when they made "slamming" comments about status and power inequities between men and women. For example, a joke was made that whenever a group of women had a meeting, the men concluded it was a "men-hater's group." Someone in the group of women quipped, "How egocentric is that?" Another woman chimed in saying that that is what the men always think, "It must be about us!" At that, the whole group of women joined in laughter at the (absent) men's narcissism. As we are discussing, the authors observe that one role of slamming in group laughter may be "to build and solidify the collective self-identity of those present" (p. 186), establishing group solidarity in the face of gender-based workplace oppression.

Non-Duchenne laughter is sometimes described as "voluntary," though it seems as though we seldom plan, execute, or control it consciously. Illustrating this point, the audience at Hofstra University for the 2008 Obama/McCain presidential campaign debate had been instructed to remain silent, including, specifically, no laughter. They complied with the instructions completely, except for laughter. The following excerpt from the transcription is one example among many that occurred throughout the evening.

> Sen. Obama: Now, with respect to a couple of things Senator McCain said, the notion that I voted for a tax increase for people making $42,000 a year has been disputed by everybody who's looked at this claim that Senator McCain keeps on making. Even Fox News disputes it, and—and—[*laughter*]—and—and that doesn't happen very often when it comes to accusations about me. (Sweet, 2008)

I am assuming that the audience at the debate was conscientiously trying to follow the directives. Their non-Duchenne laughter, however, could not be so easily turned off, even in the face of an explicit instruction to inhibit it.

Laughter Linked to Other Systems of Behavior

Both Duchenne and non-Duchenne laughter crop up as we discuss the laughter that bridges from attachment to a number of other behavioral systems. I am speculating that Duchenne laughter is almost purely positive attachment behavior, bridging to exploration/play and to the pro-social behavioral systems such as affiliation and sex/mating. Non-Duchenne laughter is attachment-based as well, but it may, in some instances, be stripped of positive affect and its beneficial, pro-social, connecting properties. It may both signal and create affect dysregulation. It will, in all probability, be the type of laughter most often associated with the conflict/aggression and fear/wariness systems.

Exploration/Play System

Duchenne laughter encourages us to embrace novelty and incongruity throughout life, thereby enhancing our flexibility and our ability to adapt to change. A secure base for exploration continues to be important even in adulthood, enabling us to embrace exploration and play in the company of safe, loving, and "fun" companions. As adults, we can lose the robust playful that is typically present and breeds so much laughter in childhood, and become instead overly anxious or serious when tackling a new idea, skill, or activity.

Still, there are delightful times, usually in the company of others, when a mutual surprise or incongruity may erupt in laughter, as it did for me in the Laughter Yoga exercises when I made eye contact with a friend in the group. Imagine, too, the group hilarity my friend reported as fellow travelers in her tour group in Egypt tried to get up on a camel's back, unquestionably a new activity for most of them. Even going to a comedy club to listen to the latest routines is a new experience, challenging our grasp of popular culture, current events, innuendo, and mental gymnastics, as we "get" the jokes and laugh in delight with the crowd.

Sociability/Affiliative System

As mentioned in earlier discussions, the link between laughter in the attachment system and in the sociability/affiliative system is a natural one. Having recently relocated to a new city, my partner and I were pleased to receive a call from a group of old friends during a lull in their garage sale. With six of us on speaker phone, I told a story about how Lori had gone to taste wine at the farmer's market in our new city and came back 10 minutes later saying, "They offered me a job!" I told the story in a way that made "they offered me a job" sound like a punch line. As we all laughed together, we felt close in our common bond of understanding and appreciating the impact of her infectious enthusiasm. Those brief, friendly, chuckles solidified a closeness that spanned the geographical distance and helped to regulate our sadness about our recent separation.

When a group of friends share an "in-joke," it affirms the power of nonlinear laughter to cement group affiliations. Even the term "in-joke" implies that it is a private, bonding ritual amusing only to those "in the know" and on the inside of the affiliated group. The social fabric of my cohort in college, as I mentioned earlier, was woven out around what we called "mocking." Some new indignity would come to our attention, and all one of us had to do was to say, "*Un*believeable!" with our patented inflection, and we would all shake our heads and laugh. Another easy laugh would come by repeating the stock phrase of the tall, slender, bespectacled professor who earnestly tried to teach us critical thinking: "On the one hand ... " gesturing to the left, and "on the other hand ... " gesturing to the right. Mocking his words, tone of voice, and mannerisms was an endless source of amusement. Even now, all these years later, I still feel the warmth of our closeness and the fun we had regulating each other's affect in those painful years when we were trying to break free of our childhood selves and establish our own identities as adults in the context of our close, safe, like-minded cohort. I even feel connected with our much-maligned professor and grateful for the important impression he made on us about not assuming a one-sided viewpoint.

Caregiving System

Caregiving in adulthood, as in infancy, is about the ways in which we help our close loved ones regulate affect, thereby building intimacy and solidifying closeness. Teacher Thomas O'Brien (2003) was having a rough day. It began when he overslept in the morning, and was followed by mishaps and stressors throughout the day, raining down on him with the bad weather. When he finally dragged himself home, frustrated and exhausted, there was one final indignity: he dropped all his school papers on the wet stairs and his coat in a puddle. It would have been the last straw, except that this time his wife and son were there, saw his predicament, and immediately burst out laughing. "At that moment" he writes, "all the things that had gone wrong during the day didn't seem as troubling. My wife and son's laughter made me realize that a bad day is not the end of the world" (p. 41). Even though technically he was being "laughed at," still the love, compassion, and sense of being home with loved ones who cared and understood served to regulate his affect.

In this example are echoes of the evolutionary theory about laughter being an adaptive signal to help down-regulate lingering negative arousal (Gervais & Wilson, 2005). Once O'Brien reached the safety and security of his home at the end of the day, the loving laughs of his wife and son, serving as caregiving behaviors, cued him in to the change in circumstances and regulated his affect accordingly.

Sexual/Mating Systems

The *San Francisco Chronicle* ran a column called "On the Couch," which profiled couples' relationship histories (Rafkin, 2009). One told the story of Clark and Theresa, who were preparing for their upcoming wedding. Clark spoke about his initial attraction to Theresa at a time in his life when he had not even been looking for a partner. What caught his attention, he said, was that "she laughed at my jokes...even the ones that weren't terribly funny." He added that the "trust between them started immediately" (p. N2).

I like this story because it combines laughter, attachment (trust), and elements of flirting and sexual chemistry. From its attachment origins, laughter travels well into the complex arena of romantic/sexual relationships. There is apparently a mysterious yet clear progression from the attachment/caregiving behavior of mothers hugging babies, to the attachment behavior of loved ones hugging each other in affection, to the hugs and kisses of mating/reproductive behavior with a romantic/sexual partner. Junkins (2002), writing about the role of laughter in intimate relationships, says, "When coupled with other biological forces urging us to connect with other human beings, laughter makes us feel safer and adds the qualities of fun and playfulness to our attraction for one another" (p. 6).

Laughter, Junkins (2002) also writes, has a place in sexual play. She says that it can help smooth out awkward sexual moments as "when our bodies don't cooperate, we say the wrong thing, or fumble at a crucial moment ... allowing such personal, embarrassing idiosyncrasies to become special, intimate elements of love" (p. 125). She gives an example of a couple that invented a sexual game called "You Move, You Lose" in which one would kiss the other all over in an effort to make the other person wiggle or twitch, with the loser being obliged to provide the winner with one of his or her heart's desires. Here, laughter bridges the attachment (safety and security), play, and mating systems in joyous harmony.

While doing a bit of popular culture research on the link between laughter and sex, I was interested to find a term new to me in the online Urban Dictionary (2011): "laughter interruptus." It is defined as what happens "when the act of sexual intercourse is interrupted by the laughter of one or both participants." As Junkins (2002) put it, "Sex and fun are a great combination," and if couples are able to put laughter and play into their sex life, "It not only becomes more exciting to do but much easier to talk about" (p. 131). Of course, laughter at the wrong time during a sexual encounter might disrupt the moment and create a quite different scenario and set of feelings in the couple.

Conflict/Aggression/Appeasement System

"Aggressive" or hostile laughter can range from friendly "joshing" to outright disdain. At its best, it is good-humored teasing contributing to attachment and affiliation, and at its worst it moves into the hostile terrain of bullying. In the childhood chapter, we referred to Jade's (personal communication, December 30, 2011) categories for distinguishing between the various types: nonhostile teasing with positive results, nonhostile teasing with negative results, and hostile teasing and bullying. In addition to these three types and subtypes, self-deprecating laughter and two subtypes of appeasement laughter are also included to round out some of the possible links between laughter in the attachment system and the conflict/aggression system.

Nonhostile Teasing With Positive Results Sitting outside a Northampton, Massachusetts, sidewalk café a few summers ago, I saw a man pull up in a big SUV and yell hello to his friends who were together enjoying a cup of coffee. Their immediate response was to start making comments about his driving. They laughed and he laughed and off he drove. It is hard to say how he really felt about this laughter, but from all appearances it looked to be friendly and bonding on both sides, "derisive" though it may have been in content. Linguistically we have terms

to describe good-humored, put-down laughter: joshing, teasing, heckling, ribbing, razzing, or giving somebody a hard time.

Keltner, Young, Heerey, Oemig, and Monarch (1998) studied teasing between fraternity brothers based on status (low-status pledges and high-status long-term members), and between romantic couples. The teasing consisted of making up nicknames for each other, and telling embarrassing stories that gave the backstories for the nicknames. The researchers were interested in understanding how the "aggressive yet playful elements of teasing work together" (p. 1234).

In the case of the fraternity brothers, the teasing, "although humiliating, generated laughter and smiling, and in the end, teasing partners evaluated each other more favorably than fraternity members whom they did not tease, suggesting that [the willingness to engage in] teasing may enhance bonds" (Keltner et al., 1998, p. 1238). The same-status teasing partners were the most playful and evoked the most positive emotions, however, suggesting that "familiarity, or the lack of status-related concerns enhances the pleasure of teasing" (p. 1238).

Teasing that is, as Keltner et al. describe, "aggressive yet playful" or "humiliating," can cross the line from nonhostile to hostile teasing. In cases where the recipient "plays along," even if by feigning jocularity so as not to lose face or act like a victim, the teasing then might be categorized as "hostile teasing with positive results," though we might ask, "positive" from whose perspective?

In the study of romantic couples' teasing, the nicknames focused, as might be expected, on personality traits, personal habits, sex, and other intimate relationship-impacting qualities. The teasing, especially when the jibes were considered prosocial or affectionate, produced increased positive emotion, suggesting that it also increased the couple's sense of closeness. When teasing led to negative arousal (e.g., nonhostile teasing with negative results or hostile teasing), hostility and distance increased, as might be expected.

Nonhostile Teasing with Negative Results Some teasing, not intended by the instigator as hostile, is perceived and reacted to as if it were by the target. As we have discussed, this may be due to the target's difficulty in correctly reading intent or to a deep sensitivity to criticism often related to preoccupied attachment. On the other hand, some ostensibly "nonhostile teasing" can contain disguised derision that the instigator does not recognize or want to admit. Rather than "greasing the wheels" of social interaction, this kind of teasing can cause them to grind and even come to a halt. These mismatches can occur, for instance, when a speaker's message is unconsciously hostile and the target accurately picks up the hostility, even though the speaker may deny it. Alternatively, mismatches occur when a listener mishears or misreads the speaker's intent and is offended or feels attacked, even though the speaker honestly states that he was "only joking." Though these teasing ruptures happen to all of us at one time or another, they can also represent characteristic patterns of interpersonal affect arousal and regulation based on attachment wounds and defenses that will be discussed more fully in Chapter 10.

One way of describing the difference between hostile versus nonhostile intent and delivery in ironic humor (the saying of the opposite of what is meant in order to deliver a criticism) is known as the "tinge" hypothesis (Dewes & Winner, 1995). Dewes and Winner found that certain nonverbal cues color or "tinge" the literal words communicated in such a way as to convey the intended meaning to the target. Colston (1997), however, found the opposite among participants in his study: Ironic humor, rather than "coating the pill," appeared to "salt the wound" and make the sting of criticism worse. The struggle to uncover the exact ways in which ironic humor does and does not work effectively in bringing people closer and avoiding conflict brings us directly to the mysteries of the multilayered, nonconscious subtleties of implicit communication. Looking at the patterns of laughter and uses of humor related to attachment style in the next chapter may suggest some further theories about when, why, and with whom ironic humor and affectionate teasing work.

Hostile Teasing with Positive Results Another example of laughter linking the conflict/aggression system is derisive laughter, which may or may not have positive results. The political arena is one place where derisive laughter frequently occurs. It may even be an occupational hazard for politicians and celebrities. Much of the time, such laughter seems aimed at conveying disbelief and a level of hostility or aggression. Ross Mirkarimi, a San Francisco supervisor representing the Haight-Ashbury neighborhood, was trying to walk a tightrope between protecting the rights of homeless people to sit and lie on the sidewalk, and a clamoring neighborhood group tired of being intimidated in their own neighborhood. An aide spoke on his behalf saying that Mirkarimi was "really looking" at options, at which point "derisive laughter rippled through the crowd" (Nevius, 2010, p. C4). The constituents were discounting his claim that he was really looking at options, indicating that they were angry at his delaying tactics and ready for action.

A transcript from the campaign debate between Obama and McCain shows the following example of derisive laughter of one politician toward another:

Sen. Obama: If I can answer the question, number one, I want to cut taxes for 95 percent of Americans. Now, it is true that my friend and supporter Warren Buffett, for example, could afford to pay a little more in taxes in order—

Sen. McCain: We're talking about Joe the plumber. [*Laughs.*]

Sen. Obama: He's been watching some ads of Senator McCain's. (Sweet, 2008)

McCain's derisive, critical laugh here implies that he was accusing Obama of changing the subject and ignoring "Joe the plumber." McCain's laughter served as a "polite" way of expressing disagreement, saying in effect, "Your assertion is laughable." It was "polite" because it served to criticize Obama without resorting to a direct, hostile, verbalized attack. If delivered in a mean-spirited way, or to a thin-skinned target, however, the results could have been quite different, as we will discuss in the following clinical section.

Hostile Teasing with Negative Results: Dark, Detached, Dissociated Laughter

Even though laughter is at heart an attachment behavior, it also clearly has what has been called a "dark side" (Panksepp, 2000). This usually mirthless laughter is used for ridicule, put-downs, establishing dominance, bullying, cruelty, mocking, scapegoating, shaming, and scorn. Dark laughter occurs in aggressive, nervous, or hierarchical contexts, functioning to manipulate, exclude, judge, deride, or subvert. Some dark-side laughter may also be trauma-based, dissociated affect, sheared off from its original attachment function in order to defensively deflect, derail, or numb unbearable fear and pain. While not all non-Duchenne laughter belongs to the dark side, all detached and dissociated laughter would seem to be non-Duchenne (Gervais & Wilson, 2005; Keltner & Bonanno, 1997). Certain traumatic, dissociated "hysterical" laughter expressed in frightening, humiliating, or shameful situations outwardly resembles Duchenne laughter, but clearly lacks the characteristic positive arousal associated with it. We will discuss examples of this latter type in Chapter 10.

The laughter of the Joker in the film *Batman*, and its sequel *The Dark Knight*, epitomizes detached and dissociated, dark, non-Duchenne laughter. It is a sinister, evil cackle delivered with a frozen smile. When the Joker gains control of Gotham City and delivers his sinister and powerful laughter, darkness prevails in all its forms—weather, mood, and behaviors between people. His malevolent "jokes" are powerful and lead to violent injuries and deaths.

The Joker knowingly uses laughter to down-regulate positive affect and up-regulate negative affect as a means of establishing control. It is a powerful form of negative contagion that impacts the characters in the film as well as the audience. In the hands of gifted actors such as Jack Nicholson, who played the Joker in *Batman*, and the late Heath Ledger, who played the role in *The Dark Knight*, the intensity of this evil force resonates powerfully, in the plot as well as among those who subject themselves to it for entertainment. Nicholson has said that playing the role took a toll on him personally, and that he had warned Ledger about its possible impact. More than one person commented on a possible link between Ledger's untimely death and his having played the role of the Joker in the film.

There is no widely accepted backstory about the Joker, other than that in the past he had fallen into a vat of chemicals while being pursued by Batman. One oft-cited explanation comes from the graphic novel *The Killing Joke* (A. Moore, 1988). According to Alan Moore, the Joker had been a chemical engineer who quit his job to become a stand-up comic, but failed miserably. He was forced into a life of crime to support his pregnant wife. He then suffered a series of traumatic losses—including the death of his wife and daughter and culminating in his disfiguring facial injury. His catastrophic fall into the vat of chemicals created his signature "frozen smile," and he finally went insane.

Part of Nicholson's and Ledger's brilliance in playing this character was their ability to display different types of laughter, including, on some occasions, laughter that conveys a universally resonating experience of deep attachment connection and grief. Most of the time, however, the attachment aspects of the Joker's laughter are corrupted and layered over with what appears to be and feels like its opposite: detachment and dissociation. Ultimately, the Joker's detached, hostile-seeming laughter may be a symbolic representation of perverted protest grief. His traumatic attachment injuries and losses may have been too great to be grieved and transformed in the context of love, and therefore remain forever locked in the black depths of hopeless loss, only to resurface in the frozen smile and the detached, dissociated laughter.

Self-Deprecating Laughter

This kind of laughter is so ubiquitous that it often fails to register with the instigator or the listener. A speaker slips it into a conversation in order to help shape the direction of the listener's response. The following example would also probably have gone unnoticed, if it weren't for Ken Auletta's (2011) attention to detail when writing a *New Yorker* profile.

Mo Ibrahim, the subject of the profile, is a Sudanese-born billionaire who founded a successful mobile phone network on the African continent. Ibrahim has used some of the proceeds from his business to create a substantial monetary reward for ethical government leaders in African nations. When Auletta asked whether Ibrahim had foreseen that his business success might become "a weapon to achieve better government" (p. 55), there was this response: "'No, I wish I had,' he said, laughing. 'We never imagined the magnitude of that development. I wish I could say I'm so smart'" (Auletta, 2011, p. 55).

Ibrahim's laughter, along with his words, seems to say that he is pleased to be given so much credit by the speaker, feels awkward about the implied praise, and wants to appear humble about his accomplishments. The final comment, "I wish I could say I'm so smart," reinforces the multilayered message in words. There is no record of whether Auletta laughed in response. In general, speakers laugh 46% more frequently than their listeners (Provine, 2000), which could be seen as indicating that speakers have a vested interest in coaching listeners on how to interpret what is being said. Throwaway laughs or self-deprecating chuckles such as these add layers of valuable, though sometimes confusing, nonverbal cues to the intended meaning of our words. Sometimes the non–Duchenne laugh substitutes for words altogether, as when someone asks an embarrassing question (How much did that cost?) and gets only a laugh for an answer. Here it is the listener who has the vested interest in conveying without using words, "That was a rude thing to ask."

Appeasement/Coaching/Shaping Laughter

I recently overheard a fragment of one side of a cell phone conversation on the street. A man said, "I'm glad to hear things are going all right. Stay in touch. Then I won't keep on bugging you," and he trailed off with a laugh. Putting myself in the laugher's shoes, I sensed he was trying to tip off the listener that he knew he might be seen as a nuisance, but if the listener would stay more in touch, they could avoid this.

Had I been the listener, I would have either felt guilty, embarrassed, or irritated, depending on my relationship with the person and my feelings about my own behavior. Alternatively, I might simply have taken the point or tried to reassure the laugher that he was not "bugging" me with his calls. No way, however, would that comment and laughter make me laugh in response. It was delivered as a bit of implicit, indirect coaching. To my ears, it seemed aimed at trying to intensify the listener's negative arousal in a friendly way so that the listener would feel guilt and offer real or feigned reassurance to the speaker. It seemed a means of offering appeasement, in the same breath as offering criticism, enabling the speaker to say something confrontive without jeopardizing the relationship. On other hand, the speaker may simply have been trying to lightheartedly elicit information: for example, should I keep calling or not?

The problem with trying to identify, let alone make course-corrections in, our nonconscious, right-brain, nonverbal laughter signals is that we are often unaware of our own intent. Non-Duchenne laughter—the kind that greases our conversational wheels so effectively—is almost too complex for our left-brain linear minds to perceive and explain. We seldom bother trying, and we don't need to, unless something goes awry, and even then it can be difficult. Our right brains are far more efficient at this kind of translation than our word-bound left-brains could ever be.

Appeasement A young Peace Corps volunteer in Mongolia wrote of encountering a group of young boys being abusive to a camel (Ogasawara, 2003). Not wanting to be perceived as controlling or aggressive, and realizing that any intervention she tried to make could easily inflame the boys more, she simply began chatting with them, asking questions about the camel. After she succeeded in distracting them a bit, she suggested a group photo. "Now I look at the picture and see the camel standing off to the side, looking faintly relieved. The boys and I lean in together, laughing at the camera like friends" (p. 41).

This laughter represents the bond she was able to forge with the boys in that precarious situation, and the interpersonal regulation of all of their affect, spurred on by her concern for the camel. The non-Duchenne laughter they shared was not the source of the transformation from conflict/aggression to affiliation, but it was a clear signal that appeasement had taken place.

Fear/Wariness System

Though anxious non-Duchenne laughter is a common way of easing nervous or embarrassed social awkwardness, at times it may be transformed into something closer to affiliation or attachment. Ann Garcia (2003) was invited to stay at the home of a high school girlfriend during their 45th high school reunion. Though they had not seen each other in the intervening years, she recalled their intense adolescent giggles with fondness. Nonetheless, she worried that their differing adult politics and lifestyles would lead to awkwardness and distance, and at the beginning of the visit it seemed to do. Then the zipper of Garcia's purse got caught on her friend's fancy bedspread. In their joint slapstick efforts to free it, she said, the bedspread starting "jumping up and down." "'It wants to stay here,' I tell her and we giggle wildly. Hysterical, we both fall onto the bed, my purse between us. My friend puts out her hand, and I take it. Our hands are warm" (p. 35). Here the laughter progressed from embarrassed, fear-wariness, non-Duchenne laughter to over-the-top, bonding Duchenne laughter. It both helped to reestablish the former closeness and signaled its return.

Laughter as Defense Against Anxiety In the next chapter, looking at adult laughter from a clinical perspective, we will discuss a type of dissociative laughter that is associated with disorganized/disoriented attachment in adults. However, a more benign version of defensive laughter also occurs in adults with secure or organized insecure attachment styles. In some instances, such as the following, the anxious laughter seems to be an attachment appeal for help in regulating negative arousal, almost like crying.

In May 2011, it was Disability Awareness Day at a Boston Red Sox game. A young autistic man was chosen to sing the National Anthem before a crowd of 40,000 people. He made a good start, but about a quarter of the way through he got the giggles—perhaps it was a case of nerves in front of all those people, or maybe it was because that song is so hard to sing a cappella. At first the crowd just cheered a bit to encourage him, but when he kept laughing more hysterically, they spontaneously joined together to support him. In the same key, at the same moment, and as one voice, they chimed in singing together with him on the line, "and the rockets red glare." They sang with him all the way to the end, as his shoulders continued to shake with laughter. On viewing the various YouTube postings of the event (Bells, 2011), many people comment that they first start smiling but end up crying as they realize how, as one blogger put it, using an appropriate baseball analogy, "People stepped up to the plate" to support the singer. I know I cry every time I watch it. His laughter acted as an attachment appeal and 40,000 people "got it" and stepped up as caregivers to keep him from failing and feeling bad.

After spending decades looking at crying through an attachment lens, I find it easy to explain how crying at a story like this binds us all together in the human community. What makes this story unusual is that the young man's appeal for help was expressed through his laughter and perceived as such by a crowd of 45,000 people. This simple, unplanned behavior communicated his distress without words in a most appealing way and brought this amazing response from the audience. We can all empathize at being seized with uncontrollable laughter at the wrong moment, but even more, they could see he was struggling and nervous and excited, and they wanted to help regulate his affect. They wanted this to be a positive experience, not a humiliating one. They were uncomfortable for him and with him. By "stepping up to the plate," and joining him in song, everyone's affect was regulated back to a comfort level. Beyond that, however, his laughter triggered something transformative in that crowd: they were no longer a group of impatient individuals waiting for the opening pitch; they were a caregiving community of fans rising as one to help a young man in need.

Laughter as Protest Grief Laughter and grief are often connected. In fact, one of the most common examples of this type of laughter is during bereavement (Keltner & Bonanno, 1997). While this laughter may certainly be seen as a defense against the pain of loss, I believe that it can also be part of the expression of protest grief (Nelson, 2005), an expression of the wish to undo the loss and restore the presence of the loved one. On the other hand, laughter can also be part of the reorganization process, contributing to the realignment of the internal attachment connection to the lost loved one that is part of the healing process. Laughter in grief, like crying, belongs to the attachment system. If there were no attachment between the deceased and survivors, there would be no pain, anxiety, and suffering created by the separation and loss. The following examples illustrate the ways in which laughter can be protest grief, pushing against acknowledging the pain of the loss, while simultaneously representing the attachment to the lost loved one in a positive way.

Three sisters whose father lay dying in the hospital were called home to be with him. Their father had been known for using laughter to regulate affect, and he apparently passed it along to his daughters.

> We met at a restaurant and proceeded to have the most raucous evening I can remember. We laughed so hard that people at other tables stared. At one point, the waitress asked us what was so funny. We were quiet for a moment. Then one of my sisters said, "Our father is dying," and the four of us burst out laughing. (London, 2003, p. 41)

The laughter was contagious among the sisters, though not among onlookers who related more to the loss. Laughter helped the sisters to bond and grieve, but in a way that kept sadness and despair decidedly at bay. Laughter such as this can defend against negative arousal, and bring mourners closer together to share in their pain.

Many people, myself included, have had this odd experience in reaction to the death of a close loved one. Marlo Thomas (2010), actress and daughter of comedian Danny Thomas, describes such laughter at her father's funeral.

> It started when Mother's lipstick fell out of her purse, hitting the ground with a noisy clack, then began rolling across the floor. Terre, Tony and

I watched it roll and started to giggle. As it made its way past the grand-kids...they started to giggle too. And trying as hard as we could, none of us could stop, until we were all laughing hysterically. It was terrible. Our bodies were shaking, tears of laughter streaming down our faces. We must have looked crazy. We were. (pp. 353–354)

Their laughter as protest and emotional/grief overload may indeed have been dissociated, or "crazy" as she calls it, but in some strange way it also seems a fitting way to mourn for the loss of a man whose professional identity was so wrapped up in laughter.

Laughter as Dissociated Anxiety In extreme situations, intense laughter may represent a dissociated anxiety/fear response. The following, for example, involves more than a hint of fear and trauma, similar to the laughter of the young teenager being sexually assaulted in public that was described in the previous chapter. An exercise teacher was volunteering for the first time to give a class at a women's prison. Scheduled to give a promotional demonstration of her class, she quickly realized she might be in trouble when she was directed to the unsuitable environment of the prison kitchen for the demonstration (Johnson, 2003). Her potential students were a group of 10 inmates. She describes her first encounter with them: "Disdain showed on their faces, and jeering obscenities issued from their mouths." She bravely persisted, even though their responses quickly became aggressively sexual. At a point when she asked them to sit on the floor, spread their legs in a "V" and touch their heads to the floor, a "muscular young woman with a light beard ... sat in front of me and threw her legs over mine." When the teacher asked what the student was doing, the woman replied, "I wanna do your exercise," and proceeded to bend over and shove her face into the teacher's crotch (p. 41).

"To this day," Johnson writes," I don't know why I started laughing, but once I did, I couldn't stop. My stomach was shaking; tears were rolling down my cheeks. My laughter must have been infectious, because the young woman and the other inmates—and even the guard—joined in" (Johnson, 2003, p. 41). The beleaguered teacher concluded the lesson and somehow found it in herself to say that they should come back together and "try this again next week," at which point she started giggling again. Somehow the anxious—even dissociated—laughter served an affiliative purpose and she was invited back and given a proper classroom, and her former tormenters participated willingly. The teacher's laughter was beyond awkward and nervous. It was a nonconscious, unplanned, physiological response to the sexual aggression, but even then, the bonding potential of laughter worked in her favor, and she was accepted and respected as a teacher.

Here the laughter as protest against humiliation and rejection seems especially clear, as does the deep realization that were she to directly express her fear and dismay, the situation would likely have worsened. Laughter provided a smokescreen that disguised her true feelings and enabled her to emerge safely from a frightening situation. "Protesting" with laughter gave her a way out that also succeeded in doing what laughter does so well: establishing and maintaining connections.

An Attachment Template for Laughter

The categories and examples in this chapter could not begin to cover all of the possible types of laughter and combinations of affect arousal each might represent. Nor can they include all of the potential links between laughter in the attachment/caregiving and other systems of behavior. The range of categories and examples, however, is aimed at providing a template for categorizing different types of laughter. Such a template can pave the way for making this non-conscious, implicit behavior more conscious. The template is built on as much existing research as I could find to support it, but it is my hope that it will invite further research as well. In the following chapter, the same template will be used to distinguish among the types of laughter that occur in the clinical hour, patterns of laughter associated with different attachment styles, and the meaning and management of laughter in the context of the therapeutic relationship.

10

LAUGHTER IN THE CLINICAL HOUR

Laughter in the clinical hour may mean many things. It may represent connection or detachment. It can invite closeness, or it can be a barrier to it. Some mutual laughter represents delight in the recognition of transformation, whereas other laughter may serve as a resistance to growth and change. Laughter, by a patient or a therapist, may represent an effective means of affect regulation, or it may signify compulsive caregiving. Laughter can also be a signal of overstimulation signaling a need for down-regulation. Laughter in the therapeutic relationship may also be a thinly veiled cover for hostility or sexual feelings. Complicating the picture still further, the complete absence of laughter in the patient and the therapist can also have multiple meanings.

As we have discussed in previous chapters, laughter is an attachment behavior that is at times linked with other behavioral systems, each of which may appear in the therapeutic context as well. In the caregiving system, laughter is sometimes a way for therapists and clients to mutually regulate affect. In the affiliative system, it is a way to establish safety in the therapeutic relationship, saying without words, "I am friendly, you can approach me." In the conflict system, laughter may be used to deliver a jab, overtly or in disguised form, or it may be a signal for avoiding conflict, as in, "I am making light of this, so do not take what I said or did as an attack." Laughter may also deliver an appeasement message such as "I am no longer angry." Flirtatious, seductive laughter that conveys sexual energy is part of the mating/sexual system of behavior and may find its way into eroticized transference or countertransference feelings. As part of the exploratory system, playful shared laughter can affirm the mutual excitement and satisfaction in discovering and creating new meanings in the course of therapy.

Most of the books and articles on laughter in psychotherapy focus on humor and what it means, and treat laughter as its by-product. While the content of humor and jokes is also of interest, in this chapter we primarily focus on laughter in order to understand its multiple relationship messages and how it may serve to strengthen or weaken the therapeutic attachment bond. Beginning with professional attitudes toward laughter in the therapeutic encounter, we continue on to explore laughter patterns typical of each different adult attachment style. Following that, we will discuss the meaning and management of laughter in the therapeutic encounter, including the challenges and enactments it may represent, along with its transformative potential.

Attitudes Toward Laughter

Attitudes toward laughter among analysts and psychodynamic and psychoanalytically oriented psychotherapists vary. While Freud was a well-known connoisseur of jokes and was known to use them in his analytic work with patients, the emphasis on analytic neutrality among classical psychoanalysts casts suspicion on laughter in an analytic hour. An exception was Grotjahn (1957), who was, according to Kuhlman (1984), "the first psychoanalyst to espouse humor as a therapeutic vehicle and still retain a reputation of eminence among his colleagues" (p. 2). Since the 1970s, the most often quoted psychoanalytic authority on the subject has been Kubie (1971).

Kubie was adamant that shared humor (laughter is implied) is not only inadvisable, but also destructive. As he put it,

> It is never fun to have a neurosis, nor is it ever fun to be in treatment. Consequently, no matter how consciously well intended the therapist's humor may be, the patient usually perceives it as heartless, cruel, and unfeeling. . . . Humor blunts the vigilance of our self-observing mechanisms and our self-correcting efforts. (pp. 39–40)

Although I disagree with Kubie's almost blanket condemnation of humor and laughter in therapy, there is much to recommend in his article by way of pointing out its possible pitfalls and enactments. A partial list of the potential enactments that he enumerates includes everything from masked hostility to false camaraderie, seductiveness and "transference wooing," confusing messages, and repetition of teasing and mockery experienced in childhood.

Kubie also accurately describes the powerful connecting properties of laughter, though for him it is a reason to avoid humor: "The sharing of humor automatically creates a powerful secret emotional involvement, just as does the sharing of grief" (p. 40). This comment underscores the feeling in the 1970s about the importance of maintaining analytic neutrality, but at the same time, it anticipates the relational components of the therapeutic dyad that are today recognized as inevitable and important. In addition, Kubie cites a number of exceptions where humor would be acceptable, or even advisable, that are also in keeping with an attachment and relational perspective. Because of the stridency of his previous arguments, however, these exceptions are seldom quoted and carry far less weight.

A colleague reported having a personal experience of a Kubie-like negative attitude toward laughter while in analytic training some years ago. Another candidate in her class asked for consultation from the senior analyst conducting their seminar because he was uncertain about having laughed in response to something a patient had said during a session. When the senior analyst responded negatively, my colleague challenged him saying, "But wouldn't anyone spontaneously laugh if someone says something funny, including in an analytic session?" The consultant looked right at her and said, "Well, *you* might," making her feel belittled and angry, and implying that a well-disciplined analyst would never laugh.

What went on behind closed doors, even during the years when analytic neutrality was in vogue, however, may have been a different matter. Another colleague has a vivid memory of being a social work student sitting in her supervisor/analyst's waiting room before their appointment. All of a sudden, she heard the supervisor and her patient laughing "loudly and deeply behind the door." The laughter surprised her, she said, but also gave her a good feeling and made her smile. Both patient and analyst emerged from the session smiling broadly. "It is interesting" she muses in retrospect, "how clear that memory is. I don't think my supervisor and I discussed it at the time, but it did leave an impression."

As psychoanalysis began to shift away from advocating a strictly neutral stance by the therapist, attitudes toward laughter also began to shift. Two articles from the 1990s, one by Ehrenberg (1990), the other by Bader (1993), stress the value of playfulness and the use of humor in the work with some patients. Ehrenberg pointed out that a change in attitude toward humor came about as psychoanalysis began to recognize the importance of more affective engagement on the part of the analyst. Bader said that another reason analyst-initiated humor had been viewed with suspicion in the past was that it was seen to be a countertransference enactment that warded off "negative affects in both analyst and patient and/or covertly expresses countertransference hostility or seductiveness" (p. 24). Both authors stress that in their view, playfulness, humor, and laughter can, at certain times with certain people, be a profound and lasting experience of connection that is both healing and growth-inducing.

Even with the shift away from viewing neutrality as a necessary stance for the analyst, however, many psychodynamic psychotherapists continue to struggle with their feelings about laughter, whether in response to the patient or initiated by the therapist. Ehrenberg, for example, describes working with a woman who was initially depressed, withdrawn, and fearful. Ehrenberg would occasionally challenge her or make interpretations in a playful way and the patient would laugh. Initially, Ehrenberg felt comfortable with using play and laughter to up-regulate the patient's extremely depressed affect. However, when the patient herself began to be more playful, clever, and funny about six years into the treatment, there was so much laughter between them that Ehrenberg began to feel guilty for "getting paid for having so much fun" (p. 86). The patient, however, disagreed, saying that being able to make her analyst laugh represented for her their ability "to make contact with each other and have so much fun together" (p. 86). Parallel to the role of successful parents who attune to positive as well as negative arousal in their infants, therapists also at times attune to—and even amplify—their patient's positive arousal, as well as negative.

Bader (1993), too, reported feeling guilty about enjoying what seemed to be a playful, "father/son" closeness with one of his male patients. Eventually, however, he realized that using "elements of an abstinent technique" was a way of colluding with the patient's "shame over his wishes for paternal strength and protection" (p. 39). With that perspective, Bader was able to be comfortable engaging in male teasing and repartee with him. On one occasion, for example, the patient was discussing his inhibition about negotiating with his girlfriend, who was critical of how he allocated his time on the weekends. Bader made a deliberately outlandish suggestion that he try "floating this proposal: that she clean your apartment while you watch sports and then the two of you can talk during the commercials!" (p. 40). The patient "roared with laughter" at this "comic articulation and caricature" and expressed amazement at how Bader had captured the essence of what was so forbidden to him. Together over time, they continued to play with the joke and laugh together about it. Bader was able to assuage his guilt as he came to understand that this joking and laughter "emboldened" the patient, "not to deny or cover up his shame over his 'dirty' masculine impulses and fantasies, but to face some of these feelings from a more secure base in our alliance" (p. 42).

The Meaning and Management of Laughter in the Therapeutic Relationship

Attachment-based laughter, beginning in infancy, is positive, mutual, spontaneous, and shared. Within the therapeutic relationship, positive affect, like negative, can also be mutually aroused. Though as therapists we may at times choose to restrain our laughter on behalf of the patient's needs, laughter is generally something that happens to us involuntarily and without forethought. Bader (1993) writes, "It does not seem quite right to say that the therapist *chooses* [italics added] to be humorous when such humor seems to be a reaction to the complex invitations and undertows of the patients' communications" (p. 46). Sometimes, indeed, the pull is so great that restraint is impossible, and although unrestrained laughter may be an enactment by the therapist that could interfere with the therapeutic connection, it may also be that the pull is a form of implicit prompting about how and when to respond to and regulate a patient's affect.

Intersubjective "Now Moments"

Certain moments of heightened affective engagement, as mentioned in Chapter 8, constitute what Stern (1998) has called "moments of meeting" or "now moments." Such moments are unpredictable, surprising, nonlinear—and often transformative—a great description of much laughter in therapy and otherwise. The prototypes for such moments occur in infancy when things are proceeding along pretty much in neutral and something unexpected (or incongruent, according to humor theory) happens. All of a sudden, infant and caregiver are laughing (though some now moments can involve anger or crying rather than joy). Without planning, the engagement "has been kicked up to a new and higher level of activation and joy" (p. 309).

Upon learning that I was writing about laughter, a former student shared with me a time when her first therapist, a woman analyst who was "very kind, somewhat reserved and definitely Freudian," dissolved in involuntary laughter that was completely out of out of character for her. The former patient writes,

> Having recently graduated from college, I had found a job as a social worker with the Salvation Army. The setting was completely alien to me. The staff wore traditional Salvation Army uniforms and called each other "Captain" and "General"—all very faux army-ish and serious. Needless to say, it was pretty gloomy.
>
> One day I was describing the scene to my therapist, going into great detail about the uniforms, the titles, and the general atmosphere of the place. I was so involved in trying to convey what it was like that I didn't notice right away that my therapist had her hand over her mouth trying to stifle her hysterical laughter. I was astonished. She kept trying to apologize but would be overcome with laughter every time she tried to pull herself together. I had never seen her lose control of herself in this way. After a minute, I, too, began laughing hysterically. I don't remember much else about my experiences with her, but the experience of our laughing together is something I'll never forget. It felt so warm and human, and even now makes me smile when I think of it.

The laughter here was initiated by the therapist and contrasted sharply with the feelings being expressed by the patient. It was "out of the blue" and the analyst felt a need to apologize. Even so, the laughter up-regulated the patient's "gloomy" affect and helped her connect to the "somewhat reserved" therapist's humanness. Even though the therapist was reluctant—and may well have suffered from guilt and remorse given the commitment to analytic neutrality in that era—her implicit procedural self took control and acted in the patient's best interest. Something transformative occurred in that moment that still resonates for the patient more than a quarter century later.

Such now moments go beyond technique and theory, and upend and transform, for better or worse, the previous intersubjective engagement. I recall a time when I also had such an experience. A depressed young mother was describing her frustration on a morning when she had been trying to seize a quiet moment for herself. She had been staring at the garden and drinking her coffee when suddenly the puppy pulled over a lamp and "pooped" on the carpet at the same moment her son came inside tracking muddy boots and lugging a leaky sprinkling can. I began chuckling involuntarily as I envisioned this chaotic, over-the-top scene, and she, like my former student and her therapist, joined in laughing with me. She said afterward that she had been so upset and irritated at the time that she "couldn't see the humor in it." My laughter was spontaneous, and, though I felt her negative arousal, rather than attuning to it, I took off in a different direction, attempting to up-regulate the depressive affect. Fortunately, she regrouped and was able to use my response to regulate and lighten her depressive mood.

When such moments can be mutually "recognized and ratified," Stern (1998) says, they will bring a "new intersubjective state," into being (p. 305). However, when the mutuality is not "recognized and ratified," the now moment will lead to a different outcome that may also impact the therapeutic process.

When I was a young mother in therapy myself, I was once describing what I considered to be ill-mannered acting out on the part of my daughter toward a fifth-grade classmate. I was mortified and upset, but my description of her behavior struck my therapist as funny, and she laughed out loud. I, on the other hand, was not at all amused and my irritation at my daughter remained. I felt a sense of judgment in my therapist's laugh, an implication that I was being too fussy as a parent and a message that I should lighten up. I was genuinely surprised that anyone could see the situation I had described as funny. It was only in retrospect that I realized how strongly it contrasted with my own mother's constant and outspoken vigilance about how my behavior looked to others. The therapist's laughter felt misattuned to my emotional state, yet the incongruity of it got my attention and created a now moment when suddenly things felt charged and different between the two of us. The connection with my therapist was strong enough to withstand a momentary misattunement. Her laughter effectively conveyed a challenge to my overactive parental superego without words, perhaps even more than a verbal interpretation might have done. Misattuned though her laughter may have felt in the moment, it eventually had far-reaching consequences, helping me to transform some of my overvigilance about conforming to social expectations.

An extremely funny *San Francisco Chronicle* columnist known as Ms. Gonick (Gonick, 2004), however, wrote of an experience early in a therapeutic relationship that was a now moment that apparently contributed to a different kind of change. She had been feeling suicidal and began seeing a therapist.

> We tried to reshape my psyche through "talking," which, for me, meant trying to make her laugh while she in turn had to stifle her laughter in order

to keep looking properly shrinkish. Then, since all that talking made me no saner and quite a bit poorer, I quit. (p. E-20)

Ms. Gonick implicitly pulled for a laugh from her therapist—perhaps using it as a quick way to affirm that she had established a connection and could positively impact someone else, or as a way to enliven herself and avoid the pull of suicide. The therapist chose to respond to the now moment by stifling her laughter and holding to her idea of the proper therapeutic persona. Although there may have been other reasons for it as well, the therapist's squelched laughter was mentioned in the line immediately before Ms. Gonick reveals that she had terminated the relationship because "talking" was not helping.

The therapist here was being asked to laugh at some very "unfunny" circumstances and symptoms. The therapist apparently felt like laughing about something that was anything but funny, which gave her some sense that a defense or a coping mechanism may have been at work. She could not bring herself to join in for understandable reasons. The now moment was confusing, the intersubjective pull unacceptable, and the moment passed without being "recognized and ratified" between therapist and patient, contributing to a rupture.

Two therapists cofacilitating a sexual trauma psychotherapy group found themselves in a similar laughter-based predicament. The eight group members shared a common "joke" about a reality show they wanted to start. The joke was that they would all move into a house together and be videotaped around the clock receiving counseling and living together in misery. The group members all laughed heartily as they described and embellished this inside joke. The group leaders, finding themselves unable to join in the laughter, tried to explore the feelings behind the joke, but encountered resistance. Eventually, the group members were able to acknowledge the deeper emotions of shame, sadness, and feeling "different" behind the humor, and the group leaders came to understand that the shared joke was a way for the group to bond around the commonality of their pain, shame, and suffering.

As Lewis pointed out, when shame is acknowledged, a joke may function to "connect in shared laughter a person who might otherwise be in a shared state of guilt or humiliation" (as cited in Retzinger, 1987, p. 165). Recognizing and ratifying the now moment in the group did not mean that the therapists joined in their laughter, but it did mean that there was attunement with all of the many feelings behind it. The now moment of group laughter was nonetheless transformative, perhaps for reasons described by Retzinger (1987). She analyzed the emotional expressions of women videotaped while discussing an experience from their personal lives, looking for markers of shame and rage. Some of the women in the group, encouraged to express their anger, laughed when talking about their resentments. Retzinger concluded, "When shame is too great . . . one feels alienated, disconnected from others, and alone in the world. Laughter serves to reconnect these severed ties, breaking the spiral of shame-rage" (p. 177).

Interpretation

Freud (1905/1983) noted that sometimes when he would make an interpretation, his patients would burst out laughing. He saw this laughter as confirmation that "I have succeeded in giving a faithful picture of their hidden unconscious to their conscious perception; and they laugh even when the content of what is unveiled would by no means justify this" (p. 170).

Laughter at the point of an interpretation such as Freud described can have many meanings—everything from joy, mutuality, and mastery to discomfort or denial. A therapist participant in Levine's (2009) study of the use of humor in psychotherapy with older adults found that couching interpretations in a humorous form made them easier to accept. Sometimes, the therapists reported, they used teasing to make their point. A 98-year-old woman, for example, was compulsively complaining about her physical problems. Finally, the therapist, in mock exasperation, made her interpretation. "Miriam! Look at me! You're 98 years old! Of course you have dry skin and problems with your hip! I'm much younger than you are and I have dry skin and problems with *my* hip" (p. 77). Miriam was surprised but began to chuckle. On subsequent occasions, she would make a complaint and then ask, "Did I just say something funny?" enjoying her ability to amuse her therapist, while also illustrating that she was gaining insight and mastery into her suffering in the context of the therapeutic connection made audible and visible in their shared laughter.

The patient's laughter at an interpretation, however, may also mark a therapeutic misattunement or an enactment that can drive a wedge between therapist and patient. It may be laughter of disbelief, or a judgment that the therapist's words are experienced as "off the wall." I can easily imagine, for example, such a laugh occurring should I attempt, in today's world, a Freudian interpretation about "penis envy" or "castration anxiety." On the other hand, laughter when a patient "gets" an interpretation and is able to take in the meaning and intent, as Freud suggested, represents a powerful bond of mutually shared understanding. Therapist and patient are traveling together on the inside track.

A clinician and former student described how gentle teasing and laughter enabled him to make an interpretation that had previously been rejected and devalued. The patient was a depressed man in his late 30s who had been hospitalized for a suicide attempt precipitated by the end of a romantic relationship. An abused, neglected, and abandoned child, he presented as preoccupied in his attachment style, with periods of disorganization. The therapist, in trying to help up-regulate the patient's positive affect and help him begin to build some reliable internal resources for self-regulation, would occasionally offer positive feedback to the patient about some of the strengths he observed in the patient. The patient was dismissive of these attempts, claiming it was just the therapist's job to say those things. Over time, the therapist found himself noting some aspect of the man's perseverance, courage, or intelligence. Instead of just noting it as before, he began to state it differently, saying something like, "You know, I'm really struck by how courageous that was of you," and then, with comedic timing would add, "Oh no, wait, I shouldn't say that because you probably won't believe me. Never mind, then," and they would laugh about this together. Gradually, the gentle teasing followed by laughter helped to ease something between them. The laughter made the predicament seem mutual rather than evoking the patient's shame. It underscored the connection between them and gradually opened the way for the patient to take in the therapist's interpretation about his unrealistic self-perceptions, as well as reflect on his view of the therapist and the therapist's role.

In a short exchange, Schimel (as cited in Kuhlman, 1984) took a similar tack with a similar patient.

Pt.: [*Complaining.*] You always point out the positive aspect of everything.
Psa. [psychoanalyst]: That isn't true.
Pt.: Then what is true?
Psa.: I simply point out the areas you habitually neglect. (p. 38)

At this point, the patient laughed. Cleverly, the analyst validated the patient's complaint, while simultaneously teasing him about it, managing to slip in a meaningful interpretation in the process.

Kuhlman (1984) points to what he calls "play signals," which alert the patient to the therapist's intent. These include such procedural coaching cues as tone of voice, twinkling eyes, a wink, a facial expression, or a "wry grin." These implicit, unplanned signals usually occur outside the therapist's conscious awareness. Nevertheless, these signals do alert the patient that what is coming next is meant to be playful, though, as in the case of interpretations, it may have an underlying serious message as well.

Interventions

The therapists in the two preceding examples provoked laughter, but did not comment on or question it. It was allowed to do its work without analysis of the behavior. Zeroing in on laughter, trying to verbalize the feelings behind it, is a matter for careful timing and thought. Laughter, whether Duchenne or non-Duchenne, is an implicit procedural, spontaneous behavior and, like trying to explain a joke, something may be lost when it's translated. Brody (1950) writes that, in analysis, "laughter is a defense best left undisturbed, for the superficial cloud of mirth that cloaks it is all too easily dissipated, leaving a substance of sadness, despair, regret, anger or hatred that may overwhelm the patient" (p. 193). Laughter may also represent as yet unacknowledged positive feelings of connection that may also overwhelm a patient, particularly one with dismissing or disorganized attachment, for whom closeness is dangerous, confusing, or threatening.

While it is often true that laughter is best left unanalyzed, the opposite may also be true. That was true, for example, in the case of the underlying grief and pain behind the laughter of the suicidal patient, Ms. Gonick, and in the case of the members of the sexual trauma survivor's group. In both of those instances, the therapists felt uncomfortable sharing a laugh with the patient, but in the first instance suppressed both the laughter and the acknowledgement of it, whereas in the second instance, it was thoroughly processed. Instances that occur early in treatment, such as these two, benefit from being openly discussed and processed. At other times, such as with Bader's patient mentioned above, processing and analyzing may make sense, but only later in treatment after the relationship is well-established. A consideration of the patient's attachment style and the accompanying patterns of affect arousal accompanying each may offer some guidance to the therapist in understanding and assessing whether laughter is a defense that needs to be respected and let be or else processed, and the timing for each.

Patterns of Laughter and Attachment Styles

There is, to my knowledge, no study that looks directly at the relationship between attachment style and laughter (Mikulincer & Shaver, 2007). Putting together a profile of the laughter patterns associated with each of the attachment styles in adulthood is therefore mostly a matter of extrapolation from the general body of research on attachment styles. Most of those look at attachment style relative to general affect arousal, defenses, and coping skills. One exception is a study by Roisman, Tsai, and Chiang (2004) that looks at affect arousal and state of mind relative to attachment of Chinese and European American college students while they were taking the Adult Attachment Interview (AAI; the AAI categories are not referred to as "attachment styles" per se). Their study included looking at "physiological responses to facial expressive behavior" as well as "self-reported emotional reflections" (p. 777).

Roisman et al. found that patterns of affect arousal during the AAI, including physiological markers, did parallel the arousal patterns associated with attachment styles in infancy and adulthood. They found that the arousal of people with secure/autonomous states of mind relative to attachment were balanced and linked to the material being discussed. As predicted, those with preoccupied states of mind showed patterns of hyperactivation of attachment affects, similar to those in the ambivalent/resistant children. Finally, the young adults in the study with dismissing states of mind demonstrated a deactivation of attachment affects, an arousal pattern associated with avoidant children. As with the children in that group, however, there were underlying physiological markers of anxiety.

I have approached the task of formulating a theory about the ways in which laughter may differ by attachment style in adult life by taking a developmental approach, beginning with the meaning of positive arousal in infancy and then childhood. Similarly, a developmental foundation is also useful for understanding experiences with laughter in the clinical hour based on attachment style. These attachment-based patterns of laughter provide clues about the attachment/caregiving history of the patient and the clinician, and the attachment/caregiving history provides the basis for understanding instances of laughter and their meaning in the clinical relationship. An attachment perspective also helps the clinician to understand enactments and guide interventions involving humor and laughter.

Secure Attachment

As with securely attached infants and children, one expects to find that securely attached adults will have a ready laugh that is generous, appropriate, and friendly. Their laughter will offer a ready avenue for affect regulation, and an invitation to closeness and connection. If there is teasing, it will be affectionate, even if pointed at times, and used to do what has been called "coating the pill, not salting the wound" (Colston, 1997, p. 24; Dewes & Winner, 1995). In normal, nonstressful periods, laughter—in a person whose attachments are secure—would be expected to occur much more frequently than signs of negativity.

At this point, it is worth returning to the description of secure attachment as conferring a "cascade of mental and behavioral events" by Mikulincer and Shaver (2007), referenced in the childhood chapter. Adults likewise carry forward the sense of safety, and the ability to "assuage distress, and arouse positive emotions" and to "remain relatively unperturbed under stress and experience longer periods of positive affectivity" (p. 38).

Securely attached people, however, also suffer wounds, pain, and loss, and seek therapy as well. That was the case with Cal, who came in around an acute relationship crisis. His security was apparent in the way he responded so readily to my attunement and attempts to help regulate his negative arousal. He was quickly able to establish a therapeutic attachment bond and to use me as a secure base for making positive changes in his life. Ultimately, he was also able to work on some of the historical attachment wounds that made him overly available as a caregiver to others. During the first year of treatment, he often cried as he delved into sources of his pain and stress. However, from time to time he would also share the joys of a new partnership, the freedom of easing up on work assignments, the fun of travel, and the fun of family gatherings. On occasion, he brought in photos he wanted to share along with anecdotes about the funny things his grandchildren would say. Affect and attunement flowed easily in the relationship, and we shared easy laughter over many exchanges. Frustrations and mismatches were successfully processed and repaired.

A wonderful example of what sounds like laughter in another securely attached person comes from M (2003) whose mother was suffering from Alzheimer's. He describes depressing visits with his mother where he was saddened as he listened to her noncomprehending rambles. One day, however, as he kissed her goodbye, he asked absentmindedly if she needed anything. To his shock, she said, "How about a cold one next time?" He burst out laughing, and, "she looked up at me from her wheelchair and began laughing, too. From then on," he writes, "I've lived for those rare moments of laughter that connect us" (p. 40). Even though this is a brief anecdote, it points toward secure (or earned-secure) attachment between M and his mother. There is the appropriate sense of loss and grief, but there is also the ability for laughter to cut through it and connect them through positive arousal, even though his mother's mental capacity was otherwise so compromised.

Preoccupied Attachment

Hyperactivation of the attachment system and overarousal of attachment affects are the hallmarks of those who are preoccupied in their attachments. This pattern is reinforced by inconsistent early caregivers who range from intrusive to alarmist to neglectful. The child, as a result, is easily aroused and hypervigilant and has difficulties with affect regulation. While we tend to associate the overarousal with distress, there are some people with preoccupied attachment who also show hyperactivated positive arousal.

Jackie, a woman in her mid-60s with preoccupied attachment, poorly concealed her neediness behind a façade of laughter. She would begin each hour early in our relationship with engaging humor, jokes, quips, and funny stories from work, the newspaper, or the Internet. Not until after we had shared a few laughs would she raise the many dysregulations she had endured since our last meeting over cross words, impatient coworkers, demanding bosses, grouchy landlords, or unresponsive family members. Behind Jackie's laughter was a deep sense that she needed to take care of her caregivers, a role reversal common to those with preoccupied attachment. Many people with preoccupied attachment styles learn in childhood to take care of their preoccupied, hyperactivated caregivers in childhood in a variety of ways, including being cute and funny and "happy."

Jackie's sense of humor, though part of her compulsive caregiving streak, was well-developed and she could be genuinely funny. Other preoccupied people, however, overuse nervous non-Duchenne laughter in conversation, and are hyperaroused sometimes to the point of annoyance. They communicate insecurity, neediness, and embarrassment that can make other people feel, among other things, irritated, affronted, pushed away, or guilty. A *San Francisco Chronicle* columnist, for example, describes an interview with an environmental activist ensconced in a threatened oak tree on the Berkeley campus. He climbed up there to interview her and she giggled at his discomfort. "The giggle turns out to be her default reaction to almost everything and is either an infectious indication of good spirits or an annoying personal tic, depending on your point of view and stress level" (Nevius, 2006, p. A11). Though I have no idea about the woman's attachment background, the persistent non-Duchenne giggle described here is an example of how hyperactivated laughter might be presented. The woman herself discounted its importance, shrugging when the columnist asked about it and replying, "It's just my noise" (p. A 11).

Dismissing Attachment

People with dismissing attachment styles do not usually feel the need for therapy, nor do they usually have any sense that an interpersonal relationship could help them feel or function better. In general, they defend against attachment affects, in effect attempting to deactivate their attachment system and as a result the arousal of attachment affect—be it negative or positive—is muted or rare. In general, their presentation is distant and nonemotional, though some dismissing adults can be quite witty when they learn to use humor as a tool to connect with others or to regulate their own or others' affect. Because of their lack of empathy and caregiving skills, however, their humor may be inclined to misfire, either because it is too hostile or misattuned, or because it is corny and off-base for the social situation.

When a dismissing patient comes in for therapy, however, positive arousal and laughter may play an important role in establishing the therapeutic attachment bond. Corbett (2004) describes how laughter over an accidental, incongruent interaction was a key ingredient in establishing his relationship with a man whose attachment affect was deactivated, presumably due to a dismissing attachment style. Mr. B spent many initial sessions, according to Corbett, "obsessively recount[ing] the details of his divorce and his empty, yet oddly functional, work life" (p. 461). Mr. B's cutoff affect and lack of passion led Corbett, early in their relationship, to experience a sense of "dull dread" at the beginning of their sessions. During one of these seemingly interminable hours, Corbett accidentally dropped his pen and it rolled under the couch. The patient, facing away from him on the couch, heard Corbett as he tried to discreetly retrieve it with his foot, and asked what was going on. Corbett told him, and then "crawled partway under the couch" to get it back. As Corbett sat back down, the patient began to laugh and said, "I can't believe you just did that" (p. 461).

In subsequent sessions, Corbett performed a series of unplanned, slapstick-like missteps—tripping on the carpet, bumping into the couch, spilling tea, even a sneeze while taking a drink of water that managed "to spray the contents of the glass halfway across the room" (p 462). The list is so long that I began to think that Corbett might have been acting out some implicit pull toward awkwardness on behalf of building his relationship with Mr. B. To each of these incidents, Mr. B responded with amusement and derision, making jesting comments such as, "How old are you anyway!?"

Early in the work, Corbett chose not interpret these moments of Mr. B's spontaneous laughter. Gradually, Mr. B began to talk about how little he had laughed in his life, "how infrequently he had felt the pull of play with another, and how odd and even a bit frightening it felt to surrender to this newfound pleasure" (p. 463). In this way, Mr. B came to his own understanding of the importance of playfulness and laughter in the context of the therapeutic relationship.

It is interesting to note that the deactivation of Mr. B's attachment system required that he avoid positive, playful attachment behaviors as well as expressions of attachment distress. Laughter and positive arousal felt just as alien, unfamiliar, and suspect as crying or hugging. Much later, Mr. B could talk about how these silly laugh-filled moments early in the treatment were key in his struggle to overcome his wariness and trust the analyst.

Disorganized/Disoriented Attachment

Patterns of affect arousal in those adults with disorganized/disoriented attachment range from dissociated and cut off, to eruptive, unpredictable, and sometimes inappropriate, especially under stress. On the other hand, laughter, as Retzinger (1987) points out, may also sometimes serve to counteract dissociation, overcome humiliation and pain, and bring about a sense of connection with fellow sufferers, as it did with the members of the sexual abuse trauma survivor's group mentioned earlier.

Some people who are disorganized may laugh completely out of context, perhaps when they are feeling threatened or fearful. Alternatively, they may laugh hysterically and inappropriately at another person's pain and suffering. In the mid-1990s, when *Schindler's List*, a World War II Holocaust epic, was playing in the theaters, grief, loss, and suffering were understandably triggered in most of the audiences who saw it. On one occasion, however, a group of high school students attending the film began laughing at it. It was so offensive to the rest of the audience that the manager of the theater stopped the film and told the students to leave (Weston, 1994). It is, of course, impossible to know what the attachment styles or wounds of the students might have been or what the sociocultural context from which they approached the violence and trauma depicted in the film was. The feeling that their laughter evoked in the rest of the audience, however, illustrates the kind of "countertransference" reaction that a clinician—or anyone—may experience when laughter is so markedly inappropriate to the stimulus. While this audience's reaction was one of anger, another woman wrote of a different reaction while sitting with her husband and his sisters as they laughed hysterically recalling their father's violent abuse (P., 2003). She first began to shake and then cry in grief for them as they laughingly described the abuse.

The State of the Therapeutic Attachment Bond

The clinical examples above also speak to the role of laughter in the establishment and maintenance of the therapeutic attachment bond, as well as to other aspects of laughter in the clinical hour. Mr. B's laughter over Corbett's mishaps, for example, helped to establish a trusted, secure base with his therapist. Jackie likewise evoked laughter in the therapist as a caregiving behavior designed to establish the therapist as a secure base who could be trusted to withstand Jackie's severe depression.

A colleague, a therapist who under most circumstances believes that laughter interferes with the transference, describes an experience of laughter while working with a fragile and isolated female patient with a dismissing attachment style so intense that she thought of her as schizoid. During one session, the patient told the therapist that a man had showed an interest in getting to know her, but that she had rejected him. The therapist replied, "That sounds like you!" and to the therapist's surprise, the patient responded with uncharacteristic hearty laughter. The therapist, also uncharacteristically, joined in laughing with her. The therapist wrote, "I laughed and felt good with the connection...feeling that she knew I knew her." The therapist said she understood that the embodiment of shared laughter meant that the patient was not only activating the defended-against positive attachment affects, but was connecting with the analyst as well. The laughter safely conveyed what words could not yet do: that the woman was beginning to feel "connected" with her therapist. Verbalizing the therapeutic connection directly, on the other hand, would have risked overwhelming the woman's ability to tolerate closeness, given her massively deactivated attachment system.

Enactments

Genuine, spontaneous, mutual laughter in the context of the therapeutic relationship is probably in some measure always an enactment, though not necessarily one with negative consequences. It is difficult to imagine how something so implicitly embedded in the nonconscious nervous system as laughter and so deeply rooted in early attachment and caregiving experiences would not tap into the internal working models of both partners in the therapeutic dyad. While the therapist's laughter with a patient may primarily represent the therapist's deep empathic connection with the patient's attachment and caregiving needs, the intertwining mutual subjectivities of both parties mean that the therapist's attachment/caregiving system is activated as well.

The therapist has the opportunity, and perhaps the obligation, to analyze laughter enactments, particularly when they arouse something problematic or uncomfortable in either patient or therapist. If that occurs, it is incumbent upon the therapist to work toward developing an explicit understanding of the elements involved, and getting consultation if necessary. When it would be in the patient's best interest, this explicit understanding might also be shared with the patient, though there are times when the therapist will choose to keep that understanding silent.

Corbett (2004), for example, looks back at what he calls his "opening enactments" with Mr. B. These, he writes, "afforded me (paradoxically) the forbearance to endure the depression, anger, paranoia, and (more important) the psychic retreats that characterized Mr. B's efforts to ward off these states" (p. 470). Corbett, however, did not share his understanding with Mr. B, waiting instead for Mr. B to come to his own realizations about their playful contact later in analysis.

An attachment perspective is often helpful in this analysis of enactments. Corbett's understanding, for example, brings to mind Bowlby's (1969) suggestion that the early smiles and laughter of infants help parents to stay engaged during the many sieges of negative arousal in their infant. In earlier writing, I characterized smiles and laughter as "warm fuzzy" attachment behaviors that create the positive chemistry of parent/child interactions, in contrast to crying, which is an emergency distress signal designed to create negative arousal in the parent, paralleling that of the child (Nelson, 2005). We hear this idea echoed in Corbett's description of how the playful laughter enabled him to endure the depressive, obsessive monotony of the early analytic hours with Mr. B. He did not share his understanding with the patient, using it instead to make sense of his own otherwise strange and inexplicable run of clumsiness.

Returning to the example mentioned earlier, where I began chuckling during a young mother's description of her early morning frustration, I recall being struck at the time by how my laughter lacked attunement, even though the patient found a way to accept and use it for affect regulation. I began to think about my enactment later as I reflected on the initial look of surprise/shock on the patient's face when I started laughing in the middle of her tale of woe. I wondered at my strange, misattuned intrusion into her narrative. I had to wonder about why I was so ready to flip the switch over to positive arousal, right in the middle of her experience of the opposite. My thoughts went to the reason she was in therapy: her couple's therapist had referred her because her husband, feeling overburdened by continually having to up-regulate his wife's depressive affect, was seriously threatening divorce. I had taken to heart the therapist's anxiety about the future of the marriage, and also came to identify with the husband's caregiving burden. The combination of both elements led to a strong wish to help my patient learn a new style of individual affect regulation that might stave off the loss of her husband that she so feared. My incongruent laughter was aimed at affect regulation, my own as well as that of the patient, and was a four-way enactment, involving me, the patient, her husband, and the couple's therapist. The patient's panic about the threatened loss—along with the dire prediction passed along by the couple's therapist—had infected me to the point that I was unnecessarily pushing the patient ahead of her own process. I did not share my insight with the patient, but I used it as a sign that I should alter my course and back off from trying to resolve all of these issues so as to let the patient's process unfold more organically in the relationship with me.

The clinical management of laughter is tricky. It is hard to know when to trust our implicitly informed laughter responses, and when it is in the patient's best interest to override them. It is even harder to consciously evaluate the pulls we feel toward initiating playful interactions that might make the patient laugh. The following examples show, for example, how difficult it might be to gauge the meaning of a laughter response—or lack thereof—especially in a first appointment or early in the therapeutic relationship.

A colleague told me of a friend, a professional comedian, who made an initial appointment with an analyst. During his initial meeting with the analyst, the comedian interjected his customary witty remarks, and then was angered by the analyst's squelching admonition: "This is not *Saturday Night Live*." The comedian refused to make a second appointment. Contrast this patient's reaction, however, with a very funny colleague of mine who told me that some years ago she was shopping around for therapists and had a hard time finding one who would *not* laugh at her jokes.

We therapists have only our own implicit, improvisational skills, guided by our explicit knowledge about the meaning of laughter, to help us negotiate this potential minefield of competing responses. An attachment perspective, with an underpinning of neurobiology, gives us a way to help make conscious and explicit the nonconscious, at times even uncontrollable, urges to laugh or restrain from laughter. It also gives us a way to surface the issue with our patients when we are confused and in conflict about whether or not to laugh.

Knowing about our own attachment styles, including our preferred methods of affect regulation, attachment wounds, and caregiving urges is the foundation for negotiating these tricky passages. Being aware of our ability to withstand negative arousal, or tendencies toward withholding positive arousal, are also key ingredients in maintaining a degree of consciousness about our implicit procedural affect-regulating patterns. In addition, it is important to carefully observe the unfolding clues early on—even in a first hour—that tip us off as to the patient's probable attachment style, and his accompanying levels of comfort with, or defenses against, the activation of the attachment affect. Our nervous systems pick up subtle clues and signals in the therapeutic interaction that serve as our best allies in the process. Bringing to bear our explicit understanding is also necessary for dealing with such ambiguous and confusing questions as whether or not to laugh with a patient in a first hour.

Being able to get an early feel for the possible attachment style of the patient may help to guide the therapist. For example, Ms. Gonick's dark, comedic, perhaps dissociated humor in the midst of being suicidal suggests disorganized attachment, and a desperate, defensive lunge into affect regulation. Like her therapist, I would not have been comfortable laughing with a suicidal person either. What I might have done, however, would be to make my reasons for not doing so explicit. I would also consider acknowledging her wit and the pull I felt toward joining her. Maybe my implicit self would have laughed before I censored it, as did Ms. Gonick's therapist. In such an instance, the pull to laughter and the conflict about doing so could be discussed overtly from the beginning. In this way, the incongruities and conflicts would be out in the open where they could be grappled with and understood mutually, similar to the process of the therapists discussing their reactions to the "reality show" joke in the sexual trauma group.

I get an altogether different attachment read from the *Saturday Night Live* patient. Here is a person who makes his living by making people laugh. Comedy is his identity, his self-esteem, his defense, and his gift. In a first session, I would listen closely to his presenting problems and history to look for confirmatory detail that he is hiding his vulnerabilities behind intellectually generated wit in a manner most associated with a dismissing attachment style. Knowing how dangerous attachment vulnerability is to such people and how long it takes for them to be able to express it in the context of the therapeutic attachment bond, I would go ahead and laugh at his humor without processing my understanding with him. His humor-based defenses would need to be respected—even enjoyed—until there is more security in the therapeutic attachment bond.

Finally, I consider how I might react to someone like my colleague who was looking for a therapist who would not laugh at her jokes. In that one sentence, she was revealing that for her being funny was an embedded and burdensome caregiving behavior. In all likelihood, her comedic presentation developed from having to up-regulate positive arousal in a depressive caregiver in her childhood, a role reversal frequently adopted by those who develop preoccupied attachment. Were I meeting her for a first appointment, I would listen carefully to her presentation and attachment history for coaching about how to respond. If I were unsure, I might choose to raise the question with her, even in a first hour, as she was perfectly conscious of her need not to entertain. If she were so funny that I laughed in spite of myself, I would expect to feel a sense of discomfort in the patient. As soon as the therapist picks up on that discomfort, it should be acknowledged, and then processed, though no doubt mutual understanding of the attachment/caregiving dynamics would be a long time in unfolding and healing.

There are a lot of places in the clinical hour where laughter goes right and bathes the clinical attachment bond in its warm glow. There are just as many places where it can trip us up, slow us down, or derail the relationship. Then there are times when it is mixed—helping on one level, disturbing on another, as in my response to the young mother.

Laughter in psychotherapy is nothing new, nor is it something about which we can make wholesale pronouncements. Our job is to bring all of our humanity, our attachment securities and insecurities, our implicit and explicit knowledge into the room so that laughter can do its playful work—right along with its serious work—to help expose and heal the attachment wounds of our patients, and, not coincidentally, our own.

Part 5

Transcendent Laughter

11

DIVINE COMEDY

Transformation and Transcendence in Laughter, Humor, Comedy, and Wit

Laughter "frees us from vanity on the one hand, and from pessimism on the other, by keeping us larger than what we do, and greater than what can happen to us" (Penjon as cited in Morreall, 1987, p. 2). Penjon, a French philosopher, here refers to the role of laughter in the dyadic regulation of affect, but he also points out that laughter can operate at another level. It can not only help us to transform the negative, but can also help us to transcend it by elevating us to something "larger" and "greater" than our personal suffering and pain. Such laughter is akin to the aesthetic, mystical, and spiritual experiences we know from art, music, literature, and religion or spiritual practice. Laughter is both an agent and a symbol of transformation, helping to bring it about and affirming its presence.

In *Thus Spoke Zarathustra*, Nietzsche (1954/1995) distinguishes between "laughter of the herd," scornful laughter related to fitting in, and "laughter of the height," which is about what he called "eternal recurrence" (Lippitt, 1992). Zarathustra experiences the former type when first trying to share his insights and wisdom with crowds of strangers who laugh at him in derision. "There is ice in their laughter," he says (Nietzsche, 1954/1995, p. 19). Laughter of the height, on the other hand, he says, is joyous, life affirming, and redemptive. It floats us above and beyond our individual particulars to experience "eternal recurrence," enabling us to gain a different perspective on the seriousness and suffering that is also part of life.

Zarathustra comes to understand this exalted type of laughter through a vision in which he encounters a young shepherd who is desperately trying to dislodge a black snake biting him on the inside of his throat. When Zarathustra is unable to pull the snake loose, he urges the shepherd to bite off its head. When he does, a dramatic change occurs in the young man.

> No longer a shepherd, no longer a man—a transformed being, surrounded with light, *laughing!* Never yet on earth had any man laughed as he laughed! Oh my brothers, I heard a laughter that was no human laughter—and now a thirst consumes me, a longing that is never stilled. My longing for this laughter consumes me. (As cited in Lippitt, 1992, p. 41)

The grief and loss we experience in life can have a suffocating, life-threatening quality, here symbolized by the battle with the life-threatening choke hold of the snake. What is amazing here is the shepherd's transformation after killing the snake. He does more than just gasp for air and resume breathing; he exalts in his release, letting out long, expiratory laughter. The snake has been vanquished and the shepherd is bathed in light, "a transformed being." The shepherd's laugh is a resounding "joyous 'Yes' to life despite its negative side, despite its horrors and suffering" (Lippitt, 1992, p. 41).

Hellman (2007) looks at the link between laughter and survival another way. He writes, "The real fate of humanity probably rests in its ability to laugh, no matter the circumstances.... There are certainly things that are not funny, but the refusal of laughter is ultimately acquiescence to darkness, a surrender to death" (p. 1).

Transformative Laughter, Transformative Play

Laughter, according to Pejon, helps us to transcend our vanity and pessimism in another way as well, freeing us to "play." In this sense, laughter liberates us "from the strict laws of rational thinking" and frees us "to play with new ideas" (as cited in Ziv, 1989, p. 106). Laughter, in this sense, also can free us from rigid thinking and can transform the way we see our plight and hence the way we feel about it. Keltner and Bonanno (1997) write, "Duchenne laughter may be the outcome of cognitive processes in which the individual develops a new, alternative interpretation of the distressing event, which in turn brings about positive emotion" (p. 698).

The link between laughter and play, attachment and exploration can also help us to transcend the confines of our personal pain and understanding. Being drawn to the incongruent, the new, and the fun within the context of a secure base elevates us to the "heights" of human existence. In these moments of exploration and discovery, something clicks and something is transformed. There is an alchemical spontaneous combustion that results in the formation of a new compound created out of the old elements. We play and explore, we discover something new that in a flash changes how we experience the world and our place in it. The transformation becomes transcendent, moving us, as do art, poetry, and spiritual practice, from the personal to the universal.

It is in the Winnicottian (1971/2001) "potential or transitional space" that laughter bridges the attachment system and the exploratory system. In that space, we are ready to abandon logic and wander around intrigued by incongruities, synchronicities, the ironic, and the absurd. We "make fun" of reality, inspiring imagination and creative spirit without fear of reprisal or retaliation. We are hard at play, expressing awe, delight, and a sense of the magical in giggles, chuckles, guffaws, and sidesplitting belly laughs. We leave the ground of the explicit and fly above and below it, giving our implicit, nonlinear selves a chance to learn about the world anew from a place before and beyond words.

My granddaughter Aurelia laughed repeatedly in this way when she read about Tigger and Roo choosing to jump out of a tree because they were too afraid to climb back down. With delight, she soared into the world of "nonsense" watching the characters in Hundred Acre Wood risk life and limb because they did not trust themselves to descend the tree they had easily climbed. They chose to come down the harder, more painful way because fear interrupted their logic and robbed them of self-confidence. She soared in laughter at their self-defeating dilemma, certainly familiar enough to her, yet common enough even among imaginary animals that she could find it funny.

I had a different kind of experience of transcendent laughter and transcendent play recently when I read a quote from the comedian Steven Wright (as cited in Thomas, 2010). It was just two lines, but they instantly put me into my own playful transitional space, made me laugh, and changed my view of the world. As a person who has spent my life "playing" with words and language, I instantly recognized the delightful truth of Wright's words:

I was reading the dictionary.
I thought it was a poem about everything. (p. 296)

I could not stop laughing in amazement as my entire world of word play reorganized around this "joke." I copied it out and sent it along to friends. Words have meanings, and meanings beyond those meanings. They are not only symbols, but meta-symbols, connected to each other and connecting each of us. We can "know" what words mean, but there is always something more to know about them and how they are connected to each other, some mystery to reach toward. The resonance was so deep, my enjoyment so pure, the playfulness so engaging, my sense of connection with the author so palpable, that nothing could express it better than a laugh.

In a similar way, I sometimes laugh when I read a poem, sharing in a writer's implicit sense of the world, finding that when I leave the ground of my own rationality, the poet helps me play with new ways of being and sometimes even of flying. I laugh in recognition and delight at a new discovery, "a universal truth," and the laughter both creates and marks an important and life-changing realization.

When an author, such as Wright, expresses an observation in a unique way or captures an ironic moment, I am able to leap from the confines of my own linear mind, learning, playing, healing, and creating as I travel. When everything comes together just right in that instant, I also laugh out loud, registering my own playful "now moment" of connection with the author, taking pleasure in the universal, transcendent meaning he has so wittily captured in words.

Laughter and Loss

We do not often connect laughter and loss, except in seeing the former as a defense against the latter. There are times, however, when laughter is part of a healing, transformative working-through of grief and loss, rather than a defense against the pain of it. In this instance, laughter is both the means of restoring hope and a sign that hope is returning. Laughter reestablishes a sense of connection with whomever and whatever has been lost and may also help the mourner to transcend personal pain and loss and experience the connection with "eternal recurrence," and the link between loss and love.

In my previous book (Nelson, 2005), I suggested that different types of crying are related to different stages of grief: protest and despair. Protest grief resists acceptance of the loss. Though necessary at times, it can impede recovery from loss. Laughter associated with irony, sarcasm, hostility, or dissociation may be an expression of protest and support the denial of the reality of a loss or its impact.

Despair, on the other hand, is the working-through phase of grief, the necessary experience of surrender to the reality of a loss. Though, as Brody (1950) points out, laughter is most often a defense against despair, sometimes it moves us forward to a new place and a new perspective, what Bowlby (1980) called "reorganization." Laughter in despair may acknowledge our surrender to the absurdities and the incongruities of loss, exposing them to the light of day and opening the door to hope, reorganization, and transformation. Perhaps this is the real link between laughter and crying that so many philosophers have made, and that so many clowns understand as well.

I found three examples linking laughter and loss in my personal "Laugh Out Loud" file. The first two, triggered by comments in magazine and newspaper articles, are definitely linked to protest grief. My laughter did not help me to heal or reorganize around these ongoing losses, but it did help me feel a sense of affirmation and connection with others who share my views. It was validating that someone found a new way of expressing my outrage about them, satire being a powerful form of protest.

The first example comes from a review of *Dancing With the Stars* (Acocella, 2008). The lines that cracked me up were, "The women are dressed like Vegas showgirls. (Many of the outfits are little more than bits of fringe pasted over their secondary sexual characteristics)" (p. 82). Acocella's exaggerated avoidance of crude language emphasizes—and to my mind speaks out against—not only the typical references to female anatomy, but the exploitation of it as well. The understated, scientific-sounding words Acocella chose struck me as very funny, though there was no small measure of hostility in my laughter. It was clearly laughter of protest over my sense of personal—as well as cultural—grief and pain about the objectification of women.

The second example of laughter and protest grief occurred when I was reading about a political debate over same-sex marriage:

> During a debate over a "marriage protection" amendment, Mr. [Barney] Frank said he did not understand Republican arguments that gay marriages would undermine traditional marriages, as if happily married men in Indiana, Nebraska, Kansas and Mississippi, learning that same-sex marriage was legal in Massachusetts, would smack themselves in the head and declare, "Wow, I could have married a guy." ("A Way With Words," 2008, p. A17)

Frank's comment was a perfect expression of my own feelings of protest grief about the "marriage protection act," which would deny my partner and me legal recognition of our marriage. The absurdity in Frank's criticism seemed perfect to the circumstances. I felt solidarity with him and cheered on his protest before Congress on behalf of many couples. Frank's comment did not help me work though my grief; it was unabated rather than transformed. Nonetheless, the protest laughter made me feel less alone and as if my voice, too, were being heard.

On the other hand, my laughter at the following comment at a book launch party for *More Old Jewish Comedians* (Friedman, 2008) went a long way toward helping to transform part of my long-standing grief and despair over the breech between my parents and myself over religion. "Finally, Jerry Stiller held up a copy of *More Old Jewish Comedians* and said gently, 'If Job got a copy of this and had known these people, he'd never have written that terrible book'" (Ross, 2008, p. 44). I can say that I laughed from the depths of my soul, but not so much because it was "funny" to me, though it was that, too. Even more so, it was because I "got" what Stiller was saying on so many levels that, for me, a deep sense of personal loss was transformed into an experience of wonder and hope. In an instant, with no planning or preparation, I soared through potential space and found something new under the sun that connected with my experience, my understanding, my limitations, and my struggles, and freed me to reframe, and, to a degree, transcend them: laughter and liberation.

I will do my best to unravel the reasons this simple comment made me laugh with such a transformative outcome. I do so in the interests of tracing the role of laughter in the process of personal transformation and, further, the transcendence from personal loss to the meaning of the human condition. The story begins with my religious upbringing. I was raised in a loving Protestant Fundamentalist family, not a Jewish one. Things began to come unraveled, however, when I matured and became critical of our family's religious beliefs in ways that have often resonated with Jewish coming-of-age stories and family dynamics, Chaim Potok's (1967) *The Chosen* being one such example. As in many Jewish families, the central psychological and social importance of religion in the lives of my parents propelled me into a painful and prolonged identity struggle during adolescence, one that was ironically made possible by the Christian-based education—which they sacrificed for—that they provided for me. In the end, I was liberated from what felt to me like the emotional and intellectual straightjacket of their religion, but at the cost of wounding them and causing them to feel a sense of bewilderment, fear, and failure. In my rejection of their religion, I was not only rejecting the security of the "eternal life" promised by their beliefs, but I was, in their minds, rejecting them personally along with the security they found in their belief in life after death.

Fast forwarding to 2008, I found the comment about Job and that "terrible book he wrote" multilayered with grief and loss. The first layer of grief begins with Job's story, in the book by his name, in the Hebrew Bible that recounts the pain and suffering of this righteous man—and follows through to the grief of the Jewish people and eventually to my parents and me. The joke, however, does not end with grief. Instead, it helped me realize that loss is part of the human condition, the other side of love, that is the essence of the meaning of life. Core losses such as these, as I describe in my book on crying, are part of our attachment/grief system where the excruciating pain of separation serves as a powerful motivator to keep us in close proximity with our loved ones.

Even now, writing about the layers of loss in this humorous comment, I find myself feeling extremely sad. If I ended my analysis here, I would be crying over the pain, grief, and despair that were behind the laughter. However, the story did not end there, because of the unexpected twist that followed, the surprise ending. Stiller refers to Job's grief, loss, suffering, and then comes the clever punch line: that Job would not have needed to write "that terrible book" if he had known these Jewish comedians. That was so incongruent and unexpected, that it struck me as hilarious. Stiller's reference to Job's chronicle of suffering being "a terrible book," as if he were simply passing critical judgment on a literary memoir, not only made it funny, it was the setup for the rest of the joke. It was the next part, about how things might have been different if he could have known the comedians that made these words transformative—from grief and loss to hope and love. If, as Stiller suggested, even Job could see things differently, if Job's affect could be up-regulated after such profound suffering and loss, if Job could be healed by the comic wisdom of the elders, it would mean that there was hope for my parents. Suddenly I had hope that retrospectively and from beyond the grave, even they could, like Job, take a different position, and their grief and loss could also be transformed into some kind of joyful acceptance. We could even celebrate as a family the kind of life of emotional and intellectual liberation that they made possible for me by providing a secure, loving home and a good education. Finally, along with hope for Job and me and my parents, I also felt hope for the whole world. My laughter both signaled and helped to achieve a transformation, what Bowlby (1980) has called the "reorganization" that brings about healing after a loss (Nelson, 2008).

This brief analysis of my internal response to this humorous remark only scratches the surface of the possible meanings to be found in this short humorous sentence. There is the meaning it had to Stiller, to Lillian Ross, the author of the article, along with the much-discussed meaning of Jewish humor in general. We think, for example, of the long, proud history of Jewish comedians, Freud's collection of Jewish jokes, and the website oldjewstellingjokes.com that is linked to the group that published the *More Old Jewish Comedians* book. Then there is the meaning of Job in the Judeo-Christian tradition, the subject of volumes of deeply reflective thought on the meaning of suffering and the human condition and the role of an all-knowing, all-powerful God when bad things happen to good people. Unpacking this one simple comedic reference could fill a book, and still we would not be able to say we were being definitive. Making the implicit explicit will keep scholars and poets and novelists, as well as psychotherapists, busy into the future of humankind.

Plessner (1970), a German philosopher, writes about the relationship between laughter and crying. He finds common ground that speaks, not only to their respective roles in resolving grief, but also to their similarity in recognizing and transforming the ineffable, the implicit, and the ultimately indescribable.

> We laugh and cry only in situations for which there is no other answer. That is, to the person who takes a word, an image, or a situation in such a way that he must laugh or cry, there is no other answer, even if others do not understand his mood, take him to be silly or sentimental, and find other types of behavior more to the point. For the person who laughs or cries, the actual situation is dominated by the effective impossibility of giving it any other suitable answer. (p. 139)

Plessner beautifully describes the implicit nature of laughter and crying. Our bodies take over and answer for us when we implicitly understand something striking about love or loss that often we cannot quite put into words.

Humor

There are two ways of asking the question about why we laugh. The first is to look at why we laugh in a given instance, which evolutionary theorists call the "proximate cause." The second is to consider why we laugh as a species, which they call the "ultimate" cause. In order to understand the meaning of laughter from an attachment perspective, I have consistently looked at the question of ultimate causation, and steered away from discussion of proximate causes, or humor. Many, if not most, theorists, however, either focus exclusively on the proximate causes—usually on humor and jokes—or conflate proximate and ultimate causes, in addition to conflating humor and laughter.

Nonetheless, as a student writing a dissertation on the clinical use of humor said to me, "*Something* has to make us laugh," and it is to that "something" that scholars of humor refer. There are endless efforts to define humor, to analyze it both cognitively and dynamically—Freud's (1905/1983) *Jokes and Their Relation to the Unconscious* being among the best of the genre. In that work, Freud analyzes at great length the layers of meaning in a given instance of humor or a joke, comparing the process to analyzing dreams. I would say, too, that it is similar to trying to decipher a poem or to understand why something makes us cry. There are layers of meaning, symbols condensed from daily life, conscious memories or forgotten ones, and implicit memories that are part of us though they have never seen the light of day.

In trying to understand the pleasure that humor brings, Freud points to the sense of recognizing or rediscovering the familiar—an example of the leap, I would say, from the personal to the universal. He refers to Aristotle, who "regarded joy in recognition as the basis of the enjoyment of art" (p. 121).

The comparison between humor and art seems especially apt, because in addition to the link between the personal and the universal, they also have in common an implied interpersonal connection between the artist or humorist and the audience that responds—complexly interweaving subject and object. In looking at humor, as with dreams and art, we look for meaning in multiple layers, asking what a witty remark says about the humorist, what it says about the audience that laughs, and what it says about the context of a particular culture, about a point in historical time, and about humankind.

Approaching every witticism, joke, stand-up routine, dramatic laugh-line, or laugh-out-loud song lyric with the readiness to analyze the combination of personal experience, symbolic representation, social context, intended meaning, and audience resonance is hard work, and perhaps ultimately misses the point. Trying to articulate what is implicit in humor, for all our attempts to do so, never quite captures the whole of it, any more than do our attempts to describe a painting in words. An attachment perspective helps, as does the ability to make sense of our own inner experience and that of others, as psychotherapists—and some art critics—do. Humility helps, too, as we acknowledge that not knowing is necessarily part of the process. We understand and value the knowledge that each time we come back to a laugh, just as with each time we revisit a poem or a painting, we find something new in it. Humor, like laughter, can be entertainment, but sometimes it is as transformative, and ultimately transcendent as art.

Comedy and Comics

Comedy and comics have generated intense and long-standing interest among philosophers, psychoanalysts, and pundits. Yet, as Freud (1905/1983) wrote, "the problems of the comic have proved so complicated, and all the efforts of the philosophers at solving them so unsuccessful" (p. 181) that even he despaired of being able to do so once and for all. Looking at comedy (consciously generated or "formal" humor) and comics (purveyors of comedy) from an attachment perspective offers another avenue of insight.

Berger (1997) writes that comedy, like humor and laughter, is transcendent in two ways. The first he calls "low transcendence," representing its ability to help us rise above everyday existence by taking us to a "different reality in which the assumptions and rules of ordinary life are suspended" (p. 205). Low transcendence is what from an attachment standpoint is called the up-regulation of positive arousal. It accounts for the comedy that through incongruity, superiority, nonsense, and a variety of other techniques creates an alternate "funny" universe that lifts us up, and gives us a different and potentially transforming view of the world and our experience of it.

There is, however, another aspect of comedy that Berger says is a signal of "true redemption," that is, "of a world that has been made whole and in which the miseries of the human condition have been abolished" (p. 205). This Berger calls the transcendence "in a higher key" (p. 205), which he says are experiences that are "religious in the full proper sense of the word" (p. 205). From an attachment perspective, this kind of comedy is redemptive in that it helps us move beyond separation, grief, and loss back to connection, attachment, and love, as I did in response to Stiller's comment about Job and "that terrible book." In mystical terms, this transcendence is expressed as an encounter with the numinous, a sense of oneness with the universe, with humankind, nature, the sun, moon, and stars; in religious terms, it is expressed as a sense of attachment to a Supreme Being, feeling and sharing the power of love and connection.

Berger (1997) also points out, however, that the sense of a magically transformed world can also create a sense of danger and have a dark side. There is a threat to everyday existence and to "undermining the social order" (p. 107). In the realm of everyday laughter, this takes the form of bullying or "making fun" of people in a hostile and destructive manner. In the more cosmic sense, altering reality in this way through laughter can be dangerous, even evil, as represented by the Joker in Batman, who was discussed in an earlier chapter. In the comic, the disruptive forces may take the form of biting satire, cruel jokes at the expense of groups or individuals, parodies, caricatures, or cartoons that target groups and their sacred beliefs, or sometimes their "sacred cows." Underlying the latter is public protest grief that takes advantage of the dark power of comedy to attack and detach. Protest laughter is an attempt to reclaim what is lost rather than surrendering to despair and moving through it to reclaim love.

The novelist Michael Chabon (2001), in a short story called "The God of Dark Laughter," braves these themes. Using a parody of the detective genre, he writes in the first person voice of the county district attorney investigating the brutal murder of a circus clown. The detective work begins by trying to understand the stressors in a clown's life—travel, transience, feigned happiness, and perhaps alcohol. Next, he focuses on a clown's potential enemies, and in the process learns about "coulrophobia," a real word, and this is the definition: the "morbid, irrational fear of or aversion to clowns" (p. 118).

Further investigation, however, reveals that darker forces are at work. In the clown's hideaway, a cave, are several books that the narrator translates from the

German. In them he learns about two warring religious cults in ancient Northern Armenia. One group worshipped the onomatopoetically named "Yê-Heh," the "God of Dark Laughter," and the other, "Ai" the "God of Unbearable and Ubiquitous Sorrow" (p. 125). The followers of the God of Dark Laughter, he learned, viewed the universe as a cosmic hoax, "a place of calamity and cruel irony so overwhelming that the only possible response was a malevolent laughter" (p. 125). They mocked life, death, and "all human aspirations." Through inbreeding, their followers developed "distended grins and skin as white as chalk" (resembling, as we might guess, clowns). The followers of Ai, on the other hand, "saw the world as no less horrifying and cruel than did their archenemies, but their response to the whole mess was a more or less permanent wailing" (p. 125). Stated in other terms, these two gods represent the two phases of grief and loss: laughter in protest, and wailing in despair.

The murder of the clown is finally pinned on one of the ragtag, inbred followers of Ai, who are the wailers. Chabon ends the story with the detective's conclusion: he fears the murderers will be gravely disappointed when their god returns to explain his intentions and, "at the end of all we know and everything we have ever lost or imagined, the rafters of the world are shaken by a single, a terrible guffaw" (p. 127).

The laughter and crying in this story are not transcendent, but the message is indeed so. Chabon understands what Bergen was driving at in talking about the overarching "danger" of the magic of dark comedy and laughter. With dark laughter—or its opposite, permanent wailing—we will be stuck in protest grief (laughter) or despair (wailing) without hope of light, love, or transformation— death instead of life.

Comedians

In reading the life stories of comedians, I have repeatedly been struck by the themes of attachment and separation, love and loss, protest and despair. Of course, the biographies of each of us contain exactly these same themes: it is the stuff of life. The difference is in the ways comedians have adapted to their loves and losses, how they have used their gifts as tools to endlessly express their protest grief or as a means to regain and restore what is missing. The best of them are artists, their performances symbolizing their losses, giving them meaning, and thereby helping them—and their audiences—to transcend, moving from loss to love.

Berger (1997) believes that comedians are drawn, perhaps we might even say "called," to live their lives in service of the transcendent. He distinguishes between secular and "religious" modes of comic experience, pointing out that "the passage from one to the other requires an act of faith" (p. 205). If it did not, every comedian, he suggests, would be a "minister of God," which, he reminds us, is what Don Quixote thought himself to be.

I have been collecting biographies and articles about comedians for years—and there is no shortage of them. Comedians, like artists, fascinate us and hold us in wonder at their gifts and in thrall of their sometimes mysterious motivations. In *Growing Up Laughing: My Story and the Story of Funny*, actress Marlo Thomas (2010) writes about what it was like growing up with her famous comedian father, Danny Thomas, and his comedian friends, and of becoming a comedian herself. Her childhood was infused with professional comedy, and she followed in her father's career, yet she, too, is drawn to try to understand its mysteries. In addition to telling her own story in the book, she interviews 22 contemporary comedians, ranging from Billy Crystal and Robin Williams, to Tina Fey and Whoopi Goldberg. Coming to their stories with an attachment eye, I noticed a number of common threads.

Comic Antics as Attachment Behavior: Connection and Love

Conan O'Brien attributes his comic sensibilities to his family. All of his siblings were funny and both parents had a good sense of humor. He says he learned 95% of what he knows at the kitchen table. "We'd sit around that table and see who could make my dad laugh—and he had good taste. He wouldn't laugh at everything, so if he did laugh, you knew you had said something funny" (as cited in Thomas, 2010, p. 170). Another way of stating this would be to say that trying to get their dad to laugh was a way of trying to connect with him, which would make their laughter-bids a form of attachment behavior. Expanding their repertoire so that their dad would find something new to laugh about also linked their comedic efforts to playful exploration and learning.

In a similar vein, Stephen Colbert says that he grew up in a "*humorocracy,*" a family of 11 children where "the funny person in the room was king. Everyone had their specialty, and there was never a moment in which we didn't try to make each other laugh. We were constantly at it" (as cited in Thomas, 2010, p. 185). The prevalence of laughter as positive attachment/caregiving behavior also included his mother, who he says not only had a good sense of humor, but also other warm fuzzy attachment behaviors as she was "a big hugger, too. And for no reason...you never had to ask for a hug" (p. 185).

Audience as Attachment Figure

Steve Coogan is a successful British comedian whose comedic style is described as having "accentuated the negative and explored the comedy of embarrassment" (Lahr, 2007, p. 42). Lahr writes that people have noticed an air of "detachment" when Coogan is not performing, and that he seems "disconnected" from the world. "Comedy is one way that he makes that connection. Part of what he's doing is reshaping the world so he can fit into it" (Lahr, 2007, p. 44).

Coogan describes growing up in the television generation. Watching comedy shows, he says, was a family event "quite formative to me. Parents and children all laughing—it's a unifying thing" (p. 46). The energy of the laughter represented the family connection, even when they were not looking at each other or otherwise directly interacting. It was connection once-removed, but powerful enough, apparently, to make him seek more of it later in life. Coogan calls comedy a form of "self-medication," and once said that performing is "very liberating. It's a very calm place to be. It's like curling up in a warm blanket" (p. 49). He speaks as though he is attached to both the role and the content. Attachment—though once removed—is preferable to detachment and disconnection.

The audience for Coogan is a safe haven—a place to up-regulate his own positive arousal, whereas for other comedians, it is a secure base from which they can explore new ideas and experiences. They talk about the powerful feelings of connection they feel when an audience laughs at their jokes. A Portland stand-up comedian, Ian Karmel, puts it this way: "In stand-up, it's just you. There's no lie in a laugh. It really is acceptance" (Turnquist, 2011, C2). Mary Tyler Moore said something to the effect of (I jotted down her words from a television interview), "You get a jolt from the audience when they laugh at you...and it gives you the oomph to go out there and do another joke" (Boettcher and Trinklein, 2008). Kevin Smith, a writer/director who does some stand-up, describes playing the San Diego Comic Con, before 6,000 people, "You ever hear six thousand people laugh at a Wayne Gretzky joke you make? You feel like Jesus" (Friend, 2009, p. 30).

Communal Attachment

Robin Williams describes a sense of shared humanity that occurs when the up-regulation of positive arousal through laughter transcends the individual comedian and moves to the level of community. "With comedy you are allowed to laugh about the insanity. You realize how absurd it all is, the painful stuff and the wonderful stuff too. For a brief moment everyone is connected, and you all go 'Hey, we're human'" (Griffin, 2006, p. 113). We are all in this together, and whether in protest or despair, we find meaning in sharing our losses and our love expressed in knowing, understanding, mutual laughter.

Using Humor to Up-Regulate Positive Arousal in Caregivers

Thomas recalls a time when her father got angry because she refused to eat her vegetables. Usually an amiable, loving man, on this occasion, perhaps embarrassed by her behavior in front of his father, he pushed back his chair as if he were going to come after her. She jumped up and ran away from the table. When he finally cornered her, she said she stopped, "spun around, waved my hands in the air and yelled in my best Hungarian accent, 'Cut! Print it! Very good! We try it again!'" She was saved. Her dad "fell over laughing" (Thomas, 2010, p. 11). For Thomas, negotiating a father's bad mood was a rare occasion, but a number of the other comedians she interviewed were faced with caregivers who were chronically depressed. Comedian Joy Behar, for example, tells Marlo Thomas,

> I think if you talk to a lot of women comics, you'll find that they had mothers who were sort of depressed.... I found that my escape from all of that was to make fun of everything. I got a lot of material just watching my mother and trying to make her laugh. (As cited in Thomas, 2010, p. 41)

Comedy as Protest Grief

Using humor to improve the mood of depressed (or sometimes angry) parents is a frequent biographical thread among comedians, while another is using comedy as an expression of protest, including protest grief. I learned from Thomas's book that the standard line after a successful joke or show is, "I killed them!" The saying is ubiquitous among both male and female comedians.

Behar uses the phrase when describing her childhood experiences entertaining her extended family. She traveled from household to household as a 10-year-old, she said, doing "shtick for them all day long" (as cited in Thomas, 2010, p. 40). Oddly, and perhaps tellingly, she adds "I would just kill in these places as a kid" (as cited in Thomas, 2010, p. 41). Perhaps it felt as though no less than her ultimate survival was at stake in those laughs.

Alan Alda has a slightly different attachment and caregiving view of the reason why comedians always talk about killing. "In a sense, that's a very accurate term. When you make people laugh, you make them helpless. So, in a way, you *are* killing them" (p. 149).

Staying with the theme of killing being equated with helplessness and conquest, the late Christopher Hitchens gave an interview trying to defend himself against the furor unleashed among feminists by his article "Why Women aren't Funny" (Hitchens, 2007). He made a comment, meant to be in his defense, that he was not opposed to female laughter because it meant that he "had" a woman in his thrall, that she was then helpless, implying sexual submissiveness.

In a documentary about the culture of atheism, *The Four Horsemen of the Apocalypse* (Dawkins, Dennett, Harris, & Hitchens, 2007), Hitchens explained his own psychology in terms that make his humor sound close to protest grief. He said, "I have the faculty of humor and it has an edge, and I'm not going to repress it," referring to, among other things, his responses to the hostility aimed at his outspoken atheism by Christians and other believers. One could view his brilliant, at times wickedly caustic humor as a narrowly focused attack on detractors, or as a more generalized protest against his grievances with the world.

Sarah Silverman, another brilliant comedian with a sharp tongue, has been described as dispatching "empathy with a kind of emotional judo.... No hugs, no learning—and screw you" (Friend, 2007, p. 77). As a female comedian, Silverman challenges the culturally imposed norm that equates female and well-socialized caregiver who tries to make everyone else feel good. "At times," Friend writes, "you wonder whether you're laughing with Silverman or at her, and then you realize that she's laughing at you" (p. 77). That is genuine protest humor in action.

Speaking of protest, Joan Rivers, who is also known for being *wickedly* funny, calls her humor a "gun." Rivers admits in her interview with Thomas (2010) that she herself is fighting the age barrier (loss), yet she makes fun of older women (protest), in what she calls "cougar jokes": jokes that mercilessly target women who go out with younger men. She says, clearly using protest language, that her comedy is about "I'll show you." And further, it comes out of "You'll be sorry." Rivers implies that grief and loss are necessary ingredients for comedy: "The minute somebody is having a wonderful soft life, they're not so funny anymore" (as cited in Thomas, 2010, p. 197). She is right at least about protest humor, which definitely needs the fuel of loss and pain before it can spark.

Turning oppression upside down by using humor is a well-known weapon of protest, a way of redirecting the aggression outward. It is also a way of protesting grief and loss, demanding that what is lost be restored, reclaimed, or returned. Because laughter invites connection and exploration, this kind of protest can be a very effective one, or, if it creates new victims and more oppression, may serve more as retaliation. In that case, grief is perpetuated by laughter rather than laughter leading the audience to reconciliation and reorganization that facilitate the healing transformation back to connection and love.

Laughter in Literature

Humor and wit in literature are ubiquitous, and the list of humorous genres and devices is long: satire, spoof, parody, irony, farce, silliness, absurdity, and nonsense. The San Francisco Public Library houses the world's largest collection: the Schmulowitz Collection of Wit and Humor with upwards of 21,000 books and 230 periodical titles, and more being added each month. Nat Schmulowitz, who endowed the collection, was an attorney who represented early Hollywood film stars. He was inspired to amass his humor collection by a reference to a book of wit in Shakespeare's *Much Ado About Nothing*. It was called *The Hundred Merry Tales* and published in 1526. When Schmulowitz acquired an 1887 reprinting of that book, he was hooked on collecting more such volumes. In 1947 he began donating his collection to the library. After discovering that the Nazis considered political jokes a crime (he wrote a book called *Nazi Joke Courts*), his goal was more sociopolitical than entertainment. Schmulowitz wrote that "the man who can laugh at himself or be laughed at has taken another step towards the perfect sanity, which brings peace on Earth and goodwill to men" (Boulware, 2009, p. E2).

Humor in literature is both static and dynamic—frozen and animated. Humor, "as represented by words on a page," Triezenberg (2008) writes, "is only a dry and dead record of what the humor had been when in the wild—in this case, in the mind of the author and reader" (p. 523). Analogizing to a dried-out biological specimen affixed to a glass slide, she writes,

> Fortunately it is easy to reanimate a piece of fixed and mounted humor: it happens every time the text is read or thought about. Thus unlike the kind of everyday social humor that springs into existence and is promptly lost, literary humor can and does endure for millennia. (p. 523)

With all due respect to humor in literature, I want to focus on the much less frequently discussed topic of laughter in literature. The king of this small genre, in my mind, is *The Vale of Laughter* by De Vries (1953/1967). It is a novel that focuses on laughter in the life of Joe Sandwich, a Chicago financial advisor. Laughter is discussed from every conceivable angle on almost every one of its 251 pages, and I found it not only educational, but also entertaining and sometimes laugh-out-loud funny!

Joe Sandwich begins his narrative by describing the clowning he did as an infant. Most of his early memories about laughter, however, come from later in childhood. In particular, he describes going to confession as a young boy, but only confessing to good deeds, not bad, to the consternation of the priests. He also recounts how, as an older child, he shared his collection of funny names at his father's "death bed" (a false alarm, it turns out), where his father was (hilariously to me) obsessed with planning his last words, even though the doctor insisted he was not dying.

Joe tells us, early on, that he has learned that Freud believes all the work of wit is done by the unconscious, and that these humorous acts of his are a cover for hostility. Joe is fine with the former—wit is clearly springing from his unconscious—but categorically denies the interpretation that his humor is hostile. This kind of satire, often laden with irony, keeps coming at the reader for 251 straight pages.

While still in high school, in order to look more deeply at the psychological side of his clowning and laughter, Joe agrees to be "psychoanalyzed" by a slightly older cousin, Benny Bonner, who is majoring in psychology at the University of Chicago. "You interest me," says Benny. "I could learn a lot about the comic type, and you might get some valuable insights into yourself" (p. 23). Benny's first interpretation is that Joe is a compulsive comic, having an "absolute *need* to make a joke about everything. You can't *not* horse around" (p. 25). When Benny explains that all compulsive rituals serve to discharge anxiety, Joe asks how "horsing around" can do that. Benny replies, "What have we laughed about so far? Exhaustion, arthritis, locomotor ataxia, paresis, and insomnia. A joke is, like prayer and hand-washing, a device for resolving fear" (p. 25).

Reading these lines, I am a goner, laughter-wise. The laugh-lines are brilliant satire of our profession; they transcend the fictional Joe and Benny, and the literal Freud and psychoanalysis. When I read, "A joke is, like prayer and hand-washing, a device for resolving fear," I find it to be not only laugh-out-loud funny, but also mystical, beautiful, poetic, and awe-inspiring. I feel like laughing and crying all at once with the truth and beauty of it.

De Vries, raised and educated in the Dutch Reform Church, was a novelist, satirist, and editor of *Poetry* magazine, who was hired to work for the *New Yorker* by renowned humorist James Thurber. The religion, the poetry, the creativity, and the humor merge artistically in this book. Even the title transcends: instead of the usual Biblical reference to this world as a "vale of tears," he propels us into "the vale of laughter."

Roddy Doyle (2004), an Irish writer, richly combines gifts of storytelling and humor in such a way as to make the pain behind laughter—and its transformation to hope—palpable. In the short story "The Joke," for example, we see laughter and loss, attachment and grief, despair and hope portrayed through the internal monologue of a husband. Married 26 years, he one day overhears his wife on the telephone volunteer him, as she had done countless times over the years, to go pick up someone in need of a ride. This time, he feels put-upon, irritated, and resistant, and he begins to examine their diminished relationship, lack of togetherness, partnership, and sex. He identifies his resentment, sadness, and sense of loss, but cannot put his finger on anything specific that is wrong. He thinks of and discards many theories: time, the kids, lack of sex, age, years together.

As he anguishes, mystified about the origins of his new anger and feelings of loss, he finds himself staring at their big, new television. He remembers buying it as a way to help their marriage, even though neither of them watches much TV. As his mind wanders, however, he does concede that football is better on the big screen. In that moment, something shifts: "He felt himself smiling. Like a fight against his face. He let it through. He smiled" (p. 122).

At the same moment, fighting the impish smile at the ironic value the television has "for his marriage," he hears his wife laughing on the telephone. He is struck by memories of how he used to make her laugh: "Words used to do it. Jokes. Playacting, acting the eejit. She'd like it. She'd loved it. She'd moved closer to him when she was laughing" (p. 122). Suddenly he is on a different page. He wants to try to make her laugh again, and he thinks to himself that he could give it a try right away: "Now. A joke" (p. 122). Nervously and self-consciously, he begins rehearsing, alternately being hopeful and scared because he knows that this joke he is about to tell, "It was more than a joke. He knew that. Would she know?" (p. 122).

We are left at the end, not knowing what he did, or how she responded. "She came to the door. She stopped. He looked at her" (p. 122). The action stops there, but there is a new feeling in the air. He understood something, gained an insight, though he could not put it into words. He knew it was "more than a joke," and soon she would know that, too, just as we the readers do. Doyle captures the ineffable role that laughter serves in our interpersonal relationships—sharing intimacy, attachment, grief, and loss—and how it enables all of us to witness—and partake if we wish—in the healing it can bring.

A scene from the novel *Pearl* (Gordon, 2005) likewise uses laughter to mark the working-through of grief, especially protest grief. The scene takes place in a hospital during a mother/daughter, life/death reconciliation scene. The clincher, however, is not the usual tears we would expect. Instead, the deal is sealed with laughter.

Pearl, a student from New York, experiencing the usual late-adolescent distance from, and disdain for, her mother Maria, has left home to find herself by studying in Dublin. While there, she gets involved with a pseudo-revolutionary group spearheaded by a self-important young American. As an indirect result of one of their "actions," a young Irish man dies. Feeling responsible, Pearl chains herself to the flagpole in front of the American embassy, engages in a hunger strike, and intends to starve herself to death in penance. Near death after six weeks, she is hospitalized, angry, and determined to die.

When her mother, Maria, arrives from New York, Pearl demands that Maria go and visit the mother of the boy who died. Maria agrees without hesitation and when she returns delivers a reassuring and upbeat summary about her conversation with the boy's mother. In doing so, Maria displays the very qualities that Pearl had found to be so annoying.

> Ridiculous, her mother's sense of possibility, her endless belief in the goodness of change. An old instinct tells her that her mother must be wrong. But what if she isn't?...Her mother is a person of faith and hope....Her mother believes in change; her mother will never change. This is the sort of thing, this inconsistency, that in the past had made Pearl angry with Maria. But now her mother's combination of constancy and inconsistency amuses her, delights her. (p. 344)

Pearl looks at her mother and says, "Mama, slow down," and Maria blinks, "as if she's just heard the most intriguing sentence of her life. And then they both begin to laugh. They laugh as if what Pearl just said was the best joke in the world" (p. 345).

Pearl's earnest young doctor, fearing that mother/daughter encounter could push the fragile patient over the edge, returns to Pearl's room to find them not locked in anger or struggle, not crying, but laughing. "It's the first time she's laughed hard for a very long time, and it hurts her throat," (p. 344) (calling to mind the snake ripped from the throat of Zarathustra's shepherd). The doctor is shocked and puzzled: "In the iconography of mothers and daughters, laughter has not taken much of a place" (p. 345). There is no better place for it to happen, however, than in the bosom of the attachment relationship, as it reorganizes and finds new life after suffering the inevitable wrenching of separation and individuation by both parties. A secure base is rediscovered, exploration encouraged, if not required, and a new understanding emerges. The transformation is marked by laughter.

I reach back to my memory of my own daughters' adolescence to resurrect a story, thankfully not a life and death one like this, about laughter during a similar period of stormy adolescent transition. I can only think of one, but it still hilarious to me. Our family rule about swearing was that it was all right as long as it was purely an expletive, not directed at a person. "This test is a 'bitch,'" rather than "You are a bitch," is the sort of distinction we made. The girls were both in high school when one evening at dinner we became embroiled in a tense discussion about their wanting permission to attend some questionable upcoming post-dance beach excursion, or perhaps it was an overnight political activity in the next county. Whatever it was, we were not making much headway. Finally, there was a pause, and in a quiet voice tinged with irony, Ingrid, the oldest, said, "Fuck you" to her parents for the first time ever in her life, yet managed to do so without any force or conviction. Without a moment's hesitation, all four of us burst out laughing—hysterically. Her expletive was so incongruent and she delivered it in such a perfectly inflected tone of voice, managing to successfully flout, without challenging, the taboo. A transformation occurred as we began to integrate our shared pain at the struggles around separation with joy at the girls' approaching maturity and independence. Laughter opened the way and marked the passage: attachment, separation, loss, and gain.

Laughter in Drama and Film

Trying to isolate laughter in films is like trying to isolate it in life: It is everywhere all the time and can mean anything and everything that we have talked about in this book. It can be deep, heartfelt, body-wrenching, contagious, connecting Duchenne laughter, or it can be haughty, bullying laughter. It can be effortful, non-Duchenne laughter punctuating awkward conversations, or the coy, come-hither laughter of flirtation. It can also be the beseeching, don't-be-mad-at-me-for-this laughter of conflict avoidance.

In writing this section, I was tempted to send out a call on the Internet to my friends, family, and colleagues for their most-laughed-at movies. Instead, I Googled "funniest movies" and found a treasure trove of lists. In some instances, I had seen very few of those mentioned, while in others, I had seen most of them (probably dating both the compilers and myself). In the end, just reading through the titles and starting a list of my own was a great up-regulator of positive arousal. Reading through my list of all-time funniest movies makes me feel smiley and happy: *Spinal Tap, Annie Hall, Harold and Maud, A Mighty Wind, What About Bob?, Blues Brothers, School of Rock* (or any comedy with Jack Black), *Airplane, M*A*S*H, Blazing Saddles, The Producers, Wayne's World,* and the oft-quoted in our family, *Ghostbusters.* I notice that when I ask other people what their favorite funny movies are, they also start grinning immediately. The thought of that fun, that joy may not make us laugh out loud, but we are certainly smiling broadly, inside and out.

I am not enough of a film buff to have the knowledge, nor do I have access to script and acting details, that would enable me to flesh out an analysis of particular laughter scenes in movies, as I did above with stories and novels. I am confident, however, that in movies there are plentiful examples of the same mundane "secular" transcendence, and the same "mystical" transcendence described at the beginning of the chapter.

From an attachment standpoint, what I would like to look at instead is the phenomenon of the transcendence experienced in communal laughter in film audiences. In the section of *Seeing Through Tears* where I write about communal crying at films, I quote Lilly Tomlin's character, Trudy, the Bag Lady. When Trudy is visited by extraterrestrials, they ask her about the meaning of goose bumps. She takes them to a play and they get goose bumps, but from watching the audience, not from watching the stage. "Yeah," says Trudy, "to see a group of strangers sitting together in the dark, laughing and crying about the same things...that just knocked 'em out" (Wagner, 1986, p. 212).

Group laughter is powerful regardless of the setting, which is why public speakers and preachers often begin with a funny story. The audience is not only connected with the speaker in this way, but they all have joined in and become a community. Watching films, the flow of shared affect can also run deep. I often find myself peering down the row at strangers to watch their faces as we join in, some experiencing some incongruity or discovering some new truth that sparks laughter. When synchronized with laughter, we are exploring the world and our internal universes as one body.

My sister and several women friends have found that laughter in an empty theater is not nearly as gratifying. They often go to weekday matinees since they have retired. While it is nice not to have ticket lines, one of the things they dislike about going to a sparsely attended movie is that the shared communal aspect of a full theater laughing together is missing.

Some years ago, while living in a community where I felt personally and politically out of place, I had the opposite experience: laughing out loud in a theater when the rest of the audience was silent. Or, on the contrary, sometimes the audience would be laughing at something I found repulsive, oppressive, or disgusting. My solution was to go see certain films in a nearby town where I felt more at home. I did so because I wanted to laugh in unison—to feel that powerful and validating sense of connection even with strangers—and to leave behind the loneliness and pain of laughing out loud alone in a theater full or people or cringing when others laughed. Eventually, I moved to that town. I followed not just my politics and my heart, but also my laugh.

We may also consider the art of communal affect in films from the director's perspective. Quentin Tarantino says, of arousing his audiences to laughter,

> I like fucking with your emotions, and I like it when it's done to me. That's my thing. You're gonna laugh, you're gonna laugh, you're gonna laugh, until you're gonna stop laughing. You're gonna stop laughing, you're gonna stop laughing, you're gonna stop laughing, until boom you're gonna laugh again. The audience and the director, it's an S & M relationship, and the audience

is the M. It's exciting! When you go out and have pie afterward, you've got some shit to talk about. You went to the movies that night! (MacFarquhar, 2003, p. 155)

It is amazing to imagine the consciously applied artistry that goes into arousing affect in this way. I do often feel manipulated into feeling something, especially by a film like Tarantino's dark comedy *Pulp Fiction,* where I laughed in spite of myself ("You killed the guy, you clean up the car"). Nonetheless, this kind of humor does allow us to treat death, for example, in a casual, almost mundane way, subjecting it to the kind of petty, immature argument we see here. It is secular transcendence to be sure, though with thought and a little more (im)maturity, I might be able to find the mystical transcendence as well.

A different artist, playwright Tom Stoppard, acknowledges fussing about laughs that don't land when he intends them to do so (Singer, 2011). It goes deeper than simply wanting a witty scene to click with the audience. "I think of laughter as the sound of comprehension," he says (p. 27). In other words, when an audience "gets it," and acknowledges it with a laugh, he feels he has connected artistically— he has transcended individual experience by transforming it into something universal. It is a way to connect the audience with each other, but also with him.

Laughter and Culture

Laughter as an attachment behavior is universal. People in every culture in the world laugh in exactly the same way and for the same evolutionary reasons related to our common inborn attachment systems. Humor, however, is another matter: We may laugh the same way, but we do not laugh *at* the same things. *What* we find funny is inextricably tied into our cultural, social, and personal life experiences, values, and educational background.

Apte (1985), an anthropologist studying humor and laughter, looks at what he calls "the external stimuli of humor" and points out that humor "must have a cultural niche; it cannot occur in a vacuum" (p. 16). He is interested in cross-cultural comparisons looking at differences but also at the "shared ways in which humor stimuli are generated and humor is appreciated" (p. 15). Humor is a very difficult thing for an outsider to study, however, because it is so contextual—and, to the extent that it is verbal, also language-specific. Because of that, much of the anthropological literature focuses on outwardly observable cultural aspects of humor such as "joking relationships" and "ritual clowning."

Western anthropological studies of "joking relationships" in Africa, North America, Asia, and Melanesia go back as far as the late 1800s. They were, for example, discussed in a Radcliffe-Brown (1940/1952) publication, *Africa.* Radcliffe-Brown defined these special kinship bonds as "a relation between two persons in which one is by custom permitted, and in some instances required, to tease or make fun of the other, who in turn is required to take no offense" (p. 90). Some relationships are between equals who trade places as teaser and teased, whereas in other cultures, the teasing is unidirectional, though it may be directed to the person above or below the teaser in status.

While joking relationships combine friendliness and antagonism, the teasing is not meant to be taken seriously. "There is a pretense of hostility and a real friendliness. To put it in another way, the relationship is one of permitted disrespect" (Radcliffe-Brown, 1940/1952, p. 91). Not surprisingly, these relationships represent complex social hierarchies that depend on showing respect in the proper way to the proper person. For example, many joking relationships occur between relatives by marriage, such as between a man and his wife's sisters or brothers. The wife's parents, on the other hand, demand complete respect even to the point of avoidance. In our own prefeminist culture, comedians were almost guaranteed a laugh simply by saying the words "mother-in-law" or "wife." Henny Youngman's famous line "Take my wife [*pause*] please" is a prime example.

Radcliff-Brown describes what we would call the attachment function of joking relationships. They are designed to prevent serious hostility "by the playful antagonism of teasing," that at once acknowledges that "social disjunction is one of the essential components of the relationship," while maintaining the social conjunction "by the friendliness that takes no offense at insult" (p. 92). It is a delicate balance, but anyone in a family anywhere in the world knows that such balance is crucial and necessary. Being able to "play" with the balance through humor is a way of coping with the inevitable ambivalences that arise in close relationships.

According to Donna Goldstein, who studied laughter and humor in a Rio shantytown, the knotty problem of understanding and relating to humor as expressed by another race, class, or culture has led to much criticism of those who try. Many insist, she writes, that we "give up attempts to 'give voice' to others" because it is "pure arrogance and conceit that drives us to attempt such projects" (Goldstein as cited in Gay, 2006, p. 237). Goldstein believed that the alternative— not trying to access humor in other cultures—risks leaving the powerless and oppressed in those cultures without a broader audience, which has social and political consequences.

Humor, it has been suggested, opens a window into the feelings of oppressed peoples about the injustice of their conditions. Humor serves as a form of protest that can reveal conditions and circumstances and feelings about them that can feel closer to home than some of the more "visible and organized social movements" that are more often the subjects of study (Gay, 2006). Goldstein, in her own work, has attempted to unravel the experiences of the poor in Rio by studying their use of humor.

A study on humor in Trinidad was cowritten by James Jones, a Guggenheim scholar, and Hollis V. Liverpool (Jones & Liverpool, 1976), a school teacher there. Liverpool is also known as "The Mighty Chalkdust," in his role as a "professional calypsonian," which is defined as a combination bard, poet, singer, composer, and performer. Calypso emerged during slavery and became part of Carnival, though it permeates everyday Trinidadian life "with a thoroughness rarely seen in other societies" (p. 259). Since their beginning, Jones and Liverpool note, calypsonians have been "verbal warriors," representing the "social and racial underdog," and directing "ridicule, satire and insults at the upper classes" (p. 283). It takes place in various forms, including dance, music song, poetry, theatre, political analysis, satire, oration, and verbal battle.

Calypso compositions build on word and language play, double entendres, puns, and the audience's shared knowledge of social and political figures. One song quoted and analyzed by Jones and Liverpool is called "Soul Chick," by the calypsonian "Lord Funny." It presents two parallel stories—one about building a chicken coop, the other about sex (the word for "wood" is also the vernacular for "penis"). The repetitive refrain, mixing questions about building the chicken coop with sexual references—"How you could nail so? How you could screw so?"—became a pervasive cultural reference and laugh-line. To an inept driver, one might say, with a characteristic inflection, "How you could drive so?" A good-looking woman on the street might inspire the remark, "How you could walk so?" A variant of the same line even appeared in a newspaper headline—"How Karl could Expect So!"—next to a photograph of a pregnant bride alongside the face of Karl, the then attorney general.

Jones and Liverpool use their combined cultural perspectives to share with readers the complexities of what is going on in calypso, this pervasive and elegant humor form. The flavor definitely comes through in their analysis, though the specifics are a reach for most of us looking in from the outside. One exception might be the songs and dances that make fun of tourists at Carnival who try to sing and dance along wearing sunglasses and shorts. The shared ridicule of outsiders solidifies "the essence of being a Trinidadian," and affirms the special character of Carnival: "It is we own ting" (p. 285).

While writing this section on humor and culture, my brother-in-law, who is a third-generation child of Dutch immigrants and a humor buff, decided to download some Dutch jokes he found on the Internet. He then had them translated and failed to connect with even one glimmer of humor in what he read. Earlier, when I was doing a computer search on humor and culture, I came across the abstract of a book called *Hybrid Humour: Comedy in Transcultural Perspectives* (Dunphy & Emig, 2010), which was described as an "interdisciplinary and transcultural study of comedy in a pan-European perspective." In distilling the topics under discussion, the summary of the book points to the tangle of variables that must be considered in cross-cultural humor research.

> These range from humour in Polish poetry via jokes about Italian migrants in English-speaking TV commercials, to Turkish comedy, literature and cartoons in Germany, Turkish, Surinamese, Iranian and Moroccan literary humour in the Netherlands, Beur humour in many media in France, and Asian humour in literature, film, and TV series in Great Britain. (p. 1 of 2)

While this sentence makes me dizzy, it also gives us some idea of what we are up against in trying to bridge the culture/humor gap. It also emphasizes the point we are making here: While we all may laugh for the same human reasons, what makes us laugh is highly contextualized, not only culturally, but personally ("You had to be there").

Conclusion

Laughter can be petty and mean, grandiose and arrogant. It can also be kind and gentle, loving and supportive. In English, we have all kinds of subtle ways of expressing these variations in the words we use to describe the sounds and faces we make, and to hint about the feelings underneath them: We chortle, chuckle, titter, giggle, grin, or sneer. We also attempt to differentiate some of the functions of laughter in some of our everyday sayings. We talk about affect regulation when we say, "I laughed it off," or "I laughed to keep from crying." We recognize how our bodies respond without our conscious direction in describing something as "a belly laugh," or when we say it was "fall-down funny" (known as "FOFL"—fall on the floor laughing—on the Internet). We speak about bullying victims when we describe someone as a "laughingstock," or ourselves as getting in the last word in an argument as, "I had the last laugh." In the regional expression of my Southern relatives, they use "tickled" to equal laughter, and when something is really funny, they say, "I was tickled to death."

I came to a study of the attachment implications of laughter through my study of crying. In looking at the conclusion of that book, I find words that seem equally fitting for the end of this chapter. I quote them here, inserting laughter where before it said crying:

> In the art of laughing we have love and loss, life and death. Laughter holds the opposites: hopelessness and hope, pain and comfort, loneliness and connection. Laughter is a transformative agent, a bridge between mother and child, lover, and beloved, stranger and Good Samaritan, body and soul, secular and sacred....Laughter is, as Shelley wrote of the skylark's song, "unpremeditated art."

REFERENCES

Acocella, J. (2008, April 14). Mambo! "Dancing with the stars." *New Yorker*, 82–83.

Ainsworth, M. D. (1964). Patterns of attachment behavior shown by the infant in interaction with his mother. *Merrill-Palmer Quarterly, 10,* 51–58.

Ainsworth, M. D., & Bell, S. M. (1970). Attachment, exploration, and separation: Illustrated by the behavior of one-year-olds in a strange situation. *Child Development, 41,* 49–67.

Allen, M. W., Reid, M., & Riemenschneider, C. (2004). The role of laughter when discussing workplace barriers: Women in Information Technology jobs. *Sex Roles, 50*(3/4), 177–189.

Apte, M. L. (1985). *Humor and laughter: An anthropological approach.* Ithaca, NY, and London: Cornell University Press.

Auletta, K. (2011, March 7). "The Dictator Index: A billionaire battles a continent's legacy of misrule." *New Yorker,* 44–55.

Auslander, S. (2007, July 2). Save us: How to handle bad behavior. *New Yorker,* 36–41.

A way with words. (2008, May 13). *New York Times,* A17.

Bachorowski, J.-A., & Owren, M. J. (2001). Not all laughs are alike: Voiced but not unvoiced laughter readily elicits positive affect. *Psychological Science, 12*(3), 252–257.

Bader, M. J. (1993). The analyst's use of humor. *Psychoanalytic Quarterly, 62,* 23–50.

Beale, B. (2003, October 10). Where did laughter come from? *ABC Science Online.* Retrieved from www.abc.net.au/science/news/stories/s961420.htm

Beckman, H., Regier, N., & Young, J. (2007). Effect of workplace laughter groups on personal efficacy beliefs. *Journal of Primary Prevention, 28,* 167–182.

Beebe, B. (2003). Brief mother-infant treatment: Psychoanalytically informed video feedback. *Infant Mental Health Journal, 24*(1), 24–52.

Bells, N. (2011, May 16). Boston Red Sox fans help autistic man sing national anthem. *The Lighter Side.* Retrieved from http://ca.news.yahoo.com/blogs/good-news/boston-red-sox-fans-help-autistic-man-sing-183026419.html

Berger, P. L. (1997). *Redeeming laugher: The comic dimension of human experience.* Berlin: Walter de Gruyter & Co.

Bettes, B. A. (1988). Maternal depression and motherese: Temporal and intonational features. *Child Development, 59,* 1089–1096.

Boettcher, S. J., & Trinklein, M. J. (2008, June 19). *Pioneers of television* (4-part miniseries). Los Angeles: PBS.

Boulware, J. (2009, March 3). Fool around at the S.F. library. *San Francisco Chronicle,* E1–E2.

Bowlby, J. (1969). *Attachment* (Vol. 1). New York: Basic Books.

Bowlby, J. (1980). *Attachment and Loss* (Vol. 3). New York: Basic Books.

Brackett, C. W. (1933). Laughing and crying of preschool children. *Journal of Experimental Education, 2*(2), 119–126.

Brody, M. W. (1950). The meaning of laughter. *Psychoanalytic Quarterly, 19,* 192–201.

Bromberg, P. (2011). *The shadow of the tsunami and the growth of the relational mind.* New York: Routledge.

Brooks, R. (1994). Humor in psychotherapy: An invaluable technique with adolescents. In E. S. Buckman (Ed.), *The handbook of humor: Clinical applications in psychotherapy.* Malabar, FL: Krieger Publishing Company.

Brooks-Gunn, J., & Lewis, M. (1982). Affective exchanges between normal and handicapped infants and their mothers. In T. Field & A. Fogel (Eds.), *Emotion and early interaction* (pp. 161–188). Hillsdale, NJ: Lawrence Erlbaum.

BruBearBaby. (2011, January 24). Baby laughing hysterically at ripping paper (Video file). Retrieved from http://www.youtube.com/watch?v=RP4abiHdQpc

Buckley, F. H. (2003). *The morality of laughter.* Ann Arbor: University of Michigan Press.

C., K. (2003, November). Readers write: Laughter. *The Sun, 34*–41.

Cameron, E. L., Fox, J. D., Anderson, M. S., & Cameron, C.A. (2010). Resilient youths use humor to enhance socioemotional functioning during a day in the life. *Journal of Adolescent Research, 20*(10), 1–26.

Cameron, E. L., Gamannossi, B. A., Gillen, J., & Cameron, C. A. (2010). Humour. In J. Gillen & C. A. Cameron (Eds.), *International perspectives on early childhood research: A day in the life* (pp. 136–154). New York: Palgrave Macmillan.

Cameron, E. L., Kennedy, K. M., & Cameron, C. A. (2008). "Let me show you a trick!": A toddlers use of humor to explore, interpret and negotiate her familial environment during a day in the life. *Journal of Research in Childhood Education, 23*(1), 5–18.

Cardosa, S. H. (2001). Our ancient laughing brain. *Brain & Mind: Electronic Magazine on Neuroscience.* Retrieved from www.cerebromente.org.br/n13/mente/laughter/laughter1.html

Carlberg, G. (1997). Laughter opens the door: Turning points in child psychotherapy. *Journal of Child Psychotherapy, 23*(3), 331–349.

Cassidy, J. (2008). The nature of the child's ties. In J. Cassidy & P. Shaver (Eds.), *The handbook of attachment: Theory, research and clinical applications* (pp. 3–20). New York: Guilford.

Cassidy, J., & Shaver, P. (2008). *Handbook of attachment: Theory, research, and clinical applications.* New York: Guilford Press.

Chabon, M. (2001, April 9). The god of dark laughter. *New Yorker,* 116–127.

Chapman, A. J. (1975). Eye contact, physical proximity and laugher: A re-examination of the equilibrium model of social intimacy. *Social Behavior and Personality, 3*(2), 143–155.

Colston, H. L. (1997). Salting a wound or sugaring a pill: The pragmatic functions of ironic criticism. *Discourse Processes, 23*(1), 25–45.

Corbett, K. (2004). Cracking in: The psychotherapeutic action of comedy. *Psychoanalytic Dialogues 14*(4), 457–474.

Coser, R. L. (1960). Laughter among colleagues. *Psychiatry, 23,* 81–95.

Cousins, N. (1979). *Anatomy of an illness as perceived by the patient.* New York: W. W. Norton.

Cozolino, L. (2006). *The neuorscience of human relationships: Attachment and the developing social brain.* New York: W. W. Norton.

Creusere, M. (1999). Theores of adults' understanding and use of irony and sarcasm: Applications to and evidence from research with children. *Developmental Review, 19*, 213–262.

Dana, R. S. (1994). Humor as a diagnostic tool in child and adolescent groups. In E. S. Buckman (Ed.), *The handbook of humor: Clinical applications in psychotherapy* (pp. 41–51). Malabar, FL: Krieger Publishing Company.

Darwin, C. (1872/1965). *The expression of the emotions in man and animals.* Chicago: University of Chicago Press.

Davidson, R., & Fox, N. (1982). Asymmetrical brain activity discriminates between positive versus negative affective stimuli in human infants. *Science, 2218*(4578), 1235–1237.

Dawkins, R., Dennett, D., Harris, S. & Hitchens, C. (2007). *The four horsemen of the apocalypse* (Documentary film). Richard Dawkins Foundation for Reason and Science.

Demos, E. V. (1982). Facial expressions of infants and toddlers: A descriptive analysis. In T. Field & A. Fogel (Eds.), *Emotion and early interaction* (pp. 127–160). Hillsdale, NJ: Lawrence Erlbaum Associates.

Denham, S. (1998). *Emotional development in young children.* New York: Guilford.

DeVries, P. (1953/1967). *The vale of laughter.* Boston: Little, Brown.

Dewes, S., & Winner, E. (1995). Muting the meaning: A social function of irony. *Metaphor and Symbolic Activity, 10*(1), 3–19.

Doyle, R. (2004, November 29). The joke. *New Yorker,* 118–122.

Dunphy, G., & Emig, R. (Eds.). (2010). *Hybrid humour: Comedy in trancultural perspectives* (Abstract). Amsterdam and New York: Rodopi.

Ehrenberg, D. B. (1990). Playfulness in the psychoanalytic relationship. *Contemporary Psychoanalysis, 26,* 74–94.

Emde, R. N., Katz, E. L., & Thorpe, J. K. (1978). Emotional expression in infancy: II. Early deviations in Down's Syndrome. In M. Lewis & L. A. Rosenblum (Eds.), *The development of affect* (pp. 351–360). New York: Plenum Press.

Field, T. (1982). Affective displays of high-risk infants. In T. Field & A. Fogel (Eds.), *Emotion and early interaction* (pp. 101–125). Hillsdale, NJ: Lawrence Erlbaum.

Fischer, R., & Fisher, S. (1987). Therapeutic strategies with the comic child. In W. F. Fry & A. S. Waleed (Eds.), *Handbook of humor and psychotherapy: Advances in the clinical use of humor* (pp. 107–125). Sarasota: Professional Resource Exchange.

Foot, H., & Chapman, A. (1996). The social responsiveness of young children in humorous situations. In A. Chapman & H. Foot (Eds.), *Humor and laughter: Theory, research, and applications* (pp. 1887–1214). New Brunswick, NJ: Transaction Publishers.

Fraiberg, S. (1979). Blind infants and their mothers. In M. Bullowa (Ed.), *Before speech* (pp. 149–170). Cambridge: Cambridge University Press.

Frank, M., Ekman, P., & Friesen, W. (1993). Behavioral markers and recognizability of the smile of enjoyment. *Journal of Personality and Social Psychology, 64*(1), 83–93.

Fredrickson, B. L. (1998). What good are positive emotions? *Review of General Psychology, 2*(3), 300–319.

Freud, S. (1905/1983). *Jokes and their relation to the unconscious.* New York: W. W. Norton.

Freud, S. (1927). Humour. In *The standard edition of the complete psychological works of Sigmund Freud* (Vol. 21, pp. 160–166). London: Hogarth Press.

Friedman, Drew. (2008). *More old Jewish comedians.* Seattle: Fantagraphics Books.

Friend, T. (2007, February 2). Hostile acts: "The Sarah Silverman Program" puts the mean back in funny. *New Yorker,* 76–77.

Fudge, E. (2003). Learning to laugh: Children and being human in early modern thought. *Textual Practice, 17*(2), 277–294.

Führ, M. (2001). Some aspects of form and function of humor in adolescence. *Humor, 14*(1), 25–36.

Garcia, A. (2003). Readers write: Laughter. *The Sun, 335,* 34–41.

Gardiner, H. M., Metcalf, R. C., & Beebe-Center, J. G. (1937). *Feeling and emotion: A history of the feelings.* New York: American Book Company.

Gay, R. (2006). Donna Goldstein, laughter out of place: Race, class, violence, and sexuality in a Rio shantytown. *Qualitative Sociology, 29,* 237–239.

Gayagoy, G. (2009, May/June). Mum's the word. *Weight Watcher's Magazine,* 64.

George, C., & Solomon, J. (2008). The caregiving system: A behavioral systems approach to parenting. In J. Cassidy & P. Shaver (Eds.), *The handbook of attachment: Theory, research and clinical applications* (pp. 833–856). New York: Guilford.

Gervais, M., & Wilson, D. S. (2005). The evolution and functions of laughter and humor: A synthetic approach. *Quarterly Review of Biology, 80*(4), 395–430.

Gonick, M. (2004). It's tough living with an enzyme bent on suicide. *San Francisco Chronicle,* E-1, E-20.

Gordon, M. (2005). *Pearl.* New York: Pantheon Books.

Grammer, K. (2005). Strangers meet: Laughter and nonverbal signs of interest in opposite-sex encounters. *Journal of Nonverbal Behavior, 14*(4), 209–236.

Grandin, T., Barron, S., & Zysk, V. (Eds.). (2005). *Unwritten rules of social relationships: Decoding social mysteries through the unique perspectives of autism.* Arlington, TX: Future Horizons.

Greig, J. Y. T. (1923). *The psychology of laughter and comedy.* New York: Dodd, Mead and Company.

Griffin, N. (2006, November/December). Tour de Frantic: Robin Williams. *AARP, 66*–113.

Grossmann, K., Grossmann, K., Kindler, H., & Zimmermann, P. (2008). A wider view of attachment and exploration: The influence of mothers and fathers on the development of psychological security from infancy to young adulthood. In J. Cassidy & P. Shaver (Eds.), *Handbook of attachment: Theory, research, and clinical applications* (2nd ed., pp. 857–879). New York: Guilford.

Grotjahn, M. (1957). *Beyond laughter: Humor and the subconscious.* New York: McGraw-Hill.

Hall, C. T. (2000, January 10). Stand-up comedy: Scientist says early hominids had to walk on two legs before they could laugh. *San Francisco Chronicle,* A6.

Hall, G. S., & Allin, A. (1897). The psychology of tickling, laughing and the comic. *American Journal of Psychology, 9,* 1–41.

Halliwell, S. (1991). The uses of laughter in Greek culture. *Classical Quarterly, 41*(2), 279–296.

Hellman, D. (2007). Laughter in the face of persecution. Retrieved from articles.sfgate.com/2007–05–21/entertainment/17245270_1_max-states-laughter-kalooki-nights/3

Hitchens, C. (2007, January). Why women aren't funny. *Vanity Fair.* Retrieved from www.vanityfair.com/culture/features/2007/01/hitchens200701

Hsu, H. C., Nwokah, E. E., & Fogel, A. (1998, April). Characteristics of infant laughter during the first six months of life. *Infant Behavior and Development, 21,* 470.

Hudenko, W. J., Stone, W., & Bachorowski, J. A. (2009). Laughter differs in children with autism: An acoustic analysis of laughs produced by children with and without the disorder. *Journal of Autism and Developmental Disorders, 39,* 1392–1400.

Johnson, K. E., & Mervis, C. B. (1997). First steps in the emergence of verbal humor: A case study. *Infant Behavior and Development, 20*(2), 187–196.

Johnson, T. (2003). Readers write: Laughter. *The Sun, 335*(November), 41.

Jones, J. M., & Liverpool, H. V. (1976). Calypso humour in Trinidad. In A. J. Chapman & H. C. Foot (Eds.), *Humor and laughter: Theory, research, and applications* (pp. 259–286). New Brunswick/USA & London: Transaction Publishers.

Junkins, E. (2002). *Belly laughter in relationships.* Irving, TX: Dustin Royale.

Kataria, M. (2006, September 26). Benefits of Laughter Yoga with John Cleese (Video file). Retrieved from www.youtube.com/watch?v=yXEfjVnYkqM

Kataria, M. (2008). Laughing alone and telephone buddy. Retrieved from www.laugh teryoga.org/drkataria

Keltner, D. (2008, December 7). In defense of teasing. *New York Times,* MM52.

Keltner, D. (2009). *Born to be good: The science of a meaningful life.* New York: W. W. Norton.

Keltner, D., & Bonanno, G. (1997). A study of laughter and dissociation: Distinct correlates of laughter and smiling during bereavement. *Interpersonal Relations and Group Processes, 73*(4), 687–702.

Keltner, D., Young, R., Heerey, E., Oemig, C., & Monarch, N. (1998). Teasing in hierarchical and intimate relations. *Journal of Personality and Social Psychology, 75*(5), 1231–1247.

Krumhuber, E. G., & Manstead, A. S. R. (2009). Can Duchenne smiles be feigned? New evidence of felt and false smiles. *Emotion, 9*(6), 807–820.

Krysstel. (2009). Do children laugh more than adults? *Social Science.* Retrieved from www. mahalo.com/answers/social-science/do-children-laugh-more-than-adults

Kubie, L. S. (1971). The destructive potential of humor in psychotherapy. *American Journal of Psychiatry, 127*(7), 861–866.

Kuhlman, T. (1984). *Humor and psychotherapy.* Northvale, NJ: Jason Aronson.

Kuiper, N. A., & Martin, R. A. (1998). Laughter and stress in daily life: Relation to positive and negative affect. *Motivation and Emotion, 22*(2), 133–153.

Kulp, R. (2009, May). When I am physically sick... (web blog comment). Retrieved from autismcrisis.blogspot.com/2009/05/autistic-way-of-laughing.html

Lahr, J. (2007, November 5). Coogan's bluff: Britain's reigning king of the comedy of embarrassment. *New Yorker,* 42–49.

Lee, A. (2008, June 30). Altered state: Pennsylvania, blackness, and the art of being foreign. *New Yorker,* 36–41.

Levine, D. (2009). *Using humor in psychotherapy with older adults: An exploratory study.* Unpublished doctoral dissertation. Sanville Institute for Clinical Social Work and Psychotherapy.

Lewis, M., & Rosenblum, L. A. (1978). Introduction: Issues in affect development. In M. Lewis & L. A. Rosenblum (Eds.), *The development of affect* (pp. 1–10). New York: Plenum Press.

Lippitt, J. (1992). Nietsche, Zarathustra and the status of laughter. *British Journal of Aesthetics, 32*(1), 39–49.

Lockard, J. S., Fahrenbruch, C. E., Smith, J. L., & Morgan, C. J. (1977). Smiling and laughter: Different phyletic origins. *Bulletin of the Psychonomic Society, 10*(3), 183–188.

Loizou, E. (2006). Young children's explanation of pictorial humor. *Early Childhood Education Journal, 33*(6), 425–431.

London, M. (2003, November). Readers write: Laughter. *The Sun,* 34–42.

Lorenz, K. (1963). *On aggression.* New York: Harcourt, Brace and World.

Lowinger, J. (2005, February 3). Laughter plays tricks with your eyes. *ABC Science Online.* Retrieved from abc.net.au/science/news/stories/s1294404.htm

Lyons-Ruth, K. (1998). Implicit relational knowing: Its role in development and psychoanalytic treatment. *Infant Mental Health Journal, 19*(3), 282–289.

Lyons-Ruth, K., & Jacobvitz, D. (2008). Attachment disorganization: Genetic factors, parenting contexts, and developmental transformation from infancy to adulthood. In J. Cassidy & P. Shaver (Eds.), *Handbook of attachment: Theory, research, and clinical applications* (pp. 666–697). New York: Guilford.

Lyons-Ruth, K., Yellin, C., Melnick, S., & Atwood, G. (2003). Childhood experiences of trauma and loss have different relations to maternal unresolved and Hostile-Helpless states of mind on the AAI. *Attachment and Human Development, 5*(4), 330–414. doi:10.1 080/14616730310001633410

M., M. (2003). Readers write: Laughter. *The Sun, 335,* 34–41.

MacDonald, N. E., & Silverman, I. W. (1978). Smiling and laughter in infants as a function of level of arousal and cognitive evaluation. *Developmental Psychology, 14*(3), 235–241.

MacFarquhar, L. (2003, October 20). The movie lover: In Quentin Tarantino's mind, the projector never stops running. *New Yorker,* 147–159.

Malatesta, C. (1982). The expression and regulation of emotion: A lifespan perspective. In T. Field & A. Fogel (Eds.), *Emotion and early interaction* (pp. 1–24). Hillsdale, NJ: Lawrence Erlbaum.

Malatesta, C. Z., Culver, C., Tesman, J. R., & Shepard, B. (1989). *The development of emotion expression during the first two years of life. 54*(219), 1–136.

markgarza22. (2006). Blood (Video file). Retrieved from http://www.youtube.com/ watch?v=fVDGu82FeQ

Martin, R. A. (2010). Do children laugh more often than adults do? *Association for Applied and Therapeutic Humor.* Retrieved from www.aath.org/index.html

Marvin, R. S., & Britner, P. A. (2008). Normative development: The ontogeny of attachment. In J. Cassidy & P. Shaver (Eds.), *The attachment handbook: Theory, research and clinical applications* (pp. 269–294). New York: Guilford.

Masten, A. (1986). Humor and competence in school-aged children. *Child Development, 57,* 461–473.

McGhee, P. (1979). *Humor, its origin and development.* San Francisco: W. H. Freeman.

McGhee, P. E. (2009). Children's humor is FUNdamental to pre-K classrooms: An in-depth look at humor. *Bank Street,* 1–6. Retrieved from www.bankstreet.edu/upk/humor_ developmentl.html

McGray, D. (2009, May 11). The instigator: A crusader's plan to remake failing schools. *New Yorker,* 66–69.

Mikulincer, M., & Shaver, P. (2007). *Attachment in adulthood: Structure, dynamics, and change.* New York: Guilford Press.

Miller, A. L., & Olson, S. L. (2000). Emotional expressiveness during peer conflicts: A predictor of social maladjustment among high-risk preschoolers. *Journal of Abnormal Child Psychology, 28*(4), 339–352.

Moore, A. (1988). *Batman: The killing joke.* New York: DC Comics.

Moore, H. (2008). *The bishop's daughter: A memoir.* New York: W. W. Norton.

Moore, W. (2010). *The other Wes Moore: One name, two fates.* New York: Spiegel & Grau.

Morreall, J. (Ed.). (1987). *The philosophy of laughter and humor.* Albany: State University of New York Press.

Mulder, M. P., & Nijholt, A. (2002). *Humour research: state of the art* (No. 10–34). Enschede: Centre for Tlematics and Information Technology, University of Twente. Retrieved from http://www.ub.utwente.nl/webdocs/ctit/1/0000009e.pdf

Nelson, J. K. (2005). *Seeing through tears: Crying and attachment.* New York: Routledge.

Nelson, J. K. (2008). Laugh and the world laughs with you: An attachment perspective on the meaning of laughter in psychotherapy. *Clinical Social Work Journal, 36*(1), 41–49.

Nevius, C. W. (2006, December 23). Protesters—on one columnist—go out on a limb in Berkeley. *San Francisco Chronicle,* A1, A11.

Nevius, C. W. (2010, January 16). Haight not taking street thugs lying down. *San Francisco Chronicle,* C1 and C4.

Nietzsche, F. (1954/1995). *Thus spoke Zarathustra.* New York: Random House.

Nwokah, E. E., Hsu, H.-C., Dobrowolska, O., & Fogel, A. (1994). The development of laughter in mother-infant communication: Timing parameters and temporal sequences. *Infant Behavior and Development, 17,* 23–35.

O'Brien, T. (2003). Readers write: Laughter. *The Sun, 335,* 34–41.

Ogasawara, C. (2003, November). Readers write: Laughter. *The Sun,* 34–41.

Oldham, M. (2009). A tale of two Tonys: Taccone on Kushner. *Berkeley Rep Magazine, 10,* 16–19.

Oring, E. (1984). *The jokes of Sigmund Freud: A study in humor and Jewish identity.* Philadelphia: University of Pennsylvania Press.

Oster, H. (1978). Facial expression and affect development. In M. Lewis & L. A. Rosenblum (Eds.), *The development of affect* (pp. 43–75). New York: Plenum Press.

P., G. (2003). Readers write: Laughter. *The Sun,* 34–41.

Paddington, R. (1933). *The psychology of laughter: A study in social adaptation.* London: Figurehead.

Panksepp, J. (2000). The riddle of laugher: Neural and psychoevolutionary underpinnings of joy. *Current Directions in Psychological Science, 9*(6), 183–186.

Panksepp, J. (2001). The long-term psychobiological consequences of infant emotions: Prescriptions for the twenty-first century. *Infant Mental Health Journal, 22*(1–2), 132–173.

Panksepp, J. (2007a). Neuroevolutionary sources of laugher and social joy: Modeling primal human laugher in laboratory rats. *Behavioural brain research, 182*(2), 231–244.

Panksepp, J. (2007b). Rats laugh when you tickle them. Retrieved from http://www.youtube.com/watch?v=j-admRGFVNM

Panksepp, J., & Burgdorf, J. (2003). "Laughing rats" and the evolutionary antecedents of human joy. *Physiology and Behavior, 79,* 533–547.

Picoult, J. (2010). *House rules.* New York: Atria Books.

Plato. (360 BCE/1957). *The republic of Plato.* New York: Dutton & Co.

Plessner, H. (1970). *Laughing and crying: A study of the limits of human behavior.* Evanston, IL: Northwestern University Press.

Potok, C. (1967). *The chosen.* New York: Simon & Schuster

Provine, R. R. (1993). Laughter punctuates speech: Linguistic, social and gender contexts of laughter. *Ethology, 95,* 291–298.

Provine, R. R. (1996, January/February). Laughter. *American Scientist, 84,* 38–45.

Provine, R. R. (2000). *Laughter: A scientific investigation.* New York: Viking.

Provine, R. R., & Yong, Y. L. (1991). Laughter: A stereotyped human vocalization. *Ethology, 89,* 115–124.

Radcliffe-Brown, A. R. (1940/1952). *Structure and function in primitive society: Essays and addresses.* New York: Free Press.

Rafkin, L. (2009, September 27). Courtship was slow but steady. *San Francisco Chronicle,* N2.

Reddy, V. (2001). Infant clowns: The interpersonal creation of humour in infancy. *Enfance, 53,* 247–256. Retrieved from www.cairn.info/article.php?ID_REVUE-ENF&ID_NUMPUBLIE-ENF_533&ID_ARTICLE-ENF_533_0247

Reddy, V. (2008). *How infants know minds.* Cambridge, MA: Harvard University Press.

Retzinger, S. M. (1987). Resentment and laughter: Video studies of the shame-rage spiral. In H. B. Lewis (Ed.), *The role of shame in symptom formation* (pp. 151–181). Hillsdale, NJ: Lawrence Erlbaum.

Roismann, G. I., Tsai, J. L., & Chiang, K.-H. S. (2004). The emotional integration of childhood experience: Physiological, facial expressive, and self-reported emotional response during the Adult Attachment Interview. *Developmental Psychology, 40*(5), 776–789.

Ross, L. (2008, March 31). Still here dept.: Screams. *New Yorker,* 42–44.

Ross, L. (2011, April 4). The talk of the town: Good morning, Baghdad. *The New Yorker,* 22–23.

Sachs, L. (1973). On crying, weeping and laughing as defenses against sexual drives, with special consideration of adolescent giggling. *International Journal of Psychoanalysis, 54,* 477–484.

Sanders, H. (2007). Laugh out loud: study shows laughter improves relationships. *The Appalachian Online.* Retrieved from http://theapp.appstate.edu/content/view/1845/42/

Schore, A. N. (2003a). *Affect dysregulation and disorders of the self.* New York: W. W. Norton.

Schore, A. N. (2003b). *Affect regulation and the repair of the self.* New York: W. W. Norton.

Shammi, P., & Stuss, D. T. (1999). Humour appreciation: A role of the right frontal lobe. *Brain, 122,* 657–666.

Sherman, L. W. (1975). An ecological study of glee in small groups of preschool children. *Child Development, 46,* 53–61.

Singer, M. (2011, March 7). Revivals: Pacing it. *New Yorker,* 26–27.

Smile—and the world can hear you, even if you hide. (2008). *Science Daily.* Retrieved from www.sciencedaily.com/releases/2008/01/0801112247–45.htm

Snider, B. (2010). Clowning around: There's a comedian in every classroom. Retrieved from www.edutopia.org/clowning-around

Spacelord72. (2006). Laughing baby (Video file). Retrieved from http://www.youtube.com/watch?v=HttF5HVYtlQ

Sroufe, L. A. (1995). *Emotional development: The organization of emotional life in the early years.* New York: Cambridge University Press.

Sroufe, L. A. (2005). Attachment and development: A prospective, longitudinal study from birth to adulthood. *Attachment and Human Development, 7,* 349–367. doi:10.1080/14616730500365928

Sroufe, L. A., & Waters, E. (1976). The ontogenesis of smiling and laughter: A perspective on the organization of development in infancy. *Psychological Review, 83*(3), 173–189.

Sroufe, L. A., & Waters, E. (1977). Attachment as an organizational construct. *Child Development, 48*(4), 1184–1199.

Sroufe, L. A., & Wunsch, J. P. (1972). The development of laughter in the first year of life. *Child Development, 43,* 1326–1344.

Stern, D. (1998). The process of therapeutic change involving implicit knowledge: some implications of developmental observations for adult psychotherapy. *Infant Mental Health Journal, 19*(3), 300–308.

Sweet, L. (2008, October 15). Barack Obama John McCain debate: Oct. 15, 2008 transcript. *Chicago Sun-Times.* Retrieved from blogs.suntimes.com/sweet/2008/10

Szalavitz, M. (2011, January 31). You're kidding! Medical clown increases pregnancy rates with IVF. Retrieved from http://healthland.time.com/2011/01/31/youre-kidding-medical-clown-increases-pregnancy-rates-with-ivf/

Thomas, M. (2010). *Growing up laughing: My story and the story of funny.* New York: Hyperion.

Trevarthen, C. (1979). Communication and cooperation in early infancy: A description of primary intersubjectivity. In M. Bullowa (Ed.), *Before speech: The beginning of interpersonal communication* (pp. 321–348). New York: Cambridge University Press.

Triezenberg, K. E. (2008). Humor in literature. In V. Raskin (Ed.), *The primer of humor research* (pp. 523–542). Berlin and New York: Mouton de Gruyter.

Tronick, E. (2007). *The neurobehavioral and social-emotional development of infants and children.* New York: W. W. Norton.

Trust, W. (2006, December 13). Laugh and the whole world laughs with you: Why the brain just can't help itself. *ScienceDaily*. Retrieved from http://www.sciencedaily.com/releases/2006/12/061212213922.htm

Turnquist, K. (2011, December 10). Funny thing is, his stand-up is outstanding. *Oregonian,* C1–2.

Urban Dictionary. (2011). Laughterglow. Retrieved from www.urbandictionary.com/define.php?term=laughterglow

Van IJzendoorn, M. H., & Sagi-Schwartz, A. (2008). Cross-cultural patterns of attachment: Universal and contextual dimensions. In J. Cassidy & P. Shaver (Eds.), *Handbook of attachment: Theory research, and clinical applications* (pp. 880–205). New York: Guilford Press.

Wagner, J. (1986). *The search for signs of intelligent life in the universe.* New York: Harper and Row.

Washburn, R. W. (1929/1972). Facial expression in children: Three studies. In M. Davis (Ed.), *Body movement: Perspectives in research* (Vol. 6, pp. 420–531). New York: Arno Press.

Weston, K. (1994, January 30). Laughing instead of crying. *San Francisco Examiner,* D-2.

Wild, B., Rodden, F., Grodd, W., & Ruch, W. (2003). Neural correlates of laughter and humour. *Brain, 126,* 2121–2138.

wildminer. (2007, June 29). Twin baby boys laughing at each other (Video file). Retrieved from www.youtube.com/watch?v=X7mOzWQSnaQ&NR=1

Winnicott, D. W. (1971/2001). *Playing and reality.* Philadelphia: Brunner-Routledge.

Wolff, P. H. (1987). *Behavior states and the expression of emotions in early infancy.* Chicago: University of Chicago Press.

Zall, D. S. (1994). "Ya get it?" Children, humor, and psychotherapy. In E. S. Buckman (Ed.), *The handbook of humor: Clinical applications in psychotherapy* (pp. 25–39). Malabar, FL: Krieger Publishing Company.

Ziv, A. (1989). Using humor to develop creative thinking. In P. McGhee (Ed.), *Humor and children's development: A guide to practical applications* (Vol. 20, pp. 99–116). Binghamton, NY: Haworth Press.

INDEX